R. N. BERKI

SECURITY AND SOCIETY

REFLECTIONS ON LAW, ORDER AND POLITICS

Also for Dent by R. N. Berki

Socialism (Modern Ideologies Series), 1975
The History of Political Thought: a short introduction, 1977
On Political Realism, 1981
Insight and Vision: the problem of Communism in Marx's thought, 1983

R. N. BERKI

SECURITY AND SOCIETY

REFLECTIONS ON LAW, ORDER AND POLITICS

J. M. Dent & Sons Ltd
London and Melbourne

First published 1986

This book is set in 10½ on 12 pt Linotron Bembo Roman by
Input Typesetting Ltd, London

Made in Great Britain by
Biddles Ltd, Guildford, Surrey for
J. M. Dent & Sons Ltd
Aldine House, 33 Welbeck Street
London W1M 8LX

British Library Cataloguing in Publication Data

Berki, R. N.
Security and society: reflections on law,
order and politics.
1. Law – Philosophy
I. Title
340'.1 K230

ISBN 0-460-04655-1
ISBN 0-460-02469-8 Pbk

Contents

Preface

Honesty, probably, is the best policy: readers should be warned that despite its formal features this is not, and certainly not meant to be, an 'academic' book, in at least two accustomed senses of 'academic'. Firstly, it is not a specialist book written by an expert researcher for a pre-selected and restricted audience who might share with the author a professional vocabulary; the rather heterogeneous collection of titles in the Select Bibliography reveals this fact immediately anyway. Secondly, the 'reflections' set out in the volume were not originally inspired by any recognizable kind of intellectual curiosity or scholarly interest or a 'hypothesis' which asked to be 'tested'. On the very contrary, the original impetus was emotional, psychological, primitive, personal, stemming from the author's very real anxiety – the ordinary citizen's gut-feelings – concerning the problem of security in society. It was this basic anxiety which then led the author, in a way typical of the conditioned reflexes of a working academic, to the designing and organization of a gigantic programme of senior seminars in the Hull Politics Department in 1982–83, entitled 'Law and Order in Britain'. The author sat through, and with one exception (viz. his own contribution) chaired, some eighteen substantial seminar meetings addressed by acknowledged experts in the field; thus it happened that his original primitive gut-feelings and prejudices began to turn, under the educative, though also somewhat disturbing, influence of a series of brilliant performances, incisive arguments, cutting repartees and at times highly entertaining verbal skirmishes, into more of an intellectual interest of a respectable kind, and enabled him, at first rather tentatively and gropingly, to seek a connection between the problem of law and order and the (to him) more familiar territory of political philosophy. The gut-feelings and convictions, of course, remained much the same to the end, and the 'education' gained in the process is still perhaps a bit fragmentary. At any rate, this background helped the book assume a formally academic character, and in the context this means the (decidedly pleasurable) obligation of acknowledging the numerous personal debts incurred on the way. The author discharges this obligation with sincere gratitude, adding the tedious but here definitely warranted saving clause that he alone is responsible for the arguments advanced and conclusions reached in this effort.

Thanks, then, are extended in the first place to all the performers, commentators and audiences at the said seminar programme, who of course are too numerous to be listed separately. Nevertheless special mention should be made of Bhikhu Parekh to whom the author acted as officially designated 'discussant', and of Neil Elder who did the same honour to the author. To Philip Norton, with particular pleasure and a grateful bow, for willingly relieving the author of the vexing task of editing a selection of these same seminar papers and for fashioning them into a neat, lively, pleasing volume (*Law and Order and British Politics* – see Select Bibliography), for making such embarrassingly generous references to the present author in the same volume, for kindly granting permission to the author to use – in this venture – material already employed in a short piece, 'Considerations on Law and Order' (Hull Papers in Politics, No. 35, 1984), and for giving much-valued bibliographical assistance. To Keith Bottomley for expert advice on reading in specialized fields and for perusing and commenting on 'Considerations'. To David Miller and Allan Megill for reading, on the author's express request, 'Considerations' and for giving the author their honest opinion. To Ken Bates, Peter Keeling and Neil King for their illuminating conversation. To Alan Bairner from whose Ph.D. thesis, for which the author had the privilege of acting as supervisor some years back, the notion of the 'plural perspective' probably derives (Bairner's thesis is entitled 'The Dual Perspective: an Examination of Gramsci's Theory of the State'). To Alan James and colleagues in the University of Keele for inviting the author and kindly discussing in a senior seminar material relating to Chapter 3. To Peter Lassman and colleagues in the British Sociological Association for listening to and debating the author's paper containing a condensed version of Chapter 2. To the family at home for their advice, concern and sympathy, and to friends in the 'Narrow Boat' for their lively involvement and inspiration. To Enid Tracy, caught for the third time, for typing up the manuscript with speed and efficiency. And to Jocelyn Burton at Dent for her accustomed incisiveness in providing the editorial finish.

R.N.B.

Hull, October 1985

1 PARADOXES OF SECURITY

Human beings desire security and yet almost everywhere their lot in life is insecurity. How this predicament came about originally I cannot and will not endeavour to tell; I greatly doubt if the situation can in any way be radically altered, or if it ought to be altered. But how we can possibly come to make better sense of this seemingly contradictory, paradoxical situation, and to accept as 'legitimate' both the yearning after security and its inadequate attainment, that is a question I will attempt to answer.

The author trusts that he will be forgiven the audacity, not to say impertinence, of paraphrasing the famous opening lines of the first chapter of Rousseau's *Social Contract* as the opening lines of this – much more modest, in aspiration as well as achievement – reflective treatise. The connection with Rousseau is that it seems to me eminently arguable that the problem of 'freedom' and the problem of 'security' for human beings in society are basically the same problem, looked at from two opposite angles. That Rousseau, in the company of a great many illustrious writers in his time, and followed by generations of others, should have conceived of the underlying concern of modern society in terms of 'freedom' no doubt reflects the overall optimism and forward-looking character of the epoch in which he lived and which has been known as the Age of Enlightenment. At least this is so in so far as we can say that the writings of any author simply 'reflect' the concerns and preoccupations of his or her social and intellectual environment (indeed, in Rousseau's case, he helped to make what we call the Enlightenment) and in so far as one can so boldly, grandiosely generalize about the character of a whole age or century. But, rightly or wrongly, this is a kind of generalization we all tend to indulge in, and if the Enlightenment can at all be described in terms of youthful optimism and an underlying belief in the concrete and imminent possibility of radical social change, then the present time – the closing decades of the twentieth century – could surely be characterized as an era of slowly descending gloom and doom, of stalemate and spiritual stagnation, uncertainty, fear and professed ignorance of the future and of viable alternatives to the existing, an age of global pessimism, post-climactic fatigue, general bafflement and despondency. Or is this just a typical middle-aged, mid-positioned attitude? At any rate, it seems to be shared by a lot of people all round and their voice, their anxieties and their apparent helplessness have largely managed to set the general tone of discussion. Security, not freedom, is in the forefront today; retrenchment rather than expansion; a re-examination of 'values' instead of their replacement. As the 1960s, to focus on a different time-scale now, were an era of 'greening' revolt and protest, of radicalism and progress, so the 1980s have witnessed the ascendancy of social, political and psychological conservatism, both with a large and with a small 'c', pervading well-nigh all areas of discourse. Ours is the age of withering leaves, gathering clouds, disquieting winds coming from all directions. This theme, the ascendancy of a general atmosphere of conservatism, will receive further comment later, in Chapter 4. For now, just another brief remark concerning Rousseau who will not otherwise receive any serious attention (apart from a few *ad hoc* references) in these pages. As has been said above, Rousseau's quest and the quest undertaken here are matched in that they deal with the same underlying problem – freedom-security in human society – and that they both professedly seek to 'legitimate' a paradoxical situation. The two works differ, however, (apart from the not entirely insignificant difference in the native talent of the two authors) in that Rousseau's *Social Contract*, in spite of its classical crispness and cogency of argument, became in the event less of an effort to explain the 'legitimacy' of the 'chains' born by originally 'free men' than an enterprise in radical moral and social innovation. By contrast, the present endeavour will keep steadfastly to the paradox of security and insecurity in society; thus we begin and thus we shall conclude.

Alas, it is only too obvious that the consciousness of insecurity has become a global phenomenon. One needs no more than a cursory glance at newspapers, special reports or current affairs programmes on the media, in Britain and elsewhere, to become convinced that the attainment of personal security for ordinary men and women looms now larger as an aspiration than anything else. Personal security is the goal, personal insecurity is, by and large, the existing fact, experienced by people all over the world. What is 'personal insecurity'? We have to start, obviously, by drawing some relevant, provisional and what in academic discourse are known as 'heuristic' distinctions, in order to set the discussion in the desired direction. By 'personal' insecurity what it is intended to convey here is the threat, imminent or remote, direct or indirect, imaginary or real, posed for individuals by other people, concrete persons, identifiable groups, larger and impersonal entities like the 'system', the 'market', the 'establishment' or even 'society' in the abstract. So in the first place we shall have to exclude from consideration the danger to personal security presented by non-human 'nature' and situations of insecurity caused by individuals themselves. I do not, of course, imagine for a moment that this distinction is anything more than convenient and relative. Where, for example, would you draw a dividing line between 'nature' and 'society'? Is starvation in so many parts of the world a 'natural' phenomenon or one due to the negligence, wilful or otherwise, of people and institutions in richer countries or the peculiar character of the international system? Or, if a person, anywhere in the world, dies or becomes crippled as a result of 'self-induced' alcoholism or drug-addiction, is this the person's own making in the true sense or a consequence of 'social' conditions, like poverty, unemployment, alienation, anomie, inadequate education or broken families? Questions like this, of course, cannot be entirely left out of account in a discussion of the problem of personal security, and the reflections that follow will express some sort of attitude towards them, at least by implication. Nevertheless, these and similar problems are still marginal to the main purpose of the present discussion, and it seems to me a valid proposition that the problem of personal security in the context of insecurity caused *directly* by the actions of *others*, and not by the person whose security is in question, is a problem essentially and relevantly different from the problems of natural and self-induced insecurity. At least the former problem is different to the extent that it can be usefully discussed on its own. I will in fact proceed a step further and argue that for the purposes of political philosophy – the genre to which these reflections, possibly in a somewhat idiosyncratic manner, belong – personal security in this delimited 'social' context is much more of a basic and essential problem than the other two kinds. This, at any rate, might not be deemed too outlandish, too controversial a proposition.

I yet, however, intend to go another step further and draw a second distinction, this time within the category of society. Let us ask the question: in what way or ways does human society, at large and in the abstract, pose a threat to the personal security, safety of individuals? What are the kinds of things, actions, events usually referred to as threats to personal security in the gloom-laden discussion going on today in all parts of the globe and, more pointedly, in the intellectual, political and media circles of Western society? There are, it seems to me, *three* kinds of phenomena to be noted above all, subsuming all important varieties. In the first place, there is the phenomenon of large-scale organized violence and deliberate destruction of human lives, viz. international and armed civil conflict, or conventional 'shooting' warfare. Without a doubt war as such is the greatest threat to personal security, equally without a doubt war is a 'social' rather than a 'natural' phenomenon, and again without any serious reservations it can be stated that war today, in the global context, is the biggest actual threat to the personal safety of the highest number of people. Perhaps war in the 1980s is more ubiquitous than ever before in modern history and it is also, apart from the greatest conflagrations of our recent past (e.g. above all, World War II and Vietnam), the most destructive in terms of the actual toll of human lives and loss of health and livelihood. A special report in the *Sunday Times* (22 January 1984) claimed recently that 'a quarter of the world's nations are currently caught up in conflicts which have already claimed up to five million lives. More than four million troops are fighting each other.' The conflicts listed in the report include five wars between nations and more than thirty revolutionary and separatist insurgencies, mainly – and this is a relevant point here – involving Third World areas and countries.

In the second place, the problem of personal insecurity in society is often taken to refer to the global phenomenon of ever-deepening economic recession, the drying up of markets, declining world trade, the growing gap between rich and poor (in the international context but also domestically, within the richer countries themselves), and the resultant erosion of the living standards and even livelihood of individuals and families. People are, and feel themselves increasingly to be, 'insecure' in their accustomed life-style and expectations. Now this kind of personal insecurity, while in its effect scarcely in the same category as violent warfare (you can still 'live', after a fashion, at a lower material standard and not knowing what the next day will bring, but try it with a rocket or napalm fired at your household), on the other hand is even more widespread than the insecurity caused by inter-state war and insurgency. Obviously there is something more than faintly immoral and incongruous in any attempt to bring together under the heading of 'economic' insecurity or insecurity of livelihood the plight of starving millions in Africa, Asia and South America on the one hand, and skilled workers, managers, administrators and people in the traditional 'professions' in the affluent West having to live on the dole, or the golden handshake, and forced to accept the hardship and humiliation of cutting down on the consumption of liquor and on foreign holidays. But the point is that the feeling, the consciousness, the subjective experience of insecurity tends to be similar or converging in both cases. Or rather, since even putting it this way would sound quite presumptuous, people whose living standards and existential situations in the West are being eroded see themselves more and more as 'poor' people, just a tiny degree nearer to those whose poverty is reckoned in absolute terms. What counts, of course, is not the momentary situation but the tendency: things are pretty bad today, certainly worse than a decade or so ago, but what is more important is that they are more likely to get even worse in the future. The general gloom-and-doom syndrome mentioned above feeds not so much on existing insecurity as on anticipated and aggravated insecurity. And let us say, in line with our – partially and temporarily – suspended judgment concerning the 'social' antecedents and causes of economic insecurity, that economic insecurity is at least to some extent definitely a *social* phenomenon. The abolition of 'poverty', in the abstract, might well be a pipe-dream, an incoherent and impossible goal. But this is certainly not true of all kinds and degrees of economic hardship and uncertainty of livelihood experienced in the world today.

Third and last, the problem of personal security in the context of society is encountered at the present time in its starkest, most direct form, as the threat posed to individuals by other individuals inhabiting the same social world, in proximity and, in most instances, sharing the same overall threat of the larger, more overarching but perhaps less imminent, 'social' sources of insecurity: war and economic dislocation. It is this person-to-person direct threat to individual life, limb, health, tranquillity and possessions which has, somewhat misleadingly perhaps and with a one-sided ideological bias, been termed the problem of 'law and order', and it is this phenomenon which provides the departure and focus of the ensuing reflections. But this concentration has to be justified, especially in the light of the above remarks concerning war and economic insecurity. It could not, of course, be contended that the problem of law and order is of the same or like seriousness and magnitude, from the point of view of personal security and in the global context, as the phenomena of war and of economic dislocation and uncertainty. A lot more people die or get wounded in existing wars, and a great deal more people lose their livelihood or suffer a severe reduction in their standard of living than fall victim to crime (whether violent or not) or to domestic political disturbance and violence. However, there are other considerations as well. In the first place, though this is not perhaps a conclusive argument, the problem of law and order figures relatively more prominently in the Western world than the other two problems. Crime and political violence are obviously not confined to the rich, stable, fully industrialized, capitalist and (in most cases) 'liberal-democratic' countries of Western Europe and North America; murder for gain, assassination, grievous bodily harm, mugging, theft and destruction of property are, if anything (and in so far as we can make any proper sense of global comparative criminal statistics), more or just as rampant in Manila, Lagos, Caracas, Kingston and Hong Kong as they are in New York, Los Angeles, London, Glasgow and West Berlin. But crime and illegal politics stand out in the West more, and have caused greater public anxiety in recent years, simply because their upsurge is measured against a background of relative peace, stability and prosperity. It is the poorer parts of our globe, the Third World, as has been noted earlier, that have experienced and are still experiencing the highest number and the most destructive wars, and it is people there who die of starvation. In the West, though we live constantly under the shadow of possible large-scale war, have instant knowledge of existing lesser wars all over the world and (quite justly) fear their consequences and their possible spreading, and have on the whole to contend with greater economic hardships and insecurity than ever before in living memory, these manifestations of personal insecurity are still somewhat remote from our actual experience, projected and subjective, not lived through and suffered. But the problem of law and order is *here* and *now*: it is direct, immediate, close, inescapable, perfectly intelligible not only in terms of our cool reason and public consciousness but also, more importantly, on the level of our instincts and emotions.

This leads to my second and I believe much more telling consideration. Whether or not, in the Western world, personal insecurity in the context of hostile intentions and malevolent indifference (I shall explain this term presently) of other persons in the same environment – which is what, roughly, the problem of law and order refers to – really has the magnitude and objective importance often attributed to it in the media, it has a curious, ineluctable fascination not matched by other problems. Just a word here on magnitude and the relative importance of various natural and social phenomena for personal insecurity in the West; the following two bits of statistical information might have some illustrative value. As reported in the London daily, *The Sun* (10 January 1984), the U.S. Justice Department revealed in 1984 that in the U.S. the chances of being a victim of violent crime were greater than being hurt in a car crash, dying from cancer or being injured in a fire. And as it is stated in a book on law and order by the leading progressive criminologist, Ian Taylor (who will receive some critical attention later), relying on another *Sunday Times* report, in 1981 in America the leading cause of death for males in the 15–44 age-group was murder, ahead of cancer, heart disease and road accidents.[1] This is just, to repeat, for marginal illustration; doubtless a lot of other statistical material could be cited, demonstrating both the relative importance and the relative unimportance of criminal and political violence from the point of view of personal security (another recent author, for example, argues that in Britain at any rate more people die of motor accidents than by deliberate violence, more people kill themselves than are killed by others, and about one half of homicides are committed by the clinically insane).[2] The point for us, however, is not so much the bewildering variety of adduced and variously interpreted 'facts and figures' as the way in which they tend to be perceived by the public, viz. as showing a dramatic increase in the crime rate. And of course ultimately what interests us here is the significance of these public perceptions for our philosophical reflections about the nature of security in human society.

To return to the curious fascination and absorbing interest attached most universally to the problem of law and order: surely this is not accidental and it has a very good, relevant and commonsensical explanation. This universal and (almost) spontaneous fascination shows, I believe, that personal security in this most immediate human social context is really basic to the whole gamut of other problems concerning personal security (such as wars and economic dislocation) and indeed to most, if not all, other problems and issues traditionally considered under the label of political and social philosophy. Here, as I will attempt to show in greater detail in ensuing chapters, the surface and the depths really meet: what immediate and to some extent (but only to some extent) media-influenced perception – our ordinary common sense and our gut-reactions – tells us on the one hand, and what is disclosed in philosophical reflection and speculation on the other, suggest the same thing: that personal security is really the key to modern society, and that the problem of so-called law and order is the key to personal security. Full-scale war, it is true, if it is actually experienced, surpasses in curiosity and fascination (as well as, of course, in destructive potential) the phenomena of criminal and domestic political violence, but fortunately war is not, in the West, part of our daily lives and immediate concerns. Even then, it could be argued that war itself is a direct, demonstrable consequence of domestic arrangements; if there were no states and politically defined domestic societies, then there could be no wars as we have known them either (though of course, war-like large-scale organized violence could still occur). Therefore, fascinating or not, war cannot be as basic to the problem of personal security as problems arising in the domestic context itself. The human interest of war as heightened insecurity stems from the interest attaching to the less acute – but more widespread and enduring – forms of insecurity encountered in the domestic scene in peace time.

Another point may be added here, foreshadowing an aspect of one of our central arguments to be advanced in this book, concerning the nature of the 'criminal' and the 'political' (discussed in Chapter 3); namely that war, in principle, is on the borderline of the category properly designated as the problem of 'personal' insecurity anyway. The threat to life and health posed by war is assuredly in the last resort *to* persons and administered *by* persons but it is, it seems to me, important to note that the transaction here is no longer between persons *as* persons. More of this later. And moreover, the very extent, magnitude, technological scale of modern warfare have rendered war more and more impersonal and its destruction of lives and livelihood more like an act of 'nature' from an immediate personal point of view. The asymmetry between the concerns, interest, power and reason of the individual human subject, the citizen of states, and the overwhelming superiority and remoteness of military technology and organization has grown so great as to render war markedly less of a subject of discussion, meditation and imagination. War now, especially nuclear war, is 'unthinkable' but this is in consequence not only of the *negative* factor of potential mass destruction but also of the *positive* factor of impersonality, lack of 'contact'. Thus science-fiction and fantasy warfare (orcs, goblins, dragons) have supplanted popular war-literature. Thrill requires personal contact and a symmetry of conflicting forces.

And as regards the other endemic and ubiquitous source of personal insecurity in society – poverty, economic dislocation, uncertainty of livelihood – it requires no reflection or special insight to register the almost total lack of curiosity and fascination these phenomena provide for ordinary consciousness. Perhaps in a way this is a sad reflection on the general level of our moral awareness but it does not alter the situation; the fact is that starvation, malnutrition, unemployment and the like, though in quantitative and existential human terms they constitute a problem of truly tragic proportions, have little or marginal or only contrived personal interest *per se*, and this has always been so. The sight of emaciated children in Ethiopia only shocks, saddens, frightens the spectator; the sight of a plane-hijack, or South African blacks fleeing from the police, thrills also. I suspect, however, that callous or not ordinary consciousness has had a point here, of great and perhaps unrecognized relevance to political philosophy: while poverty and the like are underlying 'social' problems and pertain to the general quest after personal security, they yet do not directly capture the truly *personal* element here and the direct personal significance of 'society' in the context of security. Poverty is a big problem for our world; it is not its key problem.

We are now in a position to confront the notion of personal security more directly and attempt to give it, for the purposes of this discussion, at least a preliminary and tentative definition. Personal security, in the most rudimentary and primitive sense, must refer above all to the desire to live one's life in conditions which preclude effective threats to this life coming from other persons directly, persons who are identifiable and who operate in the same vicinity as the person whose security is in question. Indeed, yet another distinction has to be drawn here, so as to get even closer to this feeling or atmosphere of 'curiosity' and 'fascination' referred to above, as accompanying the law and order syndrome and as being largely absent from the areas of economic insecurity and destructive, but remote, warfare. Just as, as has been remarked earlier, *de facto* insecurity might well be greater in magnitude when self-inflicted or caused by external nature than any kind of human, deliberate, socially caused insecurity, so within the narrower and properly designated social-personal realm we might well find (and statistics seem to bear this out) that *domestic* insecurity occupies the prominent position. That is, we are more likely to experience insecurity as victims to domestic violence or self-provoked social violence (e.g. a punch-up between jealous lovers in the bedroom, aggro in the nightclub, etc.) than to violence, as it were, outside, encountering it as bare 'persons', and the same goes for fraud, theft and the like. Yet, once again, this element of curiosity and fascination is missing from or exists only in a subdued form in the domestic and similar situations: here, although one is often a totally innocent and unwilling victim, one is yet positively, substantively involved; threats are not entirely unpredictable; violence, theft, fraud, misappropriation occur in contexts which have positive, valued aspects as well; there is always at least the possibility of reciprocity. Domestic and social insecurity in this narrower sense is always two-sided: in principle the 'victim' is always, and precisely by virtue of being a contingent victim, also an 'agent'. Personal, deliberate and indeed often intense hostility accompanying this kind of fraud, theft and violence make it, if certainly not more pleasant and endurable, at least more 'familiar' and correspondingly less 'social' in the required sense; it becomes at the same time and by the same token more humdrum (less fascinating) and less threatening to personality. Hostility here involves mutuality which involves familiarity which leads to contempt.

Personal security, therefore, in the last resort has less to do with my own personal circle: resentful family members, envious friends, greedy colleagues, jealous rivals, than with *strangers*, with people who are identifiable as persons and who occupy my own social space but whose relationship to me is yet general, abstract, in a way impersonal. The threats coming to me from this last source are always, in principle, *one-sided*; I enter into the relationship only as (contingent) victim. Personal hostility – anger, envy, jealousy, resentment, vengefulness – might play a part here as well but it is subordinate and inessential. The key is *malevolent indifference* to me as a person. Malevolent indifference means not only the complete disregard meted out to me as a person but in addition also the implied feeling and intention that my interests, desires, security ought not to count at all, ought not to be in the way of this other person. I count here not just as zero but negatively: my bare existence disturbs the other whose conduct is directed towards my annihilation, if not physically then certainly in a moral sense. In this situation my being and my security become simply barriers to the other person, something to be overcome, to be brushed aside as insignificant in themselves while irritating to him. I become, in other words, a mere thing, a simple *means* to the designs of someone else who is pursuing his personal interest, whatever that might be, in total indifference to my personal security, malevolently regarding me as an obstacle in the way. As a victim I experience hostility, malevolence, but not in personal terms; my opponent does not know and recognize me as a concrete human being, and so is 'indifferent': but simultaneously my opponent hates me, despises me as a dumb, natural object. This is why this relationship typically, and one might say exclusively, involves strangers: only strangers, not acquaintances, can relate to me in this dualistic way, combining abstract malevolence and personal indifference. Here alone, and nowhere else essentially, the threat to my *personal* security is at the same time a direct negation of my basic, universal *humanity*. Strangers need not be indifferent and need not be malevolent. But they may always be both, I just don't know and have no sure means of knowing; this is why they are 'strangers', near and at the same time very far, recognizable and familiar externally as 'humans' but unfathomable in their inner, essential, concrete being as individual human persons. Our modern society, whatever else it might be, is one that contains *some* strangers, and to *some* of these an attitude of malevolent indifference towards me can always be attributed. This is what is really basic about 'society' regarded from the point of view of the individual person, this is why (and this is where – in one's relationship to strangers) the problem of personal security is an immediately 'social' problem while 'society' directly becomes a personal problem. Some political philosophers have certainly recognized the centrality of this issue, and its primary importance for a proper understanding of the modern state and society. Hobbes, who perhaps exaggerated and illegitimately generalized an historical predicament (let us reserve our judgment on this point for the time being), certainly hit the nail on the head and described a situation which, whether or not universal and perennial, is certainly and easily *recognizable* in our world today, by commenting on the basic relationship to strangers thus:

> It may seem strange to some man, that has not well weighed these things; that Nature should thus dissociate and render men apt to invade, and destroy one another: and he may therefore, not trusting to this Inference, made from the Passions, desire perhaps to have the same confirmed by Experience. Let him therefore consider with himselfe, when taking a journey, he armes himselfe, and seeks to go well accompanied; when going to sleep, he locks his dores; when even in his house he locks his chests; and this when he knowes there bee Lawes, and publike Officers, armed, to revenge all injuries shall bee done him; what opinion he has of his fellow subjects, when he rides armed; of his fellow Citizens, when he locks his dores; and of his children, and servants, when he locks his chests. Does he not there as much accuse mankind by his actions, as I do by my words?[3]

Even if we exclude 'children' and 'servants' as belonging to the relevantly different domestic situation, we can easily recognize this generalized 'accusation' in our own and others' manifest attitudes to strangers in general. Of course, Hobbes's point is that children and servants might also behave towards us *as though* they were strangers to whom malevolent indifference is at least a practical option: for him, in the last resort, all human beings are irreducibly strangers to one another, occupying a 'natural state' in which malevolent indifference is generalized. On the other hand, however, while we may not want to go as far as Hobbes in 'accusing' the whole of mankind as such, in defiance of common sense, and turning an historically encountered existential problem into an anthropological axiom, we ought it seems to me to go even further than he did, in explicitly including the 'laws' and 'armed public officers' in that general social group of strangers by whom our personal security can thus be constantly threatened. This is an important point to note. The problem of law and order as perceived today, properly understood and seen in its total depth and breadth, is really a double-sided problem, it is a problem not only *for* the forces of the law (the state) but also, at the same time and inseparably, a basic problem *of* the state and as presented *by* the state. The world of strangers, our modern society, is indeterminate as to the nature and extent of strangeness contained in it: not everybody, like loved ones and personal friends, acquaintances, is to be necessarily included, and not everybody, like bearers of the 'sovereign', is to be necessarily excluded. And here we come once again upon this elemental curiosity, interest, thrill, fascination: who are strangers? Why are there strangers in our 'own' society? Why do we find the presence of strangeness, and of strangers, in our midst so exciting and at the same time threatening? Why are people at all indifferent to me, and possibly hostile? In this chapter, later on, a preliminary view will be presented in the form of outlining some fundamental 'paradoxes of security', which relate, and perhaps explain up to a point, the perceptions and experiences referred to; in following chapters there will be further reflections dealing with this theme, connecting it with more conventionally oriented analyses of some familiar issues from the traditional arsenal of social and political philosophy.

But first a few more illustrations of the 'problem' itself might be in order. In today's Western world, Hobbes and his 'accusation' have achieved a state of prominence they do not seem to have had before, and in a more extended sense. In this relatively affluent, prosperous, industrialized, urbanized society the amount and quality of 'strangeness' characterizing personal relationships have become appreciably higher, embracing more and larger social groups and diluting families and close personal relations. A situation has been reached in which it is widely felt that the same kind (though not the same degree or amount) of personal insecurity is threatening all: men, women, young and old, the rich and powerful as well as the poor and downtrodden. And at the same time the 'state' itself – the appointed guardian of law and order – has suffered a definite lowering of estimation, in practically everybody's eye, conservative or radical. The state is now revealed as too feeble, ill-equipped to deal effectively with the threat of criminal and political violence; it is infused with misleading 'liberal' and 'progressive' principles, soft on law-breakers, indifferent to the fate of victims. But yet again the state now is itself seen as more threatening, more interfering, more in evidence as sheer power; while more people suffer today as victims of direct, individual or group-oriented lawlessness, also more people find themselves at the receiving end of legislation, administrative justice and law-enforcement, often of a petty, bureaucratic kind, typically encountered in matters relating to taxation, social security and traffic regulations. The law is both tyrannical and negligent; police 'brutality' goes with police inefficiency. Ordinary 'law-abiding' citizens think they *need* 'law-and-order' to provide protection against the malevolent indifference of strangers; but the same citizens find that their own relationship to law and order has become confused, ambiguous.

As J. E. Conklin writes in *The Impact of Crime*, referring to American cities, 'Fear of crime is fear of the stranger, the unknown person who commits an unpredictable and violent attack on a vulnerable and innocent citizen who is merely going about his regular business.' 'Fear of violence from strangers is generalized to fear of the streets . . .'[4] 'Deep-seated fears and concerns are aroused by crime, and the promise to re-establish law and order and to make the streets safe is an effective way to mobilize support. Crime is an even better target than Communism, because it affects everyone. It is both a realistic threat and a symbol of the breakdown of the social order.'[5] In J. Lea and J. Young's *What Is to Be Done about Law and Order?* we find the view expressed that the general fear and dislike of interpersonal violence have not to do just with physical injury or forfeited possessions but: 'Such crime involves another individual purposely and directly violating your property or self'.[6] 'In fact, malice is even more intentional in street crime than in war, because its individualism produces a collapse of human solidarity; in represents the palpable breakdown of the social order, or the rampant individualism of a Hobbesian war of all against all.'[7] (N.B. These two joint authors are by no means conservative 'law-and-order' protagonists but, like Ian Taylor cited earlier, criminologists of a radical persuasion.) Peter Marsh, in *Aggro: the Illusion of Violence* (again, not a conventional law-and-order treatise, quite the contrary!), has this to say concerning the current fear of burglary: 'The house becomes an extension of the family – a visible summary of its attitudes, ambitions and personal tastes. When we defend our home we defend something which is us. We defend it like we defend our own body.' 'The burglar becomes like the rapist who invades the ultimate privacy.'[8] From a more immediately recognizable conservative and Hobbesian point of view, Patricia Morgan in *Delinquent Fantasies* writes about 'the spread of what could be called a delinquent syndrome, a conglomeration of behaviour, speech, appearance and attitudes, a frightening ugliness and hostility which pervades human interaction, a flaunting of contempt for other human beings, a delight in crudity, cruelty and violence, a desire to challenge and humiliate and never, but never, to please . . .'[9] 'You may be abused for your class, your sex, your colour: that, in a way, you understand. But to be abused because you are someone who happens to be there, where even being your attacker's identical twin would not save you?'[10] Later in the same book the author also deals with the question of general public passivity in the face of delinquency. 'The simple answer is that they know to their cost that if they do [intervene], they will get no support whatever from the law and the authorities, and may even be in trouble themselves.'[11]

Just two more instances, taken from what is almost literally an ocean of public pronouncements of all possible kinds on the ubiquity and social significance of violence, crime, hostility, delinquency in this world of increasing and generalized strangeness. E. van den Haag, in *Punishing Criminals*, an insightful and sane treatise though generally classified as presenting a 'conservative' view on the current criminological spectrum, quotes from an essay by Margot Hentoff, herself a progressive writer, from the New York *Village Voice*, published in 1974. The essay is significantly entitled 'We Can't All Be Victims of Society' and the operative passage goes: '. . . An act of physical assault is a violation of that fundamental social contract which has as its basic compact the agreement that I can walk down the street and if I don't bother you, you won't bother me. If society has brutalized some people, there is no advantage in allowing the rest of us to be brutalized by the brutalized.'[12] When liberals, radicals, progressives begin to use terms like 'war of all against all' and 'basic compact', well known from the classical Hobbesian 'accusation', then one can be pretty certain that something rather strange is going on in our cosy Western world; it is, as we have been saying repeatedly, becoming more and more *strange*, strangely indifferent and strangely malevolent, as experienced in our individual lives, in the context of our own personal security – or the lack of it. And lastly under this heading let an 'ordinary' citizen speak for himself; this letter, from the *Hull Daily Mail* (28 March 1984), should perhaps be quoted in full, to get the flavour:

> I can well remember many an evening visiting the Regal Cinema right in the city centre, leaving my cycle in Ferensway and, after enjoying the show, coming out at around 10.30 p.m. clad in cycling kit, anorak, plus shorts. This in the gentle 1950s and 60s. Oh yes! There was a little titter or two – the British are well known for their reserve, modesty and rigid conservative laws. But no real trouble. Now, it seems, the boozers and troublemakers have taken over and for me to hark back to those days I would need to have a Bengal tiger on a chain, or a shotgun, or both. The violent ones who cannot visit the city centre without causing dismay and chagrin, to say the least, have practically ruined night entertainment.

As readers will have of course noted, this letter strikes a decidedly more moderate and tolerant chord than thousands of others found in the popular and local press all over the Western world; but it hence manages all the better to convey this general sense of puzzlement and estrangement that we are seeking to illustrate and comment on here. And just to furnish one instance highlighting the 'other side' of the law-and-order problem, viz. the public estimation of the state, we can refer to L. J. Macfarlane's observation in *Violence and the State* concerning erstwhile middle-class respect for state authority: '. . . this mutual respect has been somewhat undermined as increasing numbers of that class have come into conflict with the police as traffic offenders and as parents of delinquents, especially drug-offenders. Respect has been further eroded by the failure of the police to protect middle-class property and persons, and by evidence of corruption inside police forces.'[13] Gloom and doom are general.

The problem of law and order, as many writers have averred, is only one surface symptom of a much more deeply embedded malady ailing our modern Western world. Beyond visible lawlessness there are underlying and less tractable processes which have led to the problem in the first place, such as the waning of traditional authority, the decline of punishment, the virtual disappearance of religious faith and moral self-discipline, and the growth of permissive individualism. All these things, at any rate, seem to be connected in the eyes of conservative-minded writers, many of whom, be it noted, have become 'conservative' in conscious reaction to the changes they see occurring. 'Historically', as Hannah Arendt wrote back in the 1960s, 'we may say that the loss of authority is merely the final, though decisive, phase of a development which for centuries undermined primarily religion and tradition.'[14] Van den Haag has no explanation for the worldwide rise in crime rates: 'However, we do know one thing: there has been a worldwide decline in punishment and therewith of respect for law.'[15] The political scientist Ghita Ionescu, in his recent *Politics and the Pursuit of Happiness*, traces the growth of permissiveness and the resultant law-and-order problem thus:

> The main symptoms appeared in the moral and legal fields, creating a paralysis of the moral and legal norms, injunctions and institutions. The formula 'Law and Order' came to be singled out ironically as reactionary. Defiance of moral rules or legal provisions was regarded as a form of liberation. This rendered relations between authority (parents, teachers, police, judges, government) and the 'look back in anger' young men increasingly difficult. Moreover, the more difficult they became the more the demand for permissiveness grew. The political, legal or religious authorities which originally forbade 'immoral' actions or attitudes, were now urged to 'permit' them and encourage them.[16]

In a similar vein the novelist Pamela Hansford Johnson, shocked by her experience of the Moors Murder Trial in the 1960s, averred that: 'The error of the liberal humanists is that they have been unable to offer an alternative faith to the one they have renounced, except for faith in the beneficial effects of total permissiveness in every form of culture. This faith is a romantic one, even more romantic that Rousseau's. Once they ceased to believe even in the possibility of sheer iniquity and replaced this by a belief in Freud, they tore up the very stones of self-discipline and moral responsibility.'[17] Robert Nisbet finally, in *Twilight of Authority*, restates once again the Hobbesian argument: 'Of all the really fundamental desires in human life, protection is surely first: protection from the kind of violence or threat of violence that Hobbes made the very essence of the state of nature.' He goes on: 'There is irony as well as tragedy in the present relation of the political state to the maintenance of order in the hundreds, even thousands, of towns and cities in the West where today disorder has become the rule. . . .' 'In many respects this is the single greatest failing of the political community in the West at the present time . . .'[18]

None of this, of course, needs to be swallowed down entirely. If conservative views and writers – in this larger, spiritual and cultural sense of conservatism – have been given the centre of the stage in the foregoing pages, this is in order to bring home the gravity of the situation; the reality of a general, widespread 'law-and-order issue' in the Western world today, as we have seen earlier, is acknowledged also by writers of a radical predisposition. Radicals, who would by and large agree (in the 1980s, not so much in the 1960s and 1970s) with conservatives on the symptoms, obviously offer a very different diagnosis. Later on in this book, and particularly in Chapter 4, we shall take a closer look at some important views on both sides. It seems, however, that the departure – as distinguished from our destination – is more easily stated in conservative terms. The intended destination of our reflective journey – it might as well be stated now without any fudging – lies neither in adding yet another shrill voice to the law-and-order chorus nor in joining the equally vocal camp of debunkers, dismissers, dissolvers of the whole issue but in the transcendence, overcoming of one-sided, ideologically oriented opinions and perspectives. The problem of law and order, to paraphrase yet once again a well-worn cliché, is too important (and too interesting) to be left in the hands of 'professionals' in both the narrow and the wide sense: lawyers, law-enforcers, criminologists, psychiatrists, and politicians, religious leaders and writers committed to some overall definite *Weltanschauung*. The problem needs to be tackled philosophically, which means 'radically', in the proper sense, rising beyond conventional wisdoms on both left and right. Perhaps there might be a lesson here in this exercise for criminologists and other professional writers and observers with their noses close to the ground: the lesson that there is no small story without the big story, no scientific explanation without reflective probing into the 'science' itself, into underlying and unstated assumptions about the nature of human beings, human values and human society. And perhaps there is also a lesson here for traditional political philosophers, for academic thinkers with (as it has been said) 'feet firmly planted in mid-air': the lesson that there can be no big story without the small story, no adequate portrayal of morality, the state, law, order, social relationships, unless a simultaneous attempt is made to grasp these traditional concerns by focusing on what are really the key elements and the palpable, commonsensical starting point, i.e. personal security and the social-personal relationship to strangers.

Political philosophy, as understood here, is a reflective endeavour which builds on everyday views, perceptions, ordinary common sense. Concerning the problem of law and order, which we contend ought to be recognized as *the* basic problem for political philosophy (and political philosophy as *the* best appointed method whereby to make adequate sense of this problem in all its dimensions), the ground on which we must stand, and which we must become conscious of occupying, is the existential position of the ordinary, average, run-of-the-mill citizen or subject, men, women and children going about their business in our society. Law and order must in other words be brought down to this basic, elemental 'human' level and conceived as well as formulated as the problem of personal security: this is, without doubt, how it appears to the 'subject'. Thus our initial 'methodological' problem is already more or less decided for us. But if more explicit justification is needed for our taking this stand, i.e. fastening on the notion of personal security in the social context of the relationship to strangers as our departure, reference can again be made to a point already made earlier: if in nothing else, in relation to security and to the strangeness surrounding us, in relation to being 'subjects' at the receiving end of society and human actions and being contingent victims to malevolent indifference, we are today all 'equal' or at least see ourselves as being equal. Security is common to us all.

★ ★ ★ ★ ★ ★ ★ ★

The first thing then to establish – and it is time to embark on a bit of more serious 'philosophizing' – is that 'security' can well claim to be the chief human value, certainly for people as we know them and in the kind of society in which we live. Introspection, experience in communication and reflective analysis would all tend to confirm this. As the *Oxford English Dictionary* defines it, security means the condition of being protected from and not being exposed to danger; it means freedom from doubt or a state of self-assurance, certainty, well-founded confidence; and it means freedom from care, anxiety and apprehension. These are, as it were, the root meanings – protection, assurance, freedom – and they all have a positive connotation, all and together they compose a 'good', a fundamental 'value'. But let us note immediately that not all connotations of security are positive. A more archaic sense of security, also listed in the *O.E.D.* entry, is a more culpable, reprehensible absence of anxiety, i.e. carelessness. As we learnt it in Shakespeare's *Macbeth:* 'And you all know security/Is mortals' chiefest enemy' (Act III, Scene 5). And in *Julius Caesar* (Act II, Scene 3):

> There is but one mind in all these men, and it is bent against Caesar. If thou beest not immortal, look about you. Security gives way to conspiracy. The mighty gods defend thee!

This somewhat, or indeed more than somewhat, pejorative meaning of security is certainly relevant (though not immediately relevant) to our overall argument and it will be taken up again when we reach the climax of our reflective endeavour in this first chapter, namely when we come to the 'paradoxes' of security. Fastening on what have above been called the root meanings, however, it would appear quite obvious that security is the paramount value for self-conscious, rational, thinking individuals; indeed security is not just an external (and therefore contingent, optional) 'condition' of life and freedom but it is simply another word for, or another and more pointed definition of, life and freedom. Life and freedom would scarcely have any meaning without security. If security is at all to be made intelligible, it must be taken to refer to the sense, consciousness, knowledge of protection and freedom, the assurance that I can go on living as I please, an assurance in the continuation of my life-style, the carrying out of my plans, the unhindered performance of my consciously intended actions. In Patricia Morgan's pithy expression: 'Freedom lies in not having to calculate the risk to oneself on every journey outdoors . . .'[19]

The assertion that 'security' and 'life' are so intimately connected will probably not be seen as being too controversial; indeed the two terms almost appear to entail each other: 'living' means 'being in security' and 'security of life' means the 'duration, continuation of life' or simply 'life'. But the same is not true of freedom. Security is often contrasted to freedom and although I think this is ultimately a false and misleading contrast, it is to be conceded that the contrasting, the opposition, makes some immediate and superficial sense – in *one* sense of 'freedom', indeed, and although this is not the sense usually employed, it makes valid sense. This is the sense of freedom as 'unpredictability' and I shall make some comment on it later. In the main, however, the contrast usually occurs in the context of conventional political discussion where the two most commonly encountered meanings of freedom are the so-called 'negative' meaning (favoured by conservatives) and the so-called 'positive' meaning (supporting radical positions and arguments). That is, freedom usually means *either* 'absence of external constraints and coercion' *or* 'ability to perform rationally intended actions', and varieties (as well as combinations) of these two stances. There is no need to go into further detail here; we can cut a very long, tortuous and somewhat tedious story quite short. In the first place, it would seem to me to be eminently sensible to argue that a proper understanding of freedom for human beings in society requires the acceptance of *both* these senses and their real synthesis (bringing in also the sense of freedom as unpredictability). In the second place, I would contend that freedom does not properly contrast to security either in the positive or in the negative or in their combined sense, and conversely security does not negate freedom (except in the sense of unpredictability). Superficially one can understand by security a situation of restriction and confinement, of either dependence or isolation, circumstances where there are walls, in the metaphorical or literal sense, erected around the individual, providing him 'protection' from danger outside and allowing him 'freedom' within this confined area. The higher and firmer the 'walls' or vaster the distances, the better to enjoy security; and correspondingly there is less 'freedom' available.

But this superficial reasoning is false, as I hope two simple examples will show. Firstly, we can take solitary confinement in a 'top security' prison to be a relevant situation where 'security' is gained at the expense and forfeiture of freedom. The individual concerned here is certainly unfree, in that he has not the ability and opportunity to leave his cell; and I submit we ought not to quibble as to whether he would actually like to depart from his prison cell: our hypothetical subject is the rational, conscious human individual for whom both security and freedom make sense. So freedom here is largely absent, but what sort of 'security' is gained by the person in question? It should be quite obvious that the individual in prison has no security whatsoever but is on the contrary experiencing insecurity in the highest degree; the more restricted, more confined, more 'protected' from the outside he is, the more *insecure* his position becomes. High and firm walls, locked doors, solitary confinement, signify the 'security' of the prison warders and the 'society' represented by them but not the security of the prisoner. It is security *against* the individual, not *for* the individual; for the latter it is the total loss of security which is thus equivalent to the total loss of his freedom. The prisoner *might* be protected from certain things by the walls, etc. but the point about this 'protection' is that it is contingent, arbitrary, uncertain. The individual is not really protected but totally exposed and dependent, an object deprived of his power and effective rationality, a mere means to the designs and intentions of others. The door is locked but it can be opened at any time by the warders who alone have the key; the prisoner is fed regularly but food can be withheld from him at any moment; he may be left in solitude and 'peace' most of the time but there is nothing *he* can do to prevent his warders neglecting, mistreating or abusing him. Security thus, it seems, cannot very well be equated with *dependence;* the latter, whatever positive aspects it might have and even though we might concede its minimal necessity (as 'social' dependence on other individuals, of which the prison situation is merely the logically most extreme and radical example), can scarcely be regarded as a paramount value for individuals in human society.

But if total dependence cannot validly be presented as security, do we fare better with an attempt to define security in terms of total *independence?* The situation is somewhat more complicated here but I think the conclusion is the same: what might appear at first as perfect security in independent isolation, bought, similarly to the prison situation, at the price of forfeiting freedom, is not security at all but insecurity. Let us conjure up an island in the ocean, far from everywhere, inhabited by a single individual who has gone to live there by his own choice, in his quest after perfect security. It is he himself now, and not the prison builders and warders and society at large, who erects unscalable walls around the island, manufactures and instals a roof of reinforced concrete, steel doors with complicated locks, look-out towers, and in addition equips himself with an early-warning radar system and heat-seeking missiles. Certainly the person is 'free' here only in the very restricted, almost farcical sense of being able to walk around his island undisturbed and fondle his weaponry; but this 'freedom' is no more significant than the 'freedom' of the prisoner in solitary confinement to scratch his backside when itching or, if he gets shackled as well as confined, to think beautiful thoughts. In both cases, freedom in any meaningful sense is absent, lost or given away. But in what sense exactly is the person on this fortress island 'secure'? In a very contrived sense indeed, and not in the sense in which security could reasonably be held up as the chief human value, equivalent to life and freedom. Electing to go and live in this situation of unsplendid isolation, in the first place, presupposes an initial fear concerning the designs of other human beings. Even if this fear is imaginary, the person on the island will continue to lead a life of misery, constantly expecting attacks from the outside world. However strong his fortifications and armoury he will still feel insecure; the walls are a continuing reminder of the, presumably hostile, world from which he endeavoured to escape. It is *also* ultimately a situation of dependence, felt to be so. And if the person's fears were well founded in the first place, then of course his situation of insecurity will continue: no conceivable amount of fortifications and weaponry could provide for adequate protection against opponents who must be supposed to have access to similar means and in greater quantities, used not for defence but to attack. Indeed, in this hypothetical situation, the hostile world beyond the walls of the island and the expanse of the sea is infinitely more powerful than the isolated island-dweller; it can continually renew its resources, while the island will get weaker and weaker. It is merely a matter of time before fortifications crumble and the sought-after 'security' evaporates totally. So once again, freedom and security prove inseparable: if one goes, so does the other.

These two, rather contrived and sketchily described, examples might well serve to epitomize some commonly found attitudes characterizing the general quest after security in the actual world: the prisoner's situation is not entirely unlike the situation of those who hope and expect to find security under the protection of an all-powerful state, the island-dweller might be taken to resemble those 'fierce individualists' who prefer to look after themselves and have no love or care for society outside. Both these rather extreme attitudes lead to a dead end, as we shall endeavour to show later in greater detail, in the concluding part of these reflections: too much reliance on 'society' just as much as too little involvement with society are inimical to the attainment of personal security, they are both irrational and self-defeating. For now, however, two further and more basic points will have to be made, following on from the above examples and considerations, and serving to clarify a little the position we have reached up to now.

Firstly, we may have been somewhat simplistic in directly equating life and freedom on the one hand and the value of security on the other. Even if the equation works up to a point, it still does not follow that 'life' and 'freedom' have no transcendent elements or aspects which are not easily subsumable under security. Or, to put it in other words, it might appear unduly restrictive, if not downright false and contradicted at least by introspective evidence, if we simply elevated security as the 'chief' human value. What about, to confine ourselves for now to the individual person (the social dimension will be looked at later), such unquestionable values as happiness, self-fulfilment or the 'good life'? Are they not, in some important and relevant sense, higher than security and security is just a means to them? This is not, however, quite the case. It has, I hope, been established sufficiently convincingly earlier that security cannot validly be considered a mere contingent 'means' to life and freedom, since it is utterly inconceivable to live, and to act freely, in a condition of insecurity. And if a 'means' is shown to be absolutely necessary to the attainment of an 'end', then the means, as a good many philosophers have argued in the past, must be classed as an integral aspect of that end. Separation is pointless and illogical. Now up to a point this does appear to hold in relation to security and the (presumably general) end of individual happiness or self-fulfilment. In no way can you achieve a state of happiness or fulfil, realize yourself, unless your happiness is a 'state', i.e. has some duration, or unless it is possible for you to perform actions which themselves express, or go towards, the realization of yourself, your potential. And duration or continuation immediately brings in security. But this is valid only up to a point, as it is quite possible to conceive of a person who lives in freedom, i.e. has security in what he wants to do, and who yet still feels unhappy or unfulfilled. There is an extra dimension involved here which it is difficult to capture and define clearly. One way, though it is rather a bland way, not very illuminating, to deal with this is to say that while security is the 'necessary condition' of happiness and the good life, and thus inseparable, it is not a 'sufficient condition'. But this of course amounts to no more than restating the problem in different terms. Why is security not a sufficient condition? Perhaps we will get a little bit further if we approach the matter thus: security (as life and freedom) has to do with the person's *objective* world, it refers to the 'outside', its presence or absence being in principle (and for that very reason) easily ascertainable. But happiness and self-realization, though necessarily partaking of this objective, outside world, contain as values an irreducibly *subjective* element also; in the last resort 'happiness' cannot be fully explained, described, rationally communicated; it must be felt. Now this *internal* world reaches beyond security, without leaving it entirely behind; and security could then be defined, in this modified form, as the chief epitome, summarized expression, of all *external* human values, those that, as it were, help to 'frame' or 'embody' internal or subjective values, like self-fulfilment, happiness or the good life. But still, there is little point in attempting a means-end separation: security (life, freedom, continuation, assurance) is not a means to happiness but an integral part of it, though not the whole of it. The internal, subjective world rises to an opaque cloud, its external counterpart is visible and intelligible but, by the same token, appears as trimmed, truncated. Once we grasp the connection, the inseparable link between inner and outer, subjective and objective, we are well guarded against the mistake of dismissing, under-valuing the good of security.

The second and probably less abstruse point, as coming out of our examples, concerns the element of 'dependence' involved in the quest after security. In some sense and in some measure, security positively involves *society*, that is, other human beings around, and related to, the individual person. Of course, society has from the very beginning been involved *negatively* in security as we defined it: personal security has to do above all with contingent threats to the person issuing from other persons (rather than with 'natural' causes). Society thus has to be brought in to counter society – let this stand as an initial statement of the underlying 'paradoxes' of security we shall be discussing below. First, however, it has to be established that the positive involvement of other human beings *is* really necessary. Our second illustration has shown this, I think, quite convincingly (the first one, too, but in a more roundabout way). A person who, like our pitiable character on the fortified desert island, wants to attain perfect security against the threats of other people by isolating himself from human society altogether, not only sinks himself into complete dependence on finite external nature, on decaying machinery, and thus comes into a state of insecurity *vis à vis* his own objective defence apparatus (what if the radar system short-circuits?), but at the same time fails to find security against other human beings this way. The more 'independent' he becomes in this manner, the greater is his *negative* dependence on his hypothetical foes: in the last resort it is only the actual intentions of those outside which will decide whether he is left in peace or an attack is launched on the island. (Note the essential similarity to the situation of the prisoner *vis à vis* his warders.) The only way in which the island-dweller's security could *really* be achieved is by increasing his positive dependence on others and correspondingly reducing his isolation; in this case it would mean, presumably, assembling an army of bodyguards, mechanics to service his rocket-launchers, a fleet of submarines to patrol the waters around the island, spies and informers planted among his would-be enemies, PR people and propagandists to weaken aggressive resolve in the enemy camp, and finally also genuine allies whose interests coincide with his own and who therefore can be counted on to act spontaneously in his favour, i.e. staving off the otherwise inevitable attack. And in the case of the prisoner in solitary confinement, again the question to ask is how he can possibly reduce his absolute, and absolutely negative, dependence on the arbitrary and hostile power of his prison warders? Unless he is as strong as Samson or has a magic power over stone walls and locked steel doors (but he isn't and hasn't, otherwise he would not have suffered this fate), he can only do this by relying on help from and positive dependence on other human beings. 'Society' in this instance, of course, would take a rather different form: a group of cronies who organize a daring escape, insurrectionists storming the Bastille, weeping wife and children imploring the chief warder for mercy, friends launching a petition to be presented to the ministry of the interior, Amnesty International launching a campaign, etc., etc. It is instructive to see, in both these contrived and seemingly outlandish examples, how quickly and smoothly and inevitably we are led back towards the real world, gaining a glimpse of the principal ways in which personal security is *actually* sought after, managed and organized.

Security and society, then, hang together and form an existentially (if not logically) inseparable unity in at least two important positive ways. In the first instance, security expresses the highest individual human value to the outside, i.e. towards society. Our own happiness is *for us* in the last analysis 'internal' but as a social value externally it is manifested as the universal quest after security. Towards society at large, even if not towards every single human being (we don't have to go all the way with Hobbes in postulating a totally individualistic state of nature), we present ourselves as seekers after security; man as a social being is above all a security-seeking animal. And in the second instance, the individual person has an absolute, inescapable dependence on society for the attainment of his security. This dependence takes a variety of forms and correspondingly 'society' in this respect displays a great multitude of appearances and manifestations. There is a range or spectrum which leads from single individuals, like friends, comrades, kith and kin, to formalized institutions. In the world today as we know it, with special but not exclusive reference to advanced industrial and urbanized societies, larger groupings and formal institutions play, of course, a much greater role. On the one hand, we do not, for the most part, consciously stand *vis à vis* other people as isolated individuals but as 'particulars' (sharers of group identities, values and concerns) and as 'universals' (partakers of moral practices, citizens of states), and thus the quest after security (the provision of life and freedom) goes considerably beyond the aim of sheer physical survival. People in modern society, as T. R. Gurr has expressed it, have the basic need for 'power' to provide for their own security through participation in social life, in 'stable supportive groups' like the family, and 'the sense of certainty that derives from shared adherence to beliefs about the nature of society and one's place in it, and to norms governing social interaction.'[20] And on the other hand, it is in modern Western urban and industrial society precisely that an almost overwhelming and exclusive reliance in matters of personal security is placed on the state, on governmental and judicial offices, law-enforcement agencies and penal institutions. The public, as N. C. M. Elder has recently put it, see themselves primarily as 'consumers of security';[21] hence the immediate linkage between personal security and the highly general issue of 'law and order'. Perhaps, indeed, this – rather than our advanced scientific technology – is the most important distinguishing mark of our modern Western civilization as compared to others; the fact and expectation that the security of the single individual person is best left in the hands of the state, the most general, formal and abstract of all social formations. It is as though, at first appearance at any rate, the anonymous and ubiquitous threat posed by a society of strangers is being expected to be overcome by the state, this supremely 'strange' institution. Whether or not we choose to assign to the state some supererogatory functions as well (e.g. taking the view that the state owes us a living) and whether or not it is correct to look upon the state as an external and 'artificial' institution merely, one whose job and sole essential *raison d'être* is the provision of security – this would, in fact, be an incorrect view, as we shall argue later – there can be scarcely any doubt that the state is universally regarded as being *more* important in this field than any other social grouping or institution.

★ ★ ★ ★ ★ ★ ★ ★

But let us stop here and pause for a moment. Things are not as simple as they might appear, and I don't refer here merely to the immediate practicalities involved in the provision of security by 'society' in general and by the 'state' in particular. There are also difficulties, intricacies involved in the underlying values, ideas, principles themselves. There is something odd, perplexing – and also, recalling an earlier point, something definitely thrilling – in this whole situation. Already we have had definite glimpses of the peculiarities to be encountered in our passing references above to the connection between security on the one hand, and freedom and happiness on the other, and to the fact that society is both negatively and positively involved in the problem of personal security. The quest after security is not only universal: it is also universally and irreducibly *paradoxical*. What do I mean by 'paradoxical'? I mean that security, as a concept and as a value, has as it were a double or plural nature and that its ultimate sense or meaning or significance is revealed only when we approach it and endeavour to grasp it in terms of a range of conceptual oppositions. It is my view, in other words, and it will be argued throughout these reflections, that a paradoxical approach or the adoption and achievement of what I shall be calling here a *plural perspective* is ultimately the most satisfactory way in which to grasp the nature of this perplexing and fascinating problem; the paradoxical way is the only truly radical and fundamental way, the only one that remains 'philosophical' through and through. It is therefore this paradoxical quality of security that has to be got hold of first, prior to our embarking on our more detailed and concrete analyses of all the other issues involved. It seems to me, furthermore, that this basic and fascinating quality of our concept can most conveniently be presented in terms of *four* distinct dualities which will be termed here respectively the social, the moral, the political and the existential paradox.

The *social* paradox of security is the one that is immediately connoted by the term itself, as employed generally in the discussion of law and order and related issues. The departure, inevitably, is the recognition that I, as an individual person, am vulnerable to others in the society we all inhabit and share, that I must concern myself with possible threats to my life and freedom caused by the actions of others, most typically those whom I regard as 'strangers'. This basic initial situation ought not to be taken for granted and left just like that as 'datum'; it may or may not be radically alterable but in either event it has a peculiar significance now, for the present, and this has to be precisely noted and defined for the purposes of reflective philosophical analysis. The significance lies surely in the fact that my individual vulnerability is not unique to me but is an integral aspect of my 'humanity', the very species-character that I *share* with those who might pose threats to my existence. There is, as Hobbes noted in his 'state of nature', an underlying equality of human beings manifested in their mutual vulnerability; they are all not only strong and intelligent enough to be able to harm one another but also their peculiar isolation in the natural state might always make them behave with direct hostility or malevolent indifference towards their fellows. But the point can (and should) be put even more strongly than was the case with Hobbes (and his like-minded followers) who developed his insight in a metaphysical direction, operating with unitarily (non-paradoxically) defined concepts and sharp moral dichotomies. The paradoxical point, surely, is that in this hypothetical 'natural state' (which is gained by abstracting from the existing, recognizable social state its barest essential features) *common humanity* is both asserted and at the same time denied. It is asserted in the clear recognition of exposure to danger in one's universal human capacity: it is because I am essentially like others around me that I am exposed to their actions and designs; I am flesh-and-blood like them, weak and strong like them, rational and purposive like them. I recognize myself in other human beings and I can tell them as human beings only because I see, feel and know them as being like me, led by similar desires, governed by the same kind and range of emotions, controlled by the same thoughts. There would be no meaning whatever to individuality, individual self-consciousness, were it not predicated on the consciousness of common universal humanity; it is as a human being that I become conscious of myself as individual and particular, with an 'inner' life and with relative differences in life-styles, pursuits, social positions. Self-identification as belonging to the species is fundamental to individuality, to what counts as 'human' life and to freedom as the essential defining characteristic of individual self-consciousness.

Identification, however, does not go all the way but it is, as it were, denied in the very act itself. The sense of common humanity is immediately interpenetrated by the sense of difference or strangeness. Humanity is not absolute but is rent in two in its very innermost essence. Identification is self-contradictory: on one level and from one given perspective it does go all the way (in the last resort I am nothing *but* a human being, and others around me likewise) but from another, and inseparable, perspective it stumbles on the rock of recognition that there is yet a *gap* between myself as an individual person and others. Humanity is thus a unity of unity and difference. The gap belongs to it just as much as the two spreads, expanses divided by it. Being human means both being *at ease* with others, as my own extensions, images, replicas, and being *on guard* against them, so that they will not absorb me and annihilate me but remain just extensions and replicas. As we posed the question rhetorically earlier: who are strangers? Why should there be strangers in society in this fundamental sense, 'units' who are so essentially like me, on whose presence around me I absolutely rely for being what I am, a human being, and yet from whom I am divided by this unbridgeable gap? The gap is not always unbridgeable, to be sure; as has been argued above, we do not need to postulate a total Hobbesian state of nature. But it is undeniable that there *are* strangers in this sense: people whose relevant characteristic is precisely this, that with them our common humanity is not perfectly shared, and who are therefore perceived by us to be potential threats to our personal existence and the continuation of our humanity. Of some people most of the time, and of most people at least some of the time, we think and feel that they are somehow distant and thus 'imperfectly human', like us and yet more unfamiliar and different than inanimate nature or created objects. I can, at least in principle if not in practice, become reasonably familiar with the forces of nature and the qualities of artefacts, can to a certain extent control them, predict their movements and processes, deal with their contingent threats as presented to me in the pursuit of my life. Nature and objects are near, cosy, familiar because they are *unlike* me. Only human beings remain mysterious and that is because they are *like* me.

A further recognition – which will be developed more fully in the next paragraph – is that 'strangers' in this sense share with us exactly the same quality of 'strangeness' which we ourselves feel and display in our relationship with them. Either my differential individuality creates the strangeness of others or it is this gap itself which reaches into my own self-consciousness and generates an internal dimension of strangeness: I appear ultimately as a stranger to myself, a 'self' divided off from but at the same time interpenetrating my consciousness of universal humanity. Now it seems to me that we can only begin to appreciate the full significance – and curious fascination – of the problem of personal security if we first grasp this basic 'social paradox': security is an underlying problem, or *the* underlying problem, of human social existence precisely because it defines the relationship of units which are identical and yet separated in and by virtue of their common identity. I am conscious of the need for security against others because I 'know' them to be basically like myself; my relative 'ignorance' of them presupposes this elemental knowledge and sharing. In society I am exposed, not just to people who are like me, but in the last resort to my own images, my own extensions – in one succinct phrase, to myself, as projected outwards and as I appear in the guise of 'strangeness'. This is why personal security, as well as being a primal *desire* and an immediate *problem*, also suggests the *possibility* of its attainment and its solution: as my life is a continual and conscious process of trying to come to terms with my internally differentiated 'self', my humanity as shared with the species, as it is refracted through my particular identity and position within society, and as it is experienced inwardly as a unique, individual manifestation of humanity, so my conscious life is *also* an attempt to come to terms with the actual strangeness perceived in my universe, with the strangeness of myself as experienced in my relation to others. We live by this desire, with this problem, and in this perpetual hope.

Let us now turn this basic social paradox inward, and it will reveal itself to us as a *moral* paradox, also entailed in the problem of personal security. We have to focus now on the individual person as the seeker after security in society. We fear strangers on account of their relative distance, or the 'imperfect humanity' attributed to them. This imperfect humanity, involving the constant possibility of personal hostility and even more relevantly the possibility of malevolent indifference, turns out on reflection, however, to be nothing else than the *freedom* which we recognize in the being of others, as the essential defining feature of their humanity. Freedom here connotes not just the desire to be autonomous in making decisions and performing actions but also the unpredictability of individual conduct: I fear others because of their humanity and *because* (and for no other reason really) their humanity entails the possibility of their interpreting this humanity in an infinite number of ways, some more and some less advantageous from my own point of view, and some being conceived by me as in their nature 'threatening'. Seeking personal security against others means the endeavour to reduce this aspect of their freedom and make them appear, and conduct themselves, more like natural or created objects. Now the question to ask is this: who am I, as this person seeking to reduce the freedom of others? It is obvious that as a security-seeker I am in the business of endeavouring to enlarge my own freedom, at the expense of other human beings. The freer they are the more insecure I feel; the greater my security the more I can limit, circumscribe, curtail, contain the unpredictability of those to whom I am related. Of course in this whole endeavour it is presupposed that I conceive myself as a 'free' being from the very start, since I believe that the attainment of my own security is 'possible', i.e. that there is a real 'movement', as it were, from desire to purpose and thence to action and result. The main point is, however, that my own freedom entailed in my quest after security, my own unpredictability and (as it appears to others) infinite possibility of interpreting 'humanity' in more or less advantageous ways for myself, make *me* an immediate and identical threat to the security of others, to whom I manifest myself as a 'stranger'. Seeking after security for oneself and being a cause of insecurity for others are not just closely related: they are the same thing, with no chance of either logical or existential separation. As a seeker and consumer of security I am also defining myself as a producer of insecurity: that's what I am. When the chips are down – and in a sense, and to a certain degree, they are *always* down – it is 'humanity' outside, my fellow human beings in society, or it is 'humanity' inside, as represented by myself. It is my life, my freedom, my security *versus* the rest of the human race. I, too, turn hostile when I feel threatened, I too display an attitude of malevolent indifference – often without noticing it! – when I think that my situation demands it. Security, it may have seemed at first, implies only self-referential humanity (i.e. a perception of vulnerability of self by the person) but in truth it also means self-preferential humanity. Again, there is no need to extend this 'zero-sum game' of security to all other persons with whom I might come into contact – it may well be a choice between the life and freedom of 'my loved ones' and the life and freedom of others outside the charmed circle – as long as *some* differentiation is made within the larger category of humanity. It is argued here that for all relevant intents and purposes it can be taken for granted that this internal distinction *is* drawn in the general quest for personal security; that this is part and parcel of security-seeking in society as we know it; and that genuine, consistent and total humanitarianism is a pretty rare phenomenon indeed, more often encountered in rhetoric than in actual practice.

What is, however, 'moral' in this evidently paradoxical situation? Morality comes in, and one could in fact reasonably argue that here lies the simplest, most commonsensical explanation for the entry of morality into human consciousness, in so far as we begin to sense this basic discrepancy in our conduct involved in the quest after security. I contradict my own universal humanity by my effort to ensure exclusive or primary security for my own person but I also feel that this is somehow 'wrong'. Being human I 'ought' to conduct myself as a human, i.e. without any kind of internal differentiation within the species. (Extreme moral absolutists would of course want to draw the line even further and include animals, sentient beings or the whole of 'nature' in this morally protected category. This doesn't matter, as long as the category is wide enough to include *at least* the human race.) However, our inevitable natural inclination (it seems) is to do just that, to draw continually such distinctions. It is for this reason that we need some restraint, some sort of emotional and rational power within us, some voice inside which echoes the authentic voice of humanity outside, to keep our search for personal security in check. The voice of morality is inside, it is subjective, but its binding character is a result undoubtedly of its external connection, its being an inner representation of the objective world. Morality can thus be taken to be the ideal representation of humanity towards and in the consciousness of the individual person. We become aware of it as a binding 'law', issuing categorical 'commands' to be obeyed unconditionally, overriding the desire after personal security. Morality thus completes the self-awareness of humanity but at the same time it heightens the internal tension involved in this awareness. From now on the quest after security assumes a more complex character: I recognize legitimate and illegitimate, justifiable and unjustifiable, ways in which my life and freedom can be protected. I might, for example, be morally permitted to disarm a would-be attacker in the street but not seriously to injure him; it is legitimate to enhance my security by investing money in shares but illegitimate to steal or embezzle money for the same purpose. Most of us most of the time do behave 'morally' in this basic sense, i.e. in recognition of the binding character of these universal commands limiting the scope of our actions, but morality nevertheless does not entirely govern human life *in practice*. The consciousness of morality is no doubt 'natural' in the sense that it is not contingent with normal, sane human beings, and not entirely a result of education or 'socialization' (various moral norms can be taught but not an elemental sense of right and wrong). But morality is not and cannot be natural in the same sense in which the desire after personal security is; the two clash at every point. I know very well that I cannot be relied on with absolute certainty (anything approaching certainty, really) to follow the dictates of morality on every occasion in the future, and this is especially so in matters explicitly relating to my personal security. Since security is a human *value*, i.e. I feel and understand the need for it as a universal human being (as we have seen above), I know also that I ought to pursue it in a genuinely 'human' way, that is, not making an exception in my own personal case; but of course from the other side, the 'natural' side, the quest after personal security means precisely making this very exception. Thus my basic human pursuit is at the same time an inhuman or anti-human pursuit. As I cannot trust others to behave in this perfectly human way to me, so others cannot trust me, and moreover I cannot trust myself. Thus, as I have to ascribe 'imperfect humanity' to others around me in society at large, so on introspective reflection I have to attribute imperfect humanity also to myself. It is my own individual, consciously felt and rationally understood 'freedom' then which makes me into both a member and an enemy of the human race, as the formally identical freedom of others renders them simultaneously into my foes and fellows.

At this point we become aware of the third underlying duality involved with the quest after personal security, the one that I have termed the *political* paradox. The crucial point here is the internal differentiation we constantly make within the human species, a process which is involved in the quest after personal security and which, as we have seen above, is what leads directly (though paradoxically) to the experience of morality. Politics is predicated on, indeed it is the direct and concrete expression of, this process of differentiation or particularization within society, the division of human beings into – actual or potential – allies and enemies. In fact, the necessity for politics in the quest after security can be seen to arise in two ways. Firstly, from the angle of society or the social paradox: in order to attain personal security I must depend on some part of society as a bulwark against other parts of society; I must rely, for the protection of my life and limb and the playing out of my basic human quality of freedom, on some people around me most of the time and on most people some of the time. We recognize, that is, in society at large people who are close to us and who we feel can and must be 'trusted'. Here we reckon (normally) first of all members of our immediate family, our friends, everyday acquaintances, professional colleagues and others – an indefinite group – who are 'like us' in apparently important and relevant ways; furthermore we reckon here the representatives of the generalized security agencies of society; policemen, security-guards, judges, lawyers, soldiers, 'officials' of all kinds. Let us not for a moment be mistaken on this absolutely vital point; the reliance for personal security on the 'state' in general, on the 'rule of law', on principles of 'impartial justice', on the 'police', on the constitution', on our legally defined 'rights', or even on a supposed elemental 'decency' of people in the abstract, always and inevitably boils down to reliance on *some* actual individual human beings. Covenants, to paraphrase again and at the same time critically develop the Hobbesian argument, are mere words, absolutely meaningless and inconsequential willows in the wind, without the 'sword'. But the further and highly relevant point is that the 'sword' must be wielded by a *friendly* hand. Otherwise the sword won't protect me, and might even be employed directly against me, whatever 'rights' I may have on paper.

Everything in society that is usually counted a 'safeguard' between the individual person and potential threats to his life and freedom must be translated into personal terms and mediated by other persons who interpret and apply these safeguards in the required way, e.g. a policeman who actually believes my story and acts upon it, a lawyer who sympathizes with my case, a sympathetic judge or MP or newspaper reporter, etc. In the absence of this personal ring around me the constitution is worse than useless and the 'commonwealth' carries on, reproduces the most terrifying kind of 'state of nature'. A lot of people, indeed, in our civilized and ordered modern society find themselves in this situation: alone, exposed, the whole weight of the commonwealth stacked against them. There are predicaments like that suffered by Hawkins, in Godwin's *Caleb Williams:*

> It was mere madness in him to think of contesting with a man of Mr Tyrrel's eminence and fortune. It was a fawn contending with a lion. Nothing could have been more easy to predict, than that it was of no avail for him to have right on his side, when his adversary had influence and wealth, and therefore could so victoriously justify any extravagancies that he might think proper to commit. This maxim was completely illustrated in the sequel. Wealth and despotism easily know how to engage those laws as the coadjutors of their oppression, which were perhaps at first intended . . . for the safeguards of the poor.

It really ought to be obvious why politics, in the shape of generalized institutional arrangements intended (among other things) for the protection of individual life and freedom, and predicated on differential 'trust' among members of society, never works perfectly but instead presents us with yet another interesting paradox. The point is that the division of society into those who are trustworthy in the required sense and those who are not is ultimately arbitrary, uncertain, nothing more than conventional. It might at best only lessen but will not entirely eradicate the felt presence of 'strangeness' in society; if we do recognize such a thing as a Hobbesian 'state of nature', it must be recognized as being demonstrably present in the so-called civilized state. Human beings remain human beings: security-seekers themselves, free, unpredictable, with the constant option of hostility or malevolent indifference. This of course works in two ways. Complete strangers can turn friendly, supposed social rivals and greedy opponents can show an unexpected 'human' face, but likewise my closest friend and comrade-in-arms can change into my bitterest enemy, and the agencies of the state can present themselves towards me in directly contrary ways. In the last resort we do, I suppose, tend to rely on those for support and protection who are 'like us', which is really laughable: can we ever trust ourselves?

Secondly, the paradox of politics in the context of the problem of personal security comes to the fore also if approached from the angle of morality. As an individual, 'rational' human being I am normally conscious of some kind of higher moral law binding on me: I accept that I always ought to act in such a way as to produce, maintain and enhance *general* security in society, including my own and that of my 'loved ones' but not making an exception in their case or my case. I must thus act as a nameless, impartial, impersonal guardian of the 'law', keep the peace, restrain others as well as myself if they pose a threat to general security, work with and for appointed social institutions, and so on. Now let us assume that the individual person does actually intend to carry on as a proper universal moral agent and that he more or less succeeds in doing so, keeping his own personal, individual 'self' in the background and in harness. The question is: *how* does he act? What kinds of social and moral action are actually possible for him, in the concrete context of society? The answer is that in every possible instance he is confronted by politics and must therefore act politically; it is politics, or *particular* differentiation, which mediates between the universal realm of morality and the individual moral actor. I act as a 'particular': a policeman, a middle-class businessman, a liberal or socialist, a frightened mother or father, a football supporter, a foundry worker, a shop steward, a stamp collector. Now at one point – and we shall have the opportunity later to see in more concrete detail as to why, how and when – this political character will be prone to clash with and contradict the universal moral character of my action. I cannot, *in practice*, help but express differential preference, and this means in the present context a differential evaluation of the personal security of people thus divided into particular groupings. These groupings can be defined in many diverse ways (e.g. in terms of objective qualities, like gender, height, age, etc.) but essentially, in respect of their contact and relationship with other groups, they come to the fore as having different *interests* or perceived relative advantages; these interests may be dovetailing and harmonious up to a point but they may, in theory as well as in practice, also be conflicting. And this situation does make a difference to the quest after personal security, especially as regards its attainment. That is to say, on this level, as distinguished from the more abstract and fundamental level of 'strange' individuals whom we have encountered in the discussion of the 'social paradox' above, security manifests itself as a *scarce* good and it is distributed differentially. The more I or we have it, the less will remain for others. With the best intentions in the world and our impeccably universal and 'moral' standpoint, you cannot *equally* promote the security-seeking interests of stock-brokers and coalminers, of fathers and sons, of boisterous football supporters and fearful elderly spinsters inhabiting the vicinity of football grounds. Fully impartial action is impossible – or at least, we should say, highly problematic – in a situation which is *itself* 'partial', in a social world which is made up of differing and conflicting parts. It is in politics that we become aware of the difficulty. Politics thus, to conclude briefly on this point, presents us with a double-sided paradox: as a 'subject' at the receiving end of the actions and conduct of others I must always absolutely rely on those outside who are less than absolutely reliable, and as a moral 'agent' acting universally I must, by virtue of the particularity of my own existence and the existence of conflicting groups, act in such a way as will tend to negate universal morality.

And now we reach the final and most fundamental paradox of security. This, for want of a more dramatic and expressive term, I am calling here the 'existential' paradox, as it reveals most acutely the internal tension and discrepancy involved in the general and elemental 'seeking' of security itself, on the bare personal level. I do seek and desire security above everything else, since security is the external side of my very existence, it is equivalent to my life and to my freedom. Yet on probing it turns out that this primary and inescapable quest after personal security is really and just as inescapably negated by both 'life' and 'freedom'. Life means above all temporal duration, the continuation of my conscious existence. It is movement in time and space. But it is not infinite movement. For us, as finite human individuals, life not only has a definite 'conclusion', being equivalent to its cessation, but also while in movement it has the character of basic unknowability and unpredictability. We don't know when the end will come and how it will come, and we cannot be sure what the next minute holds for us. Living means being constantly exposed to dangers and contingencies, lurking around the next corner and in the next moment. Life in this fundamental sense is constant 'war', perpetual readiness against the unknown, the future, and against its own continuing movement. Existence perpetually contradicts itself and the contradiction is 'resolved' only in the termination of existence. Perfect 'security' is found only in death, in perfect repose, when of course the quest after security itself becomes completely meaningless. By wanting security, therefore, in order ostensibly (and consciously) to protect and prolong our lives, we are really courting insecurity, nay, actually engaging in the quest after *insecurity*. This plurality, as it were, of personal existence enters of course into our consciousness in many different ways but at least it does point towards an explanation as to why people are so often ready to take risks with their lives, to play with and contingently sacrifice their *overall* existence for the sake of gaining a variety of smaller, more immediate 'existences' (a phenomenon which Hobbes found incomprehensible and ascribed to irrationality). What is more worth while: to act so as to prolong *bare* life while being passively, negatively exposed to constant and ubiquitous dangers to it, or to take on risks willingly, positively, expressing thereby a preference for condensed *quality* or *intensity* of existence, as opposed to its mere duration? This is and always remains an open question. The point to realize, as Michael Laver has put it in his excellent and thought-provoking recent work, *The Crime Game*, is that 'everyone puts a different value on his or her own life. This may seem a little odd at first sight. You might think that everyone would put an infinite value on staying alive. This cannot be true, however, as everyone takes tiny risks in the course of even a mundane day-to-day existence.'[22] However far-fetched and 'metaphysical' this existential paradox might appear at first glance in the context of a discussion of law and order, we can be assured that no proper appreciation of the seemingly 'mundane' problem presented by the latter is possible without taking some cognizance of the former.

The existential paradox can also be approached from the side of freedom. The curious and fascinating thing to notice about freedom is that it is both equivalent to the quest after personal security and at the same time it transcends this quest. Freedom is the consciousness of life as *human* life, the awareness of 'will', 'purpose', 'ability', 'choices', and the recognition of obstacles in one's way. In the first instance I am 'free' (as we noted earlier) to the extent that I am not hampered by others in my actions, plans, designs, if I can act without external constraint and coercion. This also involves – very centrally, indeed – a relative reduction in the unpredictability of the intentions and actions of others, and since others are potentially just as free as I am myself, total personal freedom in society, or what is the same thing total personal security, is impossible. However, what we must explicitly note now is that the consciousness of my freedom also involves my *own* unpredictability. We may be, from a pedestrian, quasi-scientific point of view, sophisticated 'machines' or instinct-driven animal organisms, but human self-consciousness also contains a *plus*: this is freedom, connoting unpredictability of the person for the person. Freedom would not have any distinct meaning whatever, and would certainly not constitute a 'value', if I knew with absolute certainty not only what I *will* do next but also what I will *intend* to do next. Now the relevance of this recognition will become obvious once we note the incidence, indeed prevalence, of people acting, and wanting to act, against themselves as it were, endangering their lives and security. Not only 'can' I act against my security but I tend also fully to cherish this transcendent freedom, actually enjoying insecurity. Freedom is *for* life but at the same time the 'stuff' of life is excitement and I would not be completely free, completely human, without experiencing this excitement. Security means permanence, duration, assurance, continuity but the consciousness of freedom includes the permanent possibility of *change* within this continuity and it also outreaches this continuity. This is then really the same story, illuminated if you like from the subjective side, as we have already depicted in relation to the paradoxicality of 'life'. Together they express the fundamental paradox of existence, as it impinges on and defines the quest after personal security.

So much, then, about these four basic 'paradoxes of security'. In the foregoing, of course, we have done no more than offer some very rudimentary and preliminary sketches, and in the following – and more substantial – chapters an effort will be made to develop some of these points further and to relate them in a more systematic way to issues encountered in the discussion on the problem of law and order and politics. The reason why this particular approach has been adopted in the introductory chapter is constituted by the author's conviction that the paradoxicality of this specific cluster of problems (indeed, *all* problems confronted reflectively, in a philosophical manner) is really basic, in the sense of being both the proper beginning and the proper conclusion. The paradoxical nature of the quest after personal security will remain paradoxical right to the end, and any kind of short- or long-term, social and political 'solution' offered – including those contained in this book – must be understood against this background.

For now the only task remaining for us in this chapter is to expand a little bit more on the 'plural perspective' which will be employed in our ensuing reflections on the nature of the state, on the difference between the 'criminal' and the 'political' and on the conventional wisdoms of conservative and radical views concerning law, order and politics in society. This perspective is of course by no means an invention of the present author, and its pedigree and distinctive character are well recognized in philosophical literature, from the ancient pre-Socratics to modern existentialists. Sometimes and in some contexts it is called the 'dialectical' view, sometimes it is tagged (somewhat misleadingly) the 'tragic' outlook on life or the 'relativist' approach. It can, I think, also be regarded as being equivalent to a properly so designated 'realist' or 'realistic' approach to politics and society. Perhaps what is relatively novel here is our concentrated endeavour to bring this perspective, this point of view, to bear on a problem which, in spite of its centrality, has been largely neglected or glossed over or misconstrued by political philosophers. And what therefore needs initial and special emphasis is the 'plurality' of the problem we have just begun to explore, or its basic defining quality of paradoxicality, its self-disclosure in terms of opposites.

There is little point in embarking here on an extended and elaborate methodological excursus. The plural perspective will have to be seen at work, in concrete application, in order for its validity and suitability to be judged. So here we will offer just a few general pointers indicating the direction in which the ensuing reflections are intended to proceed and the principles which – more or less – govern them. Essentially, taking a plural perspective signifies our recognition of the impossibility of unitary predication of 'things' encountered in thought and in experience. Nothing in life, in consciousness, and *par excellence* in philosophical reflection, is simple or unitary. Everything *means* a lot of other things, besides the 'one' meaning we choose to attribute to it, depending on the nature of our particular inquiry. A 'table' is a man-made material object, it is also an aggregate of physical particles, a contraption to be used, an obstacle to be removed, a legal exhibit, a congealment of energy, an entity subject to chemical and mechanical laws, a source of poetic inspiration. The wind is one thing for the meteorologist, something else for the ballistics expert, yet another for the sailor and the track runner. Noise can be the conversion of energy or it can be music. The 'same' liquid is nectar and poison. And so on. There is ultimately no way in which one particular mode, idiom, vocabulary describing an object can be regarded as more 'real' or 'truer' than others. As the well known and (to our present sensitivities) somewhat vulgar joke has it, when the cannibal chief is asked what became of the missionary who had visited the village, he replies: 'dat was no missionary, dat was my supper!' Similarly, this animal is a black cat, he is Kormoska a special family favourite, also a nuisance at bed-time; that green contraption in front is my car, a source of pleasure and irritation, bread and butter for the mechanic, a curse for the household budget, a means of escape, an excuse, a companion with a definite personality. But more relevantly here we have to grasp the irreducible (and indeed most fascinating) plurality of the phenomenon or thing we call 'human' and the significance of this plurality for political philosophy in general and for the problem of personal security in particular. We have already had a glimpse of this: as a person, a unit of consciousness and an empirically distinct 'body' I am unique to myself in the first place and also, in a considerably weakened sense, to others, or an *individual*. But my uniqueness is nevertheless experienced in terms of a general humanity which I share: I recognize myself in others and others in myself, I share my fundamental desires and my rationality with others, I accept a binding moral law controlling my actions as a bare human being, therefore I am also *universal*. And thirdly my universal human consciousness as well as my unique individual consciousness are resolved and concretely mediated for me by my immediate self-recognition as a determinate kind of human being: male or female, young or old, Dutch or Eskimo, sick or healthy, a peasant or a traffic warden or a mercenary soldier, pale or dark, a lover of poetry or a lover of pushpin, and others also recognize me as such; that is, I am a *particular*. Again, there is no convincing way to argue that one dimension in human identity is more basic, more real, more central than the other two; in society they are all there together, coterminous, co-experiential, interpenetrating.

The point about this plurality of perspectives concerning human beings is, however, not just simply that the plurality is 'given' and, so it would appear, irreducible. It is also that this specific plurality in question (whatever we might want to say about tables, liquids, noise and wind) is laden with tension and is essentially conflictual. The world would be a very different place indeed if this were not so, and we would have no such thing either as a problem of 'law and order' to make us worried (as well as thrilled) or an escape route like political philosophy which might help us regain a certain amount of calm. The tense and conflictual relationship between these three aspects of human consciousness and society will receive plenty of comment in what follows, starting with the 'state' as the repository of law and order in the next chapter, and continuing with the 'negation' of the state, i.e. law-breaking and order-defiance, in the chapter after that. But it might be worth our while to stress two points right here. Firstly, to my mind it is vitally important to grasp the truth that the tension and conflict in modern society is *three-tiered*, not dichotomous, and that the problem of personal security (the problem of law and order) cannot be adequately explained by reducing it either to criminality (i.e. the conflict between individuality and universality) or to politics (i.e. the conflict between particulars); a great many departures, scientifically and/or ideologically orientated, have suffered as a result of precisely this kind of reductionist assumption (on which we shall expand in the concluding chapter). Indeed, even our tripartite perspective is no more than a convenient simplification of a 'reality' that is shot through with conflict and tension in all directions and on an immense variety of levels. Society is a perpetually moving, whirling, heaving, multi-coloured kaleidoscope. Secondly, while we have to be mindful of tension and antagonism at all points, we must not forget either that at any rate up to now (could we ever be confident enough to assert that the 'future' will be *totally* different from past and present?) this tension and this conflict have been adequately contained; in a remarkable and really fascinating manner the dimensions of universality, particularity and individuality are productive not only of trouble but also of on-going correction and accommodation.

2 THE STATE AS LAW AND ORDER

Personal security, then, as we said, becomes a problem in and for society; it connects up with the individual's relations to others in his social environment, especially strangers, and it arises out of the individual's exposure to hostility and malevolent indifference. Insecurity results from inimical, damaging, irregular and unpredictable conduct in society, from lawlessness and disorder in general. But we cannot properly comprehend the nature of lawlessness and disorder, since these are 'negative' notions whose meaning is dependent and derivative, until we make an effort first to understand their positive counterparts, viz. law and order. And again, certainly in the contemporary context, law and order derive their meaning from the *state* and without being approached from the angle of the state their meaning will remain unanchored and ambiguous. Thus we have to take what could appear at first glance a long and winding detour but indeed this is necessary; on the other hand, however, at least the discussion here can proceed more or less along the lines of the traditional concerns of political philosophy, which (after the first chapter) might well be considered an advantage.

The state, as any student of politics knows or should know, is an entity that has so far successfully resisted attempts at a simple, straightforward, untroubled definition. Endeavours to grasp the distinctive nature of the state as an enduring form of human association have most often erred by either being too restrictive or being too embracive, in neither case being able to eliminate the 'essentially contestable' character of the phenomenon they have sought to explain. It seems to me that, with our particular problem in mind, the best we can do is to seize exactly this contestable character of the state and give serious attention to both the 'narrow' and the 'broad' approaches. These, to give them an initial and summary description here, define the state essentially either in terms of *power* or in terms of *authority*. At one pole (this view, in the main, characterizes radical writers and 'social scientists') the state has been seen in terms of external, empirical features, as a discernible 'institution' within society, and inhabiting one, and a relatively small, part of society; it consists of such things as the 'government' (in some instances, indeed, the state is directly identified with 'government'), the public services, the legislature, the judiciary, the army and police, and so on – a collection or system of certain 'offices', the essential defining function of which is the exercise of force over and on behalf of 'society'. There is little else important to the state, except for various ideological trappings – Saint Augustine and Max Weber seem to agree at least on this. At the opposite pole we find the view, espoused by idealists, conservatives above all but also by (probably) a sizable section of those who even these days regard themselves as 'political philosophers', that the state essentially consists of ideas in the minds of citizens, and feelings deep in their hearts, rendering it an entity which is co-extensive with society, a spiritual presence visibly expressing the moral consciousness and preferences of the people; 'will, not force, is the basis of the state', in T. H. Green's memorable phrase. On this view the 'power' of the state, its institutional, external manifestation, is secondary and derivative; what is primary and original is its embodiment of 'authority', i.e. its moral superiority deriving (however tortuously) from the citizens' 'good will' or 'good sense'.

There is without doubt something definitely odd about both these views, in so far as they are held in a rigid, reductionist manner. On the one hand, it is ridiculous to imagine that states could have persisted over time, and generally flourished, if they had really been 'separated' off from society and maintained themselves by relying on power only, or even essentially. And on the other hand, it is just as ridiculous to assert that all or even a majority of citizens in any state we know of (from experience or from studying history) actually identify themselves with the state and positively supply it with the 'will' that constitutes the state's internal, moral authority. In what concrete and positive sense could, for instance, tramps and derelicts, hooligans on the rampage, professional criminals, Rastafarians, unemployed school-leavers, militant shop stewards and women camping on Greenham Common be called a 'part' of the state (as distinguished from being passive, and recalcitrant, subjects of the state)? Yet on the whole, on the view taken in these reflections, this so-called 'idealist' approach to the state has something to be said for it, and indeed it illuminates the problem of law and order from an angle which is more or less closed to the scientific view. But this philosophical approach needs to be restated with a very decisive difference, taking account of the truth contained in its opposite. What we require, and will endeavour to work out here, is a workable plural perspective on the state, to account for its heterogeneous, contestable, paradoxical nature; this plurality of the state, already obliquely illuminated by the paradoxes of security as seen above, will in turn shed further light on *insecurity* as actually encountered, i.e. on lawlessness and disorder. Working towards the achievement of a plural perspective will mean here the successive examination of alternative languages or vocabularies purporting to explain 'the' nature of the state, and showing how all these – *three*, in fact – vocabularies are valid and necessary, within the limits imposed by their respective philosophical assumptions.

We shall make here one large assumption ourselves but it is, I believe, a relatively and reasonably uncontroversial one; it seems, at any rate, to be shared by conservative and radical, and scientific and philosophical, writers alike. It is that the sundry states, countries, societies encountered in what we are calling the 'modern world', with the advanced industrial and urban societies of the West at its centre, share at least some essential features among themselves, and with particular reference to those aspects which relate to personal security (as defined in the previous chapter). They all have, that is to say, governments, legislatures, armies, police forces; they are all stratified societies, industrial, post-industrial or industrializing economies, with a prevalence of mixed enterprise; they share a certain 'global' culture and enjoy a comparable degree of prosperity (making them at least historically, temporally comparable, in spite of the obvious 'spatial' divide). Of course there are important differences, too, and in the context of personal security: the problem of crime, political violence and law-enforcement is, on a certain level of inquiry, very different in Norway and in Turkey, in Belfast and in Dublin, in Bedford-Stuyvesant and in Topeka, Kansas, in Kensington Palace Gardens, London and barely a mile away in Latimer Road. But – and this is not just an irresponsible sleight of hand – for the purpose of philosophical reflection these local varieties can and will have to be overlooked; they will enter our purview only as illustrations. Our plural perspective will supply all the 'concreteness' needed: it will, as far as practicable and as space allows, display the rich reality of most states and societies as they are recognized in public consciousness (and particularly in the ubiquitous 'law-and-order' literature) in terms of their shared and common internal self-contradictions, intricate paradoxes, interpenetrating oppositions, overlapping identities.

The first identity of the state, then, as described typically and most cogently in the language of traditional political philosophy, is that of moral association or a *universal* entity, characterized essentially by its 'internal', ideal features, encapsulated for the most part in such ringing terms as 'authority', 'justice', 'law', 'rights' and 'obligations'. This view is not only highly respectable, attractive and boasting of a long historical pedigree but the fact (among other things) that its typical vocabulary is commonly shared by other and self-consciously antithetical views suggests at least its partial validity. In constructing its most significant features for the purposes of our inquiry, we must start with what is without doubt the first logical step, namely a characteristic view of *morality*. As already sketchily presented in the introductory chapter, this traditional 'mainstream' Western conception of morality postulates a basic distinction between immediate natural desires and a 'higher' consciousness prescribing the 'right' course of action for people, as individuals and as groups. It will be convenient at this point to consider this traditional view under two headings, surveying its formal and substantive character separately. Formally the view elevates *humanity* as the proper subject and object of moral action; the category may be more embracing, as we have remarked earlier, opening it either 'upwards' to include super-human and super-terrestrial entities or 'downwards' to include other sentient beings, but in every case humanity is the centre and other entities are approximated to it. Man is the measure of all things, as the ancient Sophist Protagoras is supposed to have said, and this view has certainly been built into our mainstream Western moral consciousness. More to the point, of course, is to stress the *minimal* character of humanity as the basic moral category: the underlying moral view recognizes no relevant and essential differences within the human species; all individuals, persons, units of self-consciousness, are to count as of equal moral worth, to be seen as 'ends' in themselves, not a 'means' to serve the designs and objectives of other humans. As H. L. A. Hart says in *The Concept of Law*: 'Indeed so deeply embedded in modern man is the principle that *prima facie* human beings are entitled to be treated alike that almost universally where the laws do discriminate by reference to such matters as colour and race, lip-service at least is still widely paid to this principle.'[1] Moral equality means universality: individuals, morally speaking, are universally substitutable. 'My' conduct is exclusively mine only in the physical, empirical sense; on the plane of morality I act as a universal 'human' being; therefore, my 'natural' (instinctual, habitual, spontaneous) self-preference must be overriden, informed, modified, transfigured in the light of my understanding of the universal moral 'law'. This leads to our noting another important formal characteristic of this underlying Western conception of morality: moral rules have typically been conceived in legal or quasi-legal terms, as binding on all human beings whoever and wherever they are, eternal, categorical, unquestionable and indisputable, superior to contingent, varying, hypothetical and 'prudential' considerations. This view then, elements of which are to be found in Plato, Cicero, the Old Testament and the Christian Gospels but which of course received its clearest and most complete modern formulation in the philosophy of Kant, supplies on its formal side the most fundamental presupposition on which the imputed 'authority' of the modern state rests: the notion of a universal moral law and the moral equality of all human beings. It is, I hope, needless to add that the foregoing is not meant to be an exact and exhaustive presentation; the view depicted here has had a long and tortuous and conflict-ridden historical build-up, and it is definitely frayed at the edges.

A similar caution is called for when it comes to outlining the substantive features of this mainstream moral understanding, its content as distinguished from the form. This substance has a no less respectable pedigree in the Western tradition, paradigmatically formulated in such diverse documents as the mosaic Ten Commandments, the Gospels, the writings of classical and early modern natural lawyers, and the various 'human rights' charters familiar to our own age. Substantive moral commands, though demonstrably general (even going beyond the cultural confines of Western civilization), are incapable of a precise, legalistic definition, and all pedantic attempts to achieve such precision have failed and are probably bound to fail; nevertheless, as Saint Paul expressed it, they are 'written in the heart'. The primary and central reference here is obviously to life, and the sanctity of life, adjoining the very widespread and deeply held injunction that life (especially human life) should not be wantonly, irresponsibly taken, i.e. a prohibition of killing for no reason or killing for the sake of mere killing. What H. L. A. Hart describes as the 'minimum content of natural law', rests on such 'truisms' as the universally attributable human aim of going on living; hence among those basic rules making human life at all possible the ones primarily and inescapably required 'are those forbidding, or at least restricting, the free use of violence, rules requiring certain forms of honesty and truthfulness in dealings with others, and rules forbidding the destruction of tangible things or their seizure from others'.[2] According to the anthropologist, I. Eibl-Eibesfeldt, nowhere in the world, Western or non-Western, is to be found 'a general licence to kill a fellow human being.'[3] Konrad Lorenz, another famous writer whose views on human 'aggression' have created a great deal of controversy, makes an interesting and telling point concerning the special value, or sanctity, of *human* life: 'The scientist who considers himself absolutely "objective" and believes that he can free himself from the compulsion of the "merely" subjective should try – only in imagination of course – to kill in succession a lettuce, a fly, a frog, a guinea-pig, a cat, a dog, and finally a chimpanzee. He will then be aware how increasingly difficult murder becomes as the victim's level of organization rises.'[4] The point is that although irreducibly 'subjective', the moral rule forbidding the taking of human life, or life with a 'high level of organization', has held a remarkable sway over the centuries and across the globe. People do kill other people, of course, but they either justify it on grounds which are themselves ostensibly based on this general injunction or they do it in self-conscious defiance of the rule in the particular case; it is much, much rarer to find instances of this substantive command being denied *in toto*, and even rarer (although it is not unheard of) to come across views holding that killing *per se* is itself a positive moral good.

The sanctity of life obviously does not exhaust our characteristic substantive moral consciousness. Going on from this negative terminus, the mainstream Western moral view has taken cognizance of a whole vast range of other and related 'values', including very positive ones indeed. The general injunction against killing is most often accompanied by injunctions against the infliction of physical and psychological injury: maiming, harming, cruel treatment. Life, in human terms, is of course not just physical survival but includes, beyond bare health, conditions that make it worth while and satisfying: freedom or security in the pursuit of one's happiness or self-fulfilment. The 'good life' for individuals, furthermore, makes it imperative for them to recognize the equal moral right of others to partake of the same according to their sundry tastes, inclinations and empirical possibilities. Human beings are thus enjoined to display 'civility' in their general conduct, to be tolerant of variety and of differing tastes and views, to be generous and magnanimous, to be honest, upright and trustworthy, to have integrity, to show compassion, gratitude and friendship, to have rectitude and veracity, to seek peace and harmony, to be just and impartial, and so on and so on. Our transcendent, universally humanistic moral view thus, starting from the infinite value attributed to the individual person (as the sanctity of life has ultimate reference to *individual* life), issues finally in a more or less determinate kind of 'social ethic': the good life for one involves just and good relations among all. Here then we reach the level of the *state* or that form of human association which – in the idiom of traditional political philosophy – represents the crowning achievement of endeavours to see morality brought 'down to earth', concretized and embodied in society.

I am, for reasons of space mainly, skipping over a few quite important stages in the argument (e.g. lesser associations like the family, economic relations, etc.) and I am also presenting the mainstream idea of the state in the Western tradition in overwhelmingly idealist terms, in the language of Aristotle, Rousseau and above all Hegel. This might seem to be an unwarranted sleight of hand, in that this presentation apparently disregards the whole empiricist, instrumentalist, mechanist tradition. But this is by no means the case. Marx and Engels may or may not have been entirely correct in describing the Hegelian idea of the state as the most advanced and perfected formulation of the 'bourgeois' conception (this description is based on the Marxist assumption, which I do not share, that the 'bourgeois' state is historically the 'last' form of state) but what is certain is that this Hegelian conception is much more deeply embedded in modern Western political thought than it might appear at first glance. For the moment – and we shall say more about this topic later on – just note that the substitution of the word 'law' or the term 'sovereignty', as used by empiricist and mechanist writers, for the Hegelian term 'state' (or the Rousseauist term 'general will'), makes but very little substantive difference to the argument. The 'state', in its broad and deep sense, and the 'law', in its general sense (as 'legislation' or as the so-called 'rule of law'), are moral and philosophical equivalents; they mean strictly the same thing.

To go on with our skeletal reconstruction then, the state in the Western understanding has come to signify the supreme moral association, the 'concrete universal' or 'ethical substance' which is alone appointed to provide a palpable framework and expression to the moral conduct of individuals and thus enable them to pursue their own personal ends in peace and tranquillity. The state embodies the moral law and thus becomes (*vis à vis* the citizens) morally autonomous and politically self-governing. Its supreme *raison d'être* is to maintain and promote just relations among citizens, secular by its nature and tolerant of diverse views and personal tastes (within certain limits, of course), it embodies civility, stands above conflicting personal and group interests and is the only effective 'impartial' adjudicator in society. The state, if you like, thus appears as the synthetic expression of the 'formal' and 'substantive' aspects of morality, encompassing both the subjective universality of individuals (with their innate sense of 'duty' and understanding of right and wrong) and the objective, substantive commands of the law of nature, as transmitted through 'custom'. Thus and only thus, if seen as a moral entity, can the state reasonably be said to have 'authority', i.e. a morally justified, legitimate claim on the allegiance of citizens whose 'obligation' to obey the law is primarily a moral obligation.

Here we must note an important point, frequently overlooked. Is it not the case, in Western 'liberal-democratic' rhetoric at any rate, that the 'authority' of the state (meaning here 'government') derives from the actual, ascertainable will or mandate of the citizenry who make their choice through 'elections' and the like? Yes, this is so (or it is *sometimes* so) but the point is that this kind of political 'authorization' or 'legitimation' takes place *within* the state already established and presupposing its moral supremacy and legal sovereignty – indeed, 'divinity' in relation to the mass of individual citizens would not be an improper term to use here. The people who 'choose' or give their 'consent' to aspiring governments and/or governmental policies are *already* defined as 'citizens' and are themselves 'authorized' to act only as citizens; the 'constitution' of the state, abstractly conceived, may remotely derive from the 'people' but *concretely* conceived it stands above and defines the people. No amount of democratic rhetoric, couched in terms either of 'popular sovereignty' or 'parliamentary sovereignty', can nullify or substantially alter this truth. 'Parliamentary sovereignty', for example, as the point was well put in Lon L. Fuller's *The Morality of Law*, 'means, in effect, that the parliament stands above the law in the sense that it can change any law that is not to its liking. But, paradoxically, it gains this position of being above the law only by subjecting itself to law – the law of its own internal procedure. For a corporate body to pass laws it must conform to laws that will determine when a law has been passed.'[5] Although Fuller here primarily talks about what he calls the 'internal' (i.e. formal) morality of law, the point applies also in a more substantive sense. At best, or at its weakest, the authority of the state and the corresponding obligation of citizens must be seen as *circular* (or paradoxical): authority presupposes citizens with a moral consciousness and rights, and the latter in turn presuppose a moral association which endows them with a concrete expression. At worst (or strongest), authority and obligation must be seen as self-derived and self-justifying, and the state as supplying its own legitimacy through its past, constantly receding.

Another point may be made now briefly, for the special attention of students of the history of political thought. The conception of the state here outlined is not in the least 'totalitarian' or 'absolutist' in the senses usually employed in liberal-democratic literature. Those who endeavour to draw a sharp and rigid contrast between the Kantian (universalistic, humanistic, pacific) and Hegelian (statist, absolutist, diabolical) conception of morality would be rightly suspected of not divining the difference between their limb-joints and posterior. The so-called Hegelian state, which is here presented as the mainstream Western understanding of the state, is conceived as the further perfection of universal human morality, and not as its denial. The state represents humanity in a concrete form, as organization, and the universal moral law in a concrete form, as positive law and government. This point becomes apparent once we note that in this understanding the state is essentially conceived as being internally *limited*, though the limitation is self-imposed, proceeding from the moral character itself of the association. The state is not, that is to say, recognizable as a proper 'state' unless it bases itself on strict legality, constitutionality, the fundamental moral equality of human beings, impartiality and respect for rights. The state *must* have 'citizens', i.e. human beings who are defined in egalitarian moral and legal terms. Here we see, incidentally, the dialectic of the narrow and broad definitions of the state at work: the state as 'law' stands in terms of this understanding superior to the state as 'government' (when the state, in a well-known idiom, is defined as the 'rule of law'). And externally the state is also limited by its own morality: it is subject to international law, the comity of nations, treaties, its 'duty' towards colonies or (nowadays) obligation to provide material aid to 'underdeveloped nations', etc. Even Hegel, be it noted, who it is true (like Hobbes) had scant regard for international law, nevertheless subjected the state to the moral superiority of world history.

The power of the state then, to go a step further (and with apologies to readers who might feel that we have wandered too far away from the problem of personal security), rests on the state's moral authority. Or rather, to put it more accurately, the 'force' – of physical and other kinds – which is at the sole disposal of the state and which supplies the largest part of the state's external, visible manifestation, is transfigured and morally elevated to become legitimate 'power', sharply distinguished from 'violence', i.e. the unauthorized, illegitimate use of force, which is mainly directed against the state. It is the power of the state which is meant to ensure the personal security of citizens but this power, to repeat, is meant to be subsidiary to, and the derivative of, the state's moral authority which in turn, as we have seen, is logically merely the reverse side of the conscious and 'rational' morality of the people. Through the state, therefore, the citizens provide their own security: it is their law, their government, their courts of justice, their army and their police, their prisons and scaffolds. Coercion by the state is fully moral, it is legitimate. But, and this is a vitally important point, the power of the state is meant to be a last resort in the playing out of just and moral relations, to be used as rarely as possible and directly affecting only a minority of citizens. The state is a proper moral association if and only if its visible power affects most people only marginally, negligibly and indirectly, while its full might is meted out only to a relatively small (and in principle) indefinite group of 'law-breakers'. The vast majority of citizens, and most of the time, are supposed to be 'rational' and fully behind the state's law-enforcing and punitive actions. 'Coercion', as the point is excellently put by Macfarlane, 'is necessary to ensure that the majority of members of any society obey that society's rules, not in the sense that most members would not conform unless themselves under threat of coercion, but in the sense that they would not continue to conform unless coercion, or the threat of coercion, were applied to the minority who do not conform or who would not otherwise conform.'[6] As in A. P. d'Entreves' apt observation, 'the "obligatoriness" of the laws does not consist in their undoubted capacity to compel observance, but in the possibility, which does not belong to all laws, of being accepted and obeyed by the "good citizen".'[7]

This 'undoubted capacity' of the modern state to ensure that the personal security of the average citizen is being adequately looked after, rests above all on two specific institutions, both of which deserve somewhat more than a passing mention here. These are the institutions of law-enforcement and punishment. Both of them are, in modern conditions, unique in principle to the state and 'monopolized' by it, both are legitimated in terms of the moral authority of the state but both serve – significantly – to show up the delicate *margin* of state authority. That is, at the very point where the authority of the state is most explicitly needed to justify the exercise of its power, this same authority reveals itself as being relatively weak, problematic, ambiguous. Here, in the first instance, we shall have to survey briefly, as it were the 'positive' side or the ideal model of law-enforcement and punishment. As regards law-enforcement, the essential point to grasp is that the state arrogates to itself the right to elevate a certain group from among the citizenry to represent it towards those who, in whatever way, are deemed to constitute a threat to the peace and tranquillity of society and who contravene the law in a serious manner. Law-enforcement, as the term itself epitomizes, signifies the maintenance of the law *as though* it were no longer 'law' in the sublime sense (to observe which citizens have a 'moral obligation') but just an indifferent set of rules which need 'force' only, or predominantly, for its protection. Citizens appointed to serve as law-enforcement representatives of the state, the police in particular, have thus a unique authority to act *against* the express wishes and actual will (as implied by their conduct) of some other citizens. In theory in most states every citizen has, of course, the formal right to arrest and prosecute but in actual practice this right is exercised almost exclusively by the police who are, justifiably, seen as constituting a 'special' body within the state, its visible shield guarding it, and through it the whole of society as such, against domestic dangers. It is important to stress the point here – obvious, maybe, but significant – that the police are meant to provide a *special* kind of service for the *whole* of society, to every citizen irrespective of position and status, in as much as the citizen conducts himself *as* a citizen, i.e. he is acting out the law and through it the morality embedded in the state. As the state in principle is totally impartial and deemed to be above the conflicts of society (though not above society itself), so must be the police. As it is stated in Sir Robert Peel's General Instructions issued to the Metropolitan Police, at its foundation: 'He [the police officer] will be civil and attentive to all persons, of every rank and class; insolence or incivility will not be passed over.' As the state has no distinct 'interest' on its own, outside and above society, similarly the police act on everyone's behalf equally and collectively – yet in a special way.

Now one thing we ought to note at this point, as belonging to the whole subject of personal security in society, is that the curious and unique fascination characterizing this subject (as remarked on in the previous chapter) tends itself to be uniquely and curiously focused on the police. It is not a mere accident, and would be quite ridiculous to explain away by reference to 'indoctrination' and 'media manipulation', that police matters, real or fictional, are, and always have been, among the most popular in attracting public attention, captivating the mind of elderly and innocent spinsters, learned philosophers, hard-headed scientists and politicians, law-abiding citizens and self-professed 'villains' alike. Scores of accounts have been written on this phenomenon, giving a variety of psychological and sociological reasons for this well-nigh universal fascination with the 'romance' of the police, with stolid, pipe-chewing inspectors, clever superintendents, cunning detectives, daring rank-and-file, intricate mysteries solved, desperate criminals pursued and confronted, the chains of deduction, the stake-out and the shoot-out. This is of course romanticization, fictionalization, an idealized representation of a hard, prosaic 'reality' which is rather different. But then we must also realize that this so-called 'hard' reality is only a *part* of reality; it is among the most childish and 'romantic' errors to believe that romance can be eradicated from human life and consciousness or to deny it a role in the speculative endeavour of political philosophy. As regards the romance of the police, the inimitable Chesterton, master-producer of paradoxes, should here be quoted:

> While it is the constant tendency of the Old Adam to rebel against so universal and automatic a thing as civilization, to preach departure and rebellion, the romance of police activity keeps in some sense before the mind the fact that civilization itself is the most sensational of departures and the most romantic of rebellions. By dealing with the unsleeping sentinels who guard the outposts of society, it tends to remind us that we live in an armed camp, making war with a chaotic world, and that the criminals, the children of chaos, are nothing but the traitors within our gates. When the detective in a police romance stands alone, and somewhat fatuously fearless amid the knives and fists of a thieves' kitchen, it does certainly serve to make us remember that it is the agent of social justice who is the original and poetic figure, while the burglars and footpads are merely placid old cosmic conservatives, happy in the immemorial respectability of apes and wolves. The romance of the police force is thus the whole romance of man. It is based on the fact that morality is the most dark and daring of conspiracies. It reminds us that the whole noiseless and unnoticeable police management by which we are ruled and protected is only a successful knight-errantry.[8]

This is essentially a Hobbesian view, delicately ornamented, but with an important difference. Chesterton's striking expression about morality itself being a 'dark conspiracy' rightly conveys a sense (which is absent in Hobbes) of the precarious character of morality, of the ambiguity involved in the moral authority of the state, and lastly of the resultant supreme paradoxicality of law-enforcement itself. The point is, surely, that morality, though in a way natural and innate to all of us, is yet precarious and thus must constantly be defended in a non-moral, or indeed, *immoral* way. The thrill of policing therefore, it seems to me, lies precisely in this concentrated and inseparable double identity, the stark self-contradiction of moral exemption, or moral speciality, attaching to the function of law-enforcement.

It is not just that, naive and childlike, I see myself enlarged and transfigured in identifying with the police 'knight-errant', in vicariously enjoying the difficult but assured triumph of good over evil, the law over traitors within the gates; in reality I enjoy the *double* thrill of seeing morality victorious through being pushed to its very margin, to the point of embracing immorality. The police are morally permitted, nay obligated, to do things (coerce, forcibly arrest, incapacitate, injure, shoot, interrogate, etc.) which would be forbidden in ordinary circumstances and might in fact be morally reprehensible *per se*; yet at the same time its context elevates police work to become the highest embodiment and epitome of morality as such, the first-line defence of society at points where it is most vulnerable, its security against itself. Policing is both central and marginal to the state and to moral consciousness; hence its fascination.

The institution of punishment is revealed, from our point of view, as having an essentially similar character to policing. Punishment has, in some form or other, been considered absolutely necessary to the maintenance of the state, and except for committed radical anarchists and libertarians (a conspicuously tiny minority, all told) all eminent political philosophers have found for it some sort of moral justification. We have to grasp here the point that in the last resort institutionalized punishment is the *same*, whatever its form and whatever label it might bear: execution, prison, banishment, flogging, fine, psychiatric treatment or community service. In every case it signifies the pitting of the will of the state (of society in the abstract) against the individual; it is an imposition, however circumscribed, it is the infliction of *pain*, however mild or remote or, as the *threat* of pain, hypothetical. Without this ultimate threat, it is said, the state would cease to function; the sharp and heavy sword must be there in the background to enforce the 'covenant'. In Laver's succinct reasoning:

> The trouble is that a deal is not a deal if it can't be enforced. Moreover, when we *really* get down to it, fear, force and pain are the only things that work. The policemen, lawyers and judges of the straight enforcement Mafia may claim that they left fear and pain behind a century or two ago. Not so. You run a red light, and you get a traffic ticket. This might look like a civilized little fine, but it's not – it's a threat.

> Don't pay the traffic ticket and they'll take you to court. Don't pay the fine in court and sooner or later you'll face a jail sentence. Don't go to jail and they'll force you. Resist and they'll hurt you. The *very, very* bottom line is always pain.[9]

In a famous passage the conservative political philosopher Joseph de Maistre, being convinced that 'God has given sovereigns the supreme prerogative of punishing crimes', argues that in the state the most important function is that of the public executioner. Sovereignty 'results in the necessary existence of a man destined to inflict on criminals the punishments awarded by human justice'.[10] But de Maistre, despite his rigid conservatism, shows a fine sense of the marginality of punishment, too, its paradoxicality. Though the executioner's function (like that of law-enforcement) is absolutely moral, the hangman himself – a bit like the stereotyped law-enforcer – stands on the borderline of society, his own moral identity ambiguous, questionable:

> He is not a criminal, yet it is impossible to say, for example, that he *is virtuous, that he is an honest man, that he is estimable*, and so on. No moral praise can be appropriate for him, since this assumes relationships with men, and he has none.
>
> And yet all grandeur, all power, all subordination rests on the executioner: he is the horror and the bond of human association. Remove this incomprehensible agent from the world, and at that very moment order gives way to chaos, thrones topple, and society disappears.[11]

Quite a great deal, again, has been written on the rationale and justification of punishment by the state, and the respective merits and insights, as well as inadequacies, of the three most influential theories – retribution, deterrence and reformation – are pretty well known. Martin P. Golding, in *Philosophy of Law*, quite reasonably observes: 'Each theory seems entangled in difficulties. In the name of deterrence, the first theory apparently permits the punishment of the innocent and punishment out of proportion to the gravity of the offence. Retribution seems to presuppose an assessment of moral wickedness that is beyond the competence of the law to make and hence degenerates into mere revenge. Finally, it is doubtful that punishment as such can reform; it seems only to harden the criminal as an enemy of society.'[12] Nevertheless, the point should be made here that, suspect or not, the concept of *retribution* still appears to be logically and morally more central to punishment by the state than the other two concepts. Deterrence and reformation are merely consequential notions and are logically expendable: their presence might make the state's punitive actions more palatable but they cannot supply the primary moral *right* to punishment. This is by no means an original observation but, it seems to me, it is valid and highly relevant here. It *is* the case, in Golding's terms, that the state assumes this moral 'competence' to punish law-breaking from the very start; otherwise the morality and authority of the state as a whole (all state institutions and offices: government, public service, army, police, education, welfare, etc.) would be inconceivable. There is, quite simply, no coherent notion of punishment without a notion of moral competence, which in turn implies retribution: the state, or 'law', represents moral *right*, law-breaking represents moral *wrong*, and this wrong is cancelled out, obliterated by punishment which thus represents the concrete *assertion* of moral right. There is a firm assertion of moral 'quality', in other words, on behalf of the state, which alone legitimates the 'quantitative' exercise of meting out punishment to 'fit the crime'. Without the right of assertion, of retribution, there can be no right of deterrence and reformation; the latter can still be considered useful and beneficial but scarcely an exclusive prerogative of the state. In punishment the state confirms its own moral essence, its supreme duty of protecting citizens; and in the fulfilment of this duty the state can recognize no limitations other than technical ones. Smugly but perfectly consistently was the point expressed by Sir Edward Gardner, Conservative MP, in his speech moving the Death Penalty Bill in the House of Commons in 1983: '. . . it is important to those of us who believe – as I hope all hon. Members believe – that it is the inescapable duty of the State to protect its citizens in the most effective way that is available to the State from unlawful violence and death by murder.'[13]

Retribution, apart from its logical necessity for the idea of punishment by the state, also brings us face to face once again with the thrill and fascination accompanying the problem of personal security in society. It is often said, by opponents of the retributivist view, that retribution is merely, as it were, glorified 'revengc'. This may be so, to a certain extent, but of course the important point to grasp is that revenge, and the elemental desire for revenge, once again merely serve to show up the basic paradoxicality of moral consciousness, its reaching out to its very margin, and turning into its opposite. In revenge we are dimly (maybe very dimly) conscious of doing something 'wrong', but revenge is at the same time supremely satisfying and absolutely *right*, the very culmination and simultaneously the incipient negation of morality. Revenge is sweet and at the same time repulsive; the climax of moral triumph and also, in the nature of climaxes, productive of moral malaise and spontaneous self-recrimination. (The author, as a child, witnessed the public hanging of Fascist war criminals in Hungary in 1945: was the crowd's exultant shouting of 'pull the wire slowly!' to the executioner morally justified or morally reprehensible? Perhaps it was both.) Retribution is the moralization of 'marginal' immorality which, precisely because it is marginal, belongs integrally to morality itself, the elevation of at least this one 'natural' emotion onto a higher category, its legitimation. Ascribed to the 'law' (the projection as well as concrete embodiment of morality), revenge is transfigured into retribution. Golding quotes the famous and relevant remark of James Fitzjames Stephen to the effect that 'the criminal law stands to the passion of revenge in much the same relation as marriage to the sexual appetite'.[14] Golding adds, not unreasonably, that what really feeds and gives popular support to retribution is not simple and natural revenge any longer but '*moral indignation*, which is a disinterested, not a self-centered, sentiment.'[15] Pamela Hansford Johnson, confessing to a feeling of 'terror' in the presence of Myra Hindley in the court room, writes: 'Compassion is the greatest of virtues, yet the mere word has been so debased that it may be used to cover a multitude of sentimentalities. There are times in this life when we *cannot* feel it, and are so alarmed because we cannot, that we tend to cook up a story, to make us appear better people and richer in human insight.'[16] Revenge, moral indignation are merely the reverse side of the lack of compassion felt towards those punished by the law, and as Johnson correctly notes these are most uncomfortable and indeed 'alarming' emotions, however neatly justified on a rational level. To conclude on this point, let's hear the famous words of Emile Durkheim:

> In fact, it is a mistake to believe that vengeance is simply useless cruelty. It is very possible that, in itself, it consists of a mechanical and aimless reaction, an emotional and unthinking action, an irrational need to destroy; but, in reality, it does tend to destroy that which is a threat to us. It consists, then, in a true act of defence, although an instinctive and unreflective one . . . The instinct of vengeance is, in sum, only the instinct of conservation heightened by peril.
>
> And in fact, punishment has remained, at least in part, a work of vengeance. [17]
>
> What we avenge, what the criminal expiates, is the outrage to morality.[18]

The two closely related subjects of law-enforcement and punishment, then, bring us to the end of the first part of our summary survey of the state, considered in the foregoing as a moral community or universal. It has been, if you like, an examination from 'upstairs', as we have employed for the most part the state's *own* preferred vocabulary, the language of traditional mainstream political philosophy. We shall move in a minute 'down below', to look at the state also from the point of view of individuals as such, and then in the third part of this chapter we shall take a 'sideways' glance and consider the state (and society, and personal security) in terms of conflicting groups or particularities.

The best summary expression of the morality and universality of the state, it seems to me, is supplied in its identification with the 'law', in the sublime, transcendent sense of law as it has been formulated in our tradition (i.e. as natural law or the universal moral law). We have to conceive of the *state as law* when law is understood to refer, above all, to the concrete, institutionalized embodiment of universal humanity. Somewhat schematically perhaps (and making an explicit mention of some points only implied in the foregoing survey or touched upon in passing) we might be able to characterize this notion of the 'state as law' under the following five headings. Firstly, the state as law postulates merely *formal* rules of morally right conduct, 'negative' injunctions, and rules which are in principle indifferent to the various substantive aims of legal subjects in promoting their own interests and seeking their satisfactions. Secondly, the state as law recognizes only abstract persons (individuals or corporate bodies) which are all without exception deemed to be 'equal under the law' – with individuals 'sanity' is the only criterion of legal subjection or accountability. Thirdly, the state as law has absolutely no interest in, and no conception of, anything that is deeply, substantively involved in the actual practice of legal conduct, like philosophy, science, religion or politics – for legal accountability what counts is only ascertainable 'action' and 'intention' in so far as it is immediately related to action. Fourthly, the state as law has no finality, no determinate 'end' beyond its own survival – its system of customary and positive 'laws' in the concrete sense are considered as infinite and constantly moving, 'evolving'. And fifthly the state as law claims absolute moral superiority in interpreting the dictates of universal humanity, right down to the very brink of asserting the right to enforce its rules and punish those who break them.

★ ★ ★ ★ ★ ★ ★ ★

Well, there is little doubt that the above account will have struck a great many readers as little more than a fairy-tale, suitable for children, innocently 'edifying' or not so innocently obscuring the real issues behind this pleasing façade. This is, to be sure, not the view taken in these reflections and at the end of the present chapter we shall return to this idealist perspective and shall endeavour to restate it, in a somewhat modified form. But it is scarcely to be denied that the idealist account presents us with a partial, truncated and one-sided picture only, and what it leaves out in the first and most striking instance is immediate individual *experience* in living in the state. It is certainly not the case, except for rare and solemn occasions, that ordinary law-abiding individuals, inhabitants of a typical modern state and subject to its government, rules, regulations and law-enforcement, will readily identify with the state, recognizing their own innermost moral selves in the law. The state for the most part is rather endured, put up with, passively and indifferently and often grudgingly tolerated, willingly used for certain private purposes (personal security is one of them) and just as willingly cursed for laws and policies which appear to go against the interests of the individual in the given particular case. The state and its laws might well be generally accepted as 'legitimate', in the sense of being conventional, authorized in the accustomed way, but it is nonetheless 'external', with a perceived and apparently unbridgeable gap between the immediate self-consciousness of the individual person (including what this person takes to be the 'moral law' binding on him) and universal morality as embedded in the laws of the community. It is on this level perceived – hardly a sensational or novel discovery! – that the state, just as it can in the underlying, though somewhat remote, sense, do the morally right thing for society including myself, and can also do that which I find personally advantageous, can just as easily act to my disadvantage and can act generally in a morally ambiguous way. The gap between the person and the community as embodied in the state signifies that the imputed 'universality' of the state cannot be absolute and perfect; in some sense, as yet undetermined, the state is also to be revealed as an *imperfect* moral community.

But there is a crucial distinction that must be noted right here: it is one thing to resent the state's actions, to grudge against indifferent or unfriendly officials, to feel that I am being personally disadvantaged as an individual; it is quite another thing to perceive that the state in reality (as opposed to its rhetoric) is treating me partially. In the first case it is my own moral imperfection which is revealed. In the second it is that of the state itself. To put it in Hobbesian terms, in the first instance I suffer 'iniquity', and in the second I suffer 'injustice'. The argument of this book differs fundamentally from the Hobbesian view, though, in that whereas Hobbes maintains that the state cannot be 'unjust' (since justice is a function of sovereignty), here we shall insist, not only that the state can be unjust but that an aspect of injustice is built into 'the' state as such, i.e. every state. But on the other hand with Hobbes we shall contend that the injustice of the state is not the same thing as the 'iniquity' suffered by individuals. On this basic and absolutely essential distinction rests, it will be argued in these reflections, any proper understanding of the problem of 'law and order' in the modern state or of the problem of personal security. The *duality* of my relationship to the state, to my own concretized universality, must never be lost from sight: the moral quality of the state is manifested in two different and opposed ways, once in confronting me as a bare, 'natural' individual (i.e. in my pre-moral or non-moral capacity) and once in clashing with my determinate existence and identity as a particular member of society. In the latter perspective only is it the case that the moral quality of the state and my own moral quality (two forms of moral imperfection) are, in principle, exactly 'matched'.

But first we have to examine the position of the bare natural individual *vis à vis* the state. The opposition on this level is undoubtedly real: it is felt, perceived, inescapable. Individuality is never wholly absorbed by the state or transcended by the universality of the moral law. My life, in the last resort, is my life only; my freedom, my state of health and my happiness are unique to me, and I have a side to my consciousness, my own 'rationality' if you like, which sets me in opposition to my community. As a natural, immediate, flesh-and-blood, thinking and feeling self I perceive myself as being both directly threatened *in* the community, and restricted in my actions, in the pursuit of my own unique happiness, my freedom and my personal security, *by* the community. Taking the negative side first, i.e. the perceived 'threat' to my individual existence and well-being, two things above all must be noted. Firstly, and this is where the simplistic, uncorrected Hobbesian understanding is most clearly exposed for its inadequacy, it is just not true that as an individual I am meaningfully and (to me) satisfactorily 'protected' by the state, by the 'sword' of the sovereign. It is not and never has been true in actual practice and experience, and it is also flawed as a principle of political philosophy. The protection against the malevolent indifference or hostility of other individuals provided for me by the 'power' of the state is at best only partial and retrospective. I do not, except marginally, rely on the police or the courts or prisons, the whole gamut of 'deterrence', for my safety – it rests on the relative absence of *actual*, expressed hostility towards me, on malevolent indifference being more or less randomly diffused in the whole community, on my being *one* single individual among many others, on my being anonymous and being able to actually seek and find security through anonymity. Deterrence, and power in general, can work only on the assumption that it is marginal, a last resource, brought to bear only in a minority of instances, which from the point of view of the individual means that he is more protected by the statistical improbability of becoming a 'target' than by the (equally improbable) effect of deterrence working in the given case. For all the actual, visible power of the state I could be murdered, raped, injured, suffer grievous bodily harm, be burgled, mugged, cheated, defrauded, my possessions taken or vandalized, twenty-four hours a day. As an individual I stand

and falter and fall alone, and I cannot help but be conscious of inhabiting a cold, indifferent, threatening atomistic state of nature *as well as* being a member of the moral community and enjoying the protection of the power that emanates from the authority that derives from my own universal morality. The crucial point is that the state – perfectly logically from its own point of view – is able to protect me as a 'moral being' in the first place, that is as a universal, and only residually as a natural, unique, empirically existing individual. That is to say, I might (and only 'might', there is never any certainty about this) be recompensed, restituted or 'revenged' by the state; deterrence, from the point of view of the actual victim, works only retrospectively. If I am murdered, it is no great consolation to 'know' that my murderer will at some point be apprehended and 'justice' will be meted out. But even if I suffer lesser wrongs, like unprovoked grievous bodily harm or the violation of my private space, the subsequent and contingent penalty imposed by the state on the wrongdoer, and the compensation I might receive, will fail to blot out, completely nullify the experience: there is an added negative involved in being a victim which no conceivable course of action by society can eradicate. The *minus* I suffer here as a bare, natural, perpetually exposed individual, will always remain a minus in my memory and future experience, a deduction from my dignity, my self-conscious humanity. There is no proper equation by adding the 'plus' of subsequent punishment; we are dealing here with two distinct and opposed categories, two different dimensions. The universality of moral consciousness and the internal infinity of subjective self-awareness and experience are closely related; but they are not the same.

Indeed, it should appear quite obvious from the idealist account of the state itself, as adumbrated earlier, that the state as such, as the repository of justice, takes no interest in natural individuals *as such*, only in their supposed empirical *alter egos*, morally and legally defined citizens. As the authority of the state is ultimately derived from itself, from its own past, so the protective attention of the state is likewise focused on itself, on its own future (e.g. victims are 'revenged'). Individuals in their natural capacity are involved only marginally and indirectly in this situation and, as we have noted above, the supposed empirical equivalence does not hold: whether restituted and compensated or not, I *remain* a victim. In van den Haag's deadpan eloquence: 'The scales usually supported by the statue of justice symbolically suggest that society is the first victim of any crime and the individual harmed, if any, the second.'[19] In a more critical vein it is argued in R. P. Rhodes's *The Insoluble Problem of Crime*: 'Yet the victim is undoubtedly the most ignored element in the criminal justice system. The system is much more interested in the question of public order, legal guilt and innocence, punishment and rehabilitation – all of which are concerns remote from the citizen's interest in safety and protection of his property'.[20] The second and closely related point here concerns the actual limits of the protective power of the state. Even were we to allow for a genuine concern on the state's part for the security of individuals as such against the hostility and malevolent indifference of other individuals, it would not follow that the state actually *could* protect them. It is essential to note here that this limitation on power is not just empirical but logical; it follows from the very principle and justification of state power. That is, and the point is frequently overlooked in the shriller kind of law-and-order literature, the trouble is not that we haven't enough policemen on the beat or more numerous and secure prisons, harsher punitive sentences.

The assumption which legitimates state *power* (as distinguished from the moral authority of the state) is that there is a certain amount of hostility, conflict and malevolent indifference at large in society but that this amount is not overwhelming. On the one hand, therefore, state power must be silent, or absent, with the morally justified, law-abiding pursuits of citizens; it is these pursuits which state power exists to protect in the first place, so it would be illogical to interfere with them. On the other hand, and more importantly in the present context, the point to note is that the presence of state power can only be intended to keep the amount of malevolent indifference in society *in check*, but not to reduce it: for reduction it is not state *power* that is required but *positive* moral action, e.g. education, welfare services, etc. It follows therefore, and since from this sublime state perspective malevolent indifference is seen as being *randomly* distributed in society, that a quantitative increase in state power simply transfers a certain amount of societal hostility and malevolence into the machinery of the state itself. In other words, more policemen would result only in the greater likelihood of the abuse of police power, of corruption, complacency, negligence and unchecked 'brutality' – the security of the individual would not be enhanced but instead threatened now from two sides. And in the logically extreme case of the 'police state', with power being as 'total' as is empirically possible, the whole problem of personal security is played out within the confines of the state: instead of the mugger round the corner you fear the knock on the door at night, the difference between kidnapping and arrest is virtually eliminated. Finally we find ourselves all in a vast top-security prison, with our own personal security reduced to nil (as noted in our hypothetical example in Chapter 1). John Alderson puts the point succinctly in his *Policing Freedom*:

> The principle is that the price of wholly eradicating crime is too high to pay. It is too high in moral terms, as it would require punishments which a civilized society cannot accept without losing the reputation of being civilized. It is too high a price to pay in resource terms, since the enforcers would outnumber the rest of society and they would need *their* own police, and so on *ad infinitum*.[21]

The individual, therefore, is and remains in a basically unprotected position, in spite of the visible might of the state. But futhermore and still on the negative side our attention should now be focused on the threat to the individual posed directly by the state – not by any kind of totalitarian police state but by the most benign and civilized of liberal-democratic states. That is, we have at this point to return to the institution of *punishment* and augment the account offered above by attempting to highlight the meaning of punishment as seen from the point of view of the individual. As already observed, all possible forms of punishment necessarily entail some minimal infliction of 'pain' on the individual, be it physical hardship, mental discomfort and (and this is by no means necessarily the 'mildest' form of punishment) humiliation, as in psychiatric treatment. The will of the community is pitted and is victorious against the will of the individual. Now it is paramountly important to note, in the first place, that this clash of actual wills is logically implied in the whole notion of punishment, and without it punishment would be devoid of meaning and unthinkable in practice. Not only is it the case, and this is a noteworthy point on its own, that punishment does not require individual 'consent' for it to be legal, and through legality, to be morally justified. Perhaps this constitutes the most significant exception even to the self-professed rhetoric of liberal and 'consensual' democracies: you consent to the laws in general, to taxation, to economic and penal policies, maybe everything *in general*; but you don't consent to, and you are never asked to consent to (only to acquiesce in), the laws as applying negatively in your own individual case. Once again the individual *qua* individual is entirely left out of account. Precisely when it begins to count, when you are about to experience the state directly as power, your 'own' authority turns against you, and in this negative encounter, you, the actual individual, are entirely powerless and *meant* to be powerless. The point concerns, however, not just the absence of individual consent in the case of punishment, and the logical independence of punishment from this consent, but the logical necessity of the individual's actual will and desire being opposed to his experience of punishment. We all know, of course, of instances when punishment is consciously desired for its own sake (and not for the comfort it might provide, as with the proverbial old derelict who always makes sure that he is 'inside' for Christmas, or as protection against your former mates on whom you have grassed), with individuals of a somewhat topsy-turvy psychological constitution, but they can be safely discarded as being exceptions to the general rule. And so we must also discard, certainly in terms of the present perspective, any Rousseauist-Kantian fancy of the individual inwardly, morally 'willing' his own punishment. This remote and inward willing may or may not be there, and may or may not be ascertainable, and it may or may not make any difference concerning the morality, legitimacy, authority of the state as such – but with the meting out and experience of punishment this is immaterial. What *is* material is that the individual's *actual* will, and his immediate, natural inclination, should experience punishment as something unpleasant, painful, involuntary, imposed, something that – given the chance – the individual would rather avoid. The whole point of punishment is to inflict some unpleasantness and against the wishes of the person being punished; otherwise punishment would not deter, it would not be a retribution, and there would be nothing for it to 'reform' (since then the individual's will would already be supposed to have been in the right 'form').

Now a further and equally crucial point to note here is that this inescapable discrepancy between the universal 'moral will' embodied in the state and manifested in punishment, on the one hand, and the immediate will and natural desire of the punished person on the other, results in the individual's experiencing 'justice' not in its ideal, pure, moral shape but in, as it were, a soiled, diluted, imperfect form. As long as justice is opposed to my individual will and desire, that justice for me will always contain at least a minimal, residual element of externality: however just and impartial it appears even in my own eyes, it will still represent for me an irreducible modicum of societal hostility or indifference. In the last resort, to repeat, in being punished you are in the most substantial and relevant sense *alone*, and the whole weight of society presses against you. Only you, the individual, can fathom and comprehend your whole subjective being, only you have access to the internal dimension, only you can know with certitude the full 'circumstances' of your offence, the true nature of your 'motives' and the ultimate 'meaning' of your action – for 'justice' outside, you are not an individual but only an individual 'case', i.e. an instance to be dealt with according to general and previously established criteria. You may genuinely accept some kind of formal 'guilt' but this will not embrace the entire subjective comprehension of your involvement in this situation of punishment by the state; there is an extra element, a 'plus' which is closed and incomprehensible to the outside world and by virtue of which you will experience punishment *also* as a 'minus', something which, whether just or not, 'deserved' or not, will take a little bit away from your basic human dignity, and which can never be restored from the outside. The 'minus' of punishment is very similar in nature to the 'minus' suffered as a victim of crime, and if the former is not experienced as widely in society as the latter, on the other hand it weighs more heavily on the individual in the given case. There is a fundamental, essential and *double-sided* asymmetry in punishment, an irreducible element of paradox: from society's point of view a crime is never entirely blotted out by punishment and morality is never entirely restored, since the *measured* amount of justice cannot be equivalent to the *infinite* wrong perpetrated in crime (this is, by the way, a less oft-noted weakness of the retributivist theory). But from the punished individual's point of view justice always affects and might in fact destroy *more* than the offence; its measurement is made to fit a certain finite action or actions but its actual target is the whole person, with his inwardly infinite dimension.

The individual *versus* the whole weight of the law, of organized society and institutionalized morality, supported by public sentiment and opinion: this is a theme explored in its depth by all kinds of literature, fictional or otherwise. Perhaps the best medium in which to express this negative individual experience in the state, the subjection to and suppression by society outside, is imaginative literature which 'individuates' and in narrative form presents a general message. In various ways this is the message that comes forth in such seminal works over the centuries as *Antigone, Hamlet, Caleb Williams, Tess of the d'Urbervilles*, and the *Good Soldier Svejk*, and in more contemporary settings *Keep the Aspidistra Flying, 1984*, and *The Lost Honour of Katharina Blum*. But the theme also enters political literature in the more restricted sense. As the philosopher and historian of punishment, Michel Foucault, has persuasively argued for instance, punishment in early modern European history was meant to be an exercise in 'terror', giving public and ceremonial emphasis to the overwhelming power of the public as against the isolation and helplessness of the person being penalized. In public executions especially, what is deliberately brought into play is 'the dissymmetry between the subject who has dared to violate the law and the all-powerful sovereign who displays his strength.'[22] Even if public executions are no longer fashionable, generally speaking, there is a similar, though subdued, aura of 'terror' and dissymmetry accompanying single arrests at a public place and especially public trials. Proceedings of criminal courts and the trappings of the public 'administration of justice' might be entirely 'fair' from a pure and formal moral point of view, with unprejudiced lay juries, powerful defence counsels, an impartial judge and the defendant having not only the formal right but the actual opportunity to present his case in a way advantageous to him; nevertheless, the solitude of the defendant, his exposure and humiliation are essential aspects built into the situation. This is so even if the defendant is acquitted and declared innocent of the charge: the 'verdict', whether favourable or unfavourable, still comes from the outside, still and perhaps even more emphatically expressing the overwhelming superiority of the 'People' or the 'Queen' as against Joe Bloggs, the solitary individual. 'Justice must be seen to be done' – this implies not only the right but also the might of justice as embodied in and administered by the state; the public must see, and indeed they are generally delighted in seeing, the effectual display of power. It is, after all, their 'own', but of course the actualization of state power must imply that in the *one* case where it actually applies, 'ownership' and authorization are as it were suspended, cancelled out, and the individual to whom justice is 'done' is in that situation only a recipient, powerless.

So far we have been talking, rather abstractly and idealistically, about the general situation, assuming that individuals arrested and defendants sentenced are actually 'guilty' in legal terms, and thus 'immoral' in social terms. Even then, as we have attempted to show, there is at least a residual element of discrepancy, asymmetry detectable in the situation: the individual, subjectively speaking, is not entirely absorbed into the realm of justice but experiences punishment as pain, and morality as external. In the actual world, as we know, individuals can very easily fall victim to adverse circumstances and the overwhelming power of society can subdue them even *before* they reach the threshold of the state; they might well be innocent of any particular crime and yet their solitary voice is feeble and confronted by indifference and hostility on all sides. Protestations of innocence are of no avail then against the loud and confident chorus of society outside; the individual, inwardly convinced of his own justice and morality, is hidden from the world by several layers of smooth, silky, soft but unpierceable veil woven out of personal and powerful interests marshalled against him, out of the ignorance and superficial prejudices of the public, out of the natural tendency of people to gloat over the fate of the unfortunate, to turn away in indifference, to sidle up to the powerful.

This situation, again, is an extreme one and perhaps rarer in actual occurrence than the other logical extreme of society 'justly' punishing a self-professed 'criminal'. But we have to recognize gradations between the two, and the soliloquy of Caleb Williams does express, in a dramatized and somewhat exaggerated form, a predicament and sentiment which often accompany the actual workings of justice in society:

> I looked on this side and on that: I was innocent; I had a right to expect assistance; but every heart was steeled against me; every hand was ready to lend its force to make my ruin secure. No man that has not felt, in his own momentous concerns, justice, eternal truth, unalterable equity engaged in his behalf, and on the other side brute force, impenetrable obstinacy, and unfeeling insolence, can imagine the sensations that then passed through my mind. I saw treachery

> triumphant and enthroned; I saw the sinews of innocence crumbled into dust by the gripe of almighty guilt.

In between the two extremes, of the innocent being unjustly dealt with at the hands of hostile social power and the guilty dealt with justly and fairly by the moral authority of the state, there is the important case, much more and, according to a number of observers, increasingly common, of the state exacting justice by methods which are, to say the least, morally suspect. This practice – the employment of immoral or dubiously moral means in the service of morally justifiable ends – is generally known by the name 'Machiavellism' and is a familiar topic in political philosophy. Here our interest is solely with the 'small change' of Machiavellian conduct, as exhibited in the day-to-day practice of law-enforcement and the administration of criminal justice, in the practice of 'assembling' evidence, 'extracting' confessions, making 'deals', in the whole gamut of persuading, cajoling, fixing, intimidating, corner-cutting selective victimization which are all – it would seem – involved in the provision of personal security by the state. This then signifies yet one more way in which the almighty power of the state is brought to bear on the individual and which highlights the gap between the ideal and what goes on in practice. From the individual perspective, again, whether or not abstract justice is the ultimate winner, the procedure often involves elements which are bound to make justice appear imperfect and external, expressing the asymmetry between the person and society. Justice, if arrived at this way, is definitely soiled. In John Wainwright's novel, *High-Class Kill*, Assistant Commissioner Sullivan muses thus, in connection with the conduct of his own subordinates in a murder investigation:

> Sullivan watched and listened, and felt physically sickened.
>
> This bobbying lark was unclean and disgusting. This underhand conniving, to get at the truth. This twisting of the knife in the wound, in the hope of a required 'cough'.
>
> He'd done it before . . . more times than he could remember. Sometimes with grim satisfaction. Sometimes with professional pride. Sometimes with

> genuine sadness. It was part of the job. Part of making law-enforcement work.
>
> But this . . .
>
> This was different. This was one hell of a lot different. This was tantamount to taking a family – a father and his only son – and deliberately peeling away their skins to expose the festering flesh beneath. It was tantamount to making them want to excrete upon each other . . . and nobody on God's earth had the right to do that!

So far then we have indicated a few areas in which a pure and immediate individual perspective, as distinguished from the perspective of universality, can illuminate the nature of the state in the context of personal security. Of course the problem of 'individual *versus* society' is much, much larger than this, and our concern here was only to show that the state, from the personal point of view, can be and in fact is also a source of *insecurity*. The hostility and malevolent indifference of strangers confronting the individual in society should be seen to include the hostile, or at least indifferent, attitude of law-enforcers, administrators of justice and the guardians of punishment, as well as the public at large. But still up to now we have considered the relationship of the individual and the state only in *negative* terms, presenting the state as a possible threat to the security – life and freedom – of individual persons. This is, however, an incomplete and indeed incoherent characterization of the situation, unless some attention is paid to the *positive* nature of individuality as appearing in the context of personal security. We shall comment on this only briefly here, as the topic will come up again and be treated substantively in the next chapter, under the general heading of 'criminal' conduct.

The human individual, as we have argued earlier, is a 'natural' as well as a 'moral' being; neither aspect of individual consciousness could be intelligible without the other. By 'natural' is meant here precisely that aspect of individual self-consciousness which signifies the self's awareness of the gap between universal moral rules, freely and perhaps spontaneously accepted as binding, and desires, inclinations, drives, emotions which also arise spontaneously but which do not blend harmoniously with conduct circumscribed by moral rules. We are all, in one way or another, aware of this gap; otherwise there would be no meaning whatever to morality, to the notions of right and wrong, duty and obligations. As a natural self I am hemmed in by and constantly kicking against my own morality. I am conscious as a universal human being of participating in morally defined conduct, and in that way I am measured, ordered, predictable, rational; but as against this I also have, and cannot help but become conscious of, an infinite expanse of effervescence, turbulence. I have a layer of lawlessness and unpredictability within me, deep down but always wanting to rise to the surface. In my universal capacity I am (at least) a co-author of the rules governing my conduct and I am thus possessor of the realm of reason and goodness; but this authority, this treasured possession, this measured rationality still fails to embrace the whole of my personal subjectivity and I also constantly 'rebel' against reason and goodness. My freedom, in one direction, culminates in my morality: I am freest when I obey no other master (e.g. my own natural inclinations) but the universal moral law binding on me as a rational human being; however, my freedom moves *simultaneously* in the opposite direction as well, and in a sense negates and transcends morality from which I am conscious of being distanced and which I then experience also as a restriction.

Now the significant point to note here is that this basic, primary and elemental clash within the individual self is both logically, categorially *different* from various constraints and detriments concretely experienced by individuals in particular states and societies, and at the same time it is inevitably *transmitted*, mediated by these detriments and constraints. That is to say, I may, in the first instance, become conscious of my being hemmed in, restricted in society by the 'powerful' (as in the case of Caleb Williams) whom I am confronting as just one of the 'powerless', or as an abstract 'defendant' at a trial being overwhelmed and defeated by the combined might of judge, jury, counsel. But beneath these *particular* oppositions (which we shall discuss later) there is the primary opposition of individual and society which is simply the outward reflection of the tension within the individual. The opposition is always expressed in terms of particular clashes but it is not exhausted or adequately explained by any concrete form of opposition: whether I am a defendant among other defendants, or powerless in the company of others similarly placed, the experience is mine only, as unique and not as a unit. The company is contingent, expendable; it is uniqueness, individuality which *makes* the experience. It is this primary and substantial opposition which is always reproduced in an infinite variety of forms. This fundamental clash of society and the individual must always be postulated as long as we look upon and accept morality at all as the expression and introjection of universal humanity; that infinite, that expanse, that limitless belonging, can only be opposed by this absolute finitude, this self-enclosed limitation, this extreme point of *not-belonging*.

To make the point clear: we are not talking here about all and any possible kinds of human experience and consciousness but about the experience and consciousness underlying our own present world, the world of states, laws, governments, societies, citizens. It is, I submit, idle to imagine other worlds: we are here and here we will remain, moving perhaps inches this way or that way. The problem of personal security and the issue of law and order are predicated on this experience, and at the very bottom of this 'historical' experience is the underlying opposition of the individual and society, and this in turn is merely the external, objective expression of the clash between the moral self and the natural self. I see, feel, experience and understand myself as universal and transcendent, and this is precisely why, and for no other reason in the last analysis, I subjectively experience the very embodiment of this very same universality and transcendence (i.e. the state as law) as restricitive. The secular 'imperfection' of the state as the embodiment of universal morality, its involvement of particular forms of 'injustice', only serve to make this situation of relative distancing and estrangement more acute; it defines its forms but does not create its substance. I am rebelling not only against my particular 'subordination' in the social order, against any specific 'role' I have to carry but against any roles and any subordination. My individuality is experienced as a distance between my 'self' and all concrete ways in which I am manifested towards the outside world. All positions in society are restrictive as such, all roles are negated by this lonely, transcendent, natural self. The absolutely limited, absolutely rebellious and absolutely subjective individual is the logical counterpart (and psychological completion) of the abstractly extended general category of the 'citizen', i.e. the universal moral subject, the co-author of the 'law' and the source of the authority embodied in the state. The point was excellently made recently, though in a different context and leading to conclusions not quite in line with the general direction of these reflections, by the political philosopher Larry Siedentop, in the course of analysing the relationship between the notion of the 'individual' in modern political thought and the notion of the abstract, 'Hobbesian' state (what we have designated here 'state as law'). The two polar opposites presuppose each other:

> That is, the right to legislate for everyone entails and helps to create a society in which the self sees itself in a newly abstract way, as distinct from any particular social roles it may in fact assume. That change in the self's relationship with its own roles marks the birth of the will in a peculiarly modern sense – the sense in which the potentialities of the self can never be exhausted in the actual, leaving an abstract 'I' over and above the social structure.[23]

And further:

> To this primary role an indefinite number of other roles may or may not be added, as the attributes of a subject. But they do not define the subject. Thus being a father, a Roman Catholic, a doctor, or a debtor may be added to (or subtracted from) an individual's identity, but the individual remains. In a society without a state that is not true.[24]

The expression 'society without a state' should perhaps be taken to refer to a 'heuristic' conceptual device, explaining the nature of the state, and not to any kind of practical possibility *for us*, in the here and now, signifying a real and attainable alternative to the state. The view taken in these reflections, already alluded to in passing and to be expounded later, is that for us 'state' and 'society' go together, and that it is idle, pointless, self-defeating and even pernicious to look towards the 'abolition' of the state in any foreseeable future. And this leads to our final comment concerning the individual perspective on the state. This comment, like our fleeting remarks just now in regard to the indestructible nature of the state, will no doubt sound quite jarring and unpalatable in radical and even mainstream 'liberal-democratic' ears but it is nonetheless a relevant, important and (as I believe at any rate) valid point, and it logically follows from our considerations earlier, leading up to it. The point is, simply, that in spite of the veritable, demonstrable, perceived opposition between state and individual, and the resultant experience and consciousness of restriction, suppression and estrangement on the part of individuals, the 'individual' as such has absolutely no 'right', no moral stand against the state. Here it seems to me traditional political philosophy (and especially Hobbesian and Hegelian political philosophy) had the correct insight. In Hobbesian language 'natural right' does pertain to 'natural individuals' but this is irrelevant, since natural right is superseded by sovereignty which stems from individual 'authorization' and thus the state comes to bear the rights, the morality of individuals. It is then in the strictest sense meaningless to postulate any kind of abstract 'natural' rights *against* the state, since the 'natural' individual is (and must be, there is no other way) defined *ab ovo* as premoral, non-moral, or even immoral, entering the realm of morality precisely at the point of entering the realm of society. Rights in the proper sense pertain to individuals only as moral beings but as moral beings they are *already* understood as 'social', i.e. subject to the universal moral law binding on them as humans and as transmitted through the state. In Hegelian terms, 'the objective ethical order, which comes on the scene in place of good in the abstract, is substance made concrete by subjectivity as infinite form.' And: 'This ethical substance and its laws and powers are on the one hand an object over against the subject, and from his point of view they *are* – "are" in the highest sense of self-subsistent being. This is an absolute authority and power infinitely more firmly established than the being of nature.'[25] 'Nature' is nothing else but 'nature'; it signifies a different category from the category of the good, rights and morality: individuals will naturally 'grumble' against the universal, they will find it positively restrictive and negatively imperfect in relation to their quest after personal security, but this grumbling and this restriction and this imperfection has no *moral* significance. One can well 'comprehend' the predicament of the natural individual and humanly 'sympathize' with him but this is very different from the arrogation of spurious absolute moral 'rights'.

Need we – perhaps we do – spell it out clearly that here reference is made exclusively and emphatically to the state *as law*? Obviously individuals in this understanding *do* have very definite rights, or should have, against particular *governments*. Here again we become mindful of the dialectical interplay between the wider and narrower – deeper and shallower – understandings of the nature of the state. The state as law, while necessarily restrictive of natural individuality, is by the same token also restrictive 'internally' as it were, in relation to (at least some) of its own concrete manifestations; actual state 'offices', like that of government, legislatures, law-enforcement agencies, are constitutionally defined, i.e. circumscribed. Being a 'citizen' means precisely having some theoretical rights *against* the government, and these are rights which are 'constitutionally' prescribed and guaranteed (whether or not they are observed in practice – this is a different question altogether). And this is the crux: since it is the basic constitution of the state (under whatever name: 'immemorial custom', Common Law, parliamentary sovereignty, Declaration of Human Rights as endorsed by legislatures, etc.) that defines these rights, there can be no rights against the basic constitution itself. It is for all practical purposes and indeed logically, impossible to go 'beyond' this basic constitution and basic law, and to assert natural individuality against it. In very few established states do we find rights against the law and if there are such, they merely refer to a higher 'law' (e.g. European Community Law as being superior to the municipal laws of member states) or, as in the speculations of philosophical jurists, to more and more profound conceptions of the 'law', and so on *ad infinitum*; the level of absolute, natural individuality is never reached.

Here we come to the recognition of another crucial point, and this will serve as the appropriate transition to our next major topic in this chapter, i.e. the state as a complex of *particularities*. To conceive of individual rights against the state as law makes sense only if we conceive of corresponding *duties* against the state, as very clearly and crucially distinguished from natural desires and inclinations being opposed to the state. It is, without the slightest doubt, possible to conceive of such duties and corresponding rights, and examples of this abound in the modern world, such as the probably best-known one of the 'right' to conscientious objection corresponding to the inwardly perceived 'duty' of pacifist conduct. (Or the 'right' not to go and fight in Vietnam, to engage in civil disobedience against the stockpiling and use of nuclear weapons, to boycott South African goods, to assassinate an odious dictator, etc., etc.) But the point here of course is that the claim to these 'rights' is asserted on behalf of *incipient particularities*, and not on behalf of natural individuals. The former, e.g. people with a pacifist or unilateralist conviction, postulate individuals who are already in a *moral* state of existence and consciousness, which the acceptance of some such underlying 'duty' implies. Here we encounter individuals who are indeed as far removed from the 'natural' state as possible, who define themselves morally as citizens, who – whether rightly or wrongly – claim to represent a higher kind of law and justice *vis à vis* the positive law which they are breaking. 'I submit', as Martin Luther King is reported to have said, 'that an individual who breaks a law that conscience tells him is unjust, and who willingly accepts the penalty of imprisonment in order to arouse the conscience of the community over its injustice, is in reality expressing the highest respect for the law.'[26] The natural individual, by definition (and, as we have tried to argue, this is by no means a haphazard and arbitrary definition) is devoid of the consciousness of duty, and therefore the natural individual, as such, has no rights. Now it is an extremely intriguing question – perhaps *the* ultimate question for political philosophy at the present time and one that is absolutely central to an understanding of the problem of law and order – as to whether, to what extent and in what conditions these particular moral rights and duties against the state can in principle be accepted as the moral equivalents of the universal moral law concretized in the state. For the moment, however, we shall leave this question open; a great deal more of reflective analysis will be required (involving the rest of this chapter and the whole of the next one) before we can even attempt to venture some sort of substantive answer. For now let us just be content with recognizing the immense complexity of this issue, which is in stark contrast to the relative logical simplicity characterizing the opposition between 'state' and 'individual'.

And so briefly to conclude on this second perspective on the state: the state as law, as the embodiment of universal morality and humanity, has now been revealed as being restrictive and oppressive of natural individuality and as being inadequate in its presumptive role of perfectly providing for personal security. As, I think, the institution of state punishment shows most clearly, the universal will of the state and the inevitable natural consciousness of the individual are necessarily opposed. The state negates individuality and is in turn negated by it. But as our further reflections should have shown, the individual opposes, negates the state only in an *abstract* and inconsequential manner; morally speaking, the individual is strictly *nothing* against the state (against the community), a mere subjectivity, indeterminate and devoid of any recognizable identity; the individual is absolute imperfection, absolute non-belonging, just a backcloth, an impenetrable darkness, a contourless and centreless ultimate context, the innermost depth of humanity (Chesterton's 'Old Adam') but simultaneously the radical absence of humanity. The presence of natural individuality in the state, therefore, fails to show up the *moral* imperfection of the state; in so far as the state appears imperfect from the perspective of the individual, this is only an accentuated mirror-image of the basic self-contradiction, paradoxicality and moral imperfection of the individual himself. The opposition of individual and state veritably exists, and it is of great importance to grasp not only the universality of this opposition but its direct and immediate relevance to the problem of law and order. However, if this problem, and through it the underlying problem of personal security in society, signified this opposition *only*, then we would, at least in point of principle, have an easy task in these reflections: all goodness, all morality, all right and all authority belong to society (i.e. the state in its deeper sense as 'law') and let individuality, figuratively speaking, perish. But we all know, or at least feel, that this is not quite the case.

★ ★ ★ ★ ★ ★ ★ ★

Now, in spite of the indubitable, introspective evidence for the existence of such a thing as 'individuality' in the sense described above, and its ineluctable clash with the state, society, the whole world outside, the story told just now also has an air of unreality about it. We do, it is true, all experience ourselves as distinct, unique and isolated individuals; it is as individuals that ultimately we experience the negative exposure to the strange might of society and state and also as individuals that we gain a consciousness of being hemmed in by universal moral rules. But basic or not, there is a large element of the fairy-tale involved here, no less than with the earlier story related, concerning the moral authority of the state and the 'human' essence of moral laws. While the latter appeared at the end as over-naive, starry-eyed, a simplistic moral tale with an edifying character, this one is definitely jarring with an exaggerated dose of stark, dark, extreme and desperate antinomianism. There is certainly no great difficulty in pointing out the limitations and incoherence of the individual perspective, just as there was little trouble discovering that the story emanating from traditional political philosophy would suffer shipwreck on the hard rock of individual existence and consciousness. But if individuality is a 'hard rock', it is also the case that in actual reality this hardness is manifested differentially, showing not merely a complex variety but a more or less clearly discernible pattern.

We are not just 'individuals' in the abstract (though we are *that* as well) but, just as immediately and fundamentally, *concrete* individuals with a determinate identity. I am conscious of myself as unique, isolated and for myself irreplaceable; *whatever* my particular self-identity might be (whether I am a millionaire or a pauper) I stand exposed to the uncertainties and perils of life; I am always in the last resort and to at least a minimal extent 'insecure' in society; and *whatever* my self-identity I experience my sublime moral 'freedom' also as a state of unfreedom. But nevertheless the whole of this experience, its negative as well as positive aspect, occurs in a context of concrete self-identity: my abstract and isolated individual self is no more than a hovering, ghost-like, untrappable presence which *itself* meets another 'hard rock' in the shape of my determinate self-consciousness connecting me to my actual social world. Individuality infuses, informs, transvalues and at certain points transcends determinate identities but it does not 'exist' without these, either in empirical, material, objective reality or in personal consciousness. Individuality is like the 'soul' to which we might validly ascribe immateriality and immortality but which we can conceive in thought only *as if* it were, or had, a finite 'body'. The same here, and the point of course concerns not only the way in which I would inevitably appear to others in society as a determinate, particular person (my 'soul' is presented to others through my living body). More fundamentally, the duality of perspective is already there, in individual consciousness: the abstract 'I' for me immediately collapses into my determinate selves and it cannot be separated – except for the purposes of reflective analysis – from all of them at the same time. There is always some basic, residual and perhaps semi-conscious and semi-amorphous 'role' I am playing or that is being played with me in all kinds of social experience. We have now to turn round the point made above, emphasizing the particular aspect. The defendant has to endure the penalty imposed by the court in his unique individual capacity; but he is in the dock nevertheless as a 'defendant', i.e. belonging to a particular category and (in this case) passively bearing a determinate 'role'; the plight of Caleb Williams pertains to him simultaneously as a unique individual and as one who has found himself in the particular predicament of powerlessness.

Of course the point about particularity itself can be pushed to reach absurd limits, in which case the concept ceases to be helpful. Not only is it the case that inwardly, for personal consciousness, the distinction at one point becomes meaningless: my own 'unique' quality is nothing ultimately but the existentially unique concentration of qualities which are by no means unique in themselves; were this not so, I would not have a 'self' consciousness. I am Joe Bloggs, thus I bear a name like other people; I have a body which is essentially similar to the bodies of other people; I have thoughts, desires, fears, emotions and aversions, like other people, all of which are mutually communicable, etc. And my own unique self is for me indistinguishable from my qualities or identities as being, let's say, a father, a stamp-collector, a music-lover, a thinker, a person with blond hair or extra large ears, a youth, a committed feminist, a hermit or a person who habitually spends his holidays in Benidorm. All these identities, without exception, are in principle *shareable*; while on the one hand their unrepeatable conjuncture expresses 'unique' individualities, on the other hand this very conjuncture itself is intelligible only as a centreless matrix of multi-directional classification. Unique individuality is only the reverse side of a complex of particularities which always relate and cross-relate to other particularities in a virtually limitless and bottomless expanse of self-recognition.

And outwardly this lack of a meaningful distinction is even more accentuated: in our recognition of other 'individuals' we cannot help but classify. Poetically and in feeling we might be able to reach the uniqueness of individuals but in *thinking* about them we conceive of them as particulars. People in society inevitably come forward as bearing the particular identities of blond people, tall people, sick people, likeable people, young or old, music-lovers or stamp-collectors, neighbours, friends, comrades, strangers, inhabitants of semi-detached houses, people with a Geordie accent, etc. There is no escaping classification and further there is no limit to classification; on one side identities are resolved into an infinite aggregation of ever more inconsequential detail (e.g. blonds are flaxen, ash, platignum, etc., music-lovers are concert-goers, gramophone-addicts, Brahms-fanatics, amateur bagpipe players, etc.) and on the other side they evaporate into a haze of vague and equally inconsequential generality.

To recognize someone as a 'friend', for example, is certainly to classify and draw a particular distinction but the quality of being a 'friend' is scarcely a mark of determinate identity useful for an understanding of society and the state. Identities like these are subjective, formless, volatile, unstable, undefinable. Other particularities, like being blond-haired or a collector of old beer-mats, are defined reasonably accurately and based on observable, objective characteristics but they are for the most part entirely inconsequential and irrelevant from a social philosophical point of view. Identities like these are petty, lightweight, arbitrarily fastened on and have little importance concerning a person's deepest self-recognition as an individual or his recognition by others as a determinate member of society. Thus the whole notion of particular identity, as distinguished from abstract and unitary individuality, is in danger of being lost. But nevertheless the universe of identities is not wholly dark or dazzling or chaotic; it is not only possible but imperative to recognize that certain forms of identity *count*, both in terms of self-consciousness and in the logically related terms of determinate *position* within society, mediating between the logical extremities of universal morality (the 'law') and individual antinomianism (estrangement and exposure). When we talk about definite 'groups' in society, like workers, blacks, women, stock-brokers, the young, the unemployed, we imply a qualitative distinction within the category of particular identity, and at least what we do is imply that these identities, unlike the petty and subjective ones mentioned above, have a decisive role in making the state itself a *particular*. To put it more accurately: a proper recognition of particular group identities within the state enables us finally to come to terms with the state as a *determinate identity* itself, beyond its image as pure law and also beyond the direct reflection of this image as pure strangeness, pure contingency, pure suppression.

The state, not only the Western liberal-democratic state but most other formations recognizable to us (with the possible exception of small and primitive tribal groupings), is constituted by people who understand themselves, and are related to one another, in terms of particular identities. The state consists of definite, identifiable groups whose complex relationships determine, and also express, the state's particular character. This, then, is the great insight gained by studying politics sociologically or through the perspective of political science. The 'real' nature of the state, it has been claimed by generations of social and political scientists, is not to be found in its universal character of law, constitution and morality, neither in the unfathomable strangeness and darkness which it presents towards the isolated natural individual. It lies rather in its embodiment of a determinate network of group-relationships. Thus both the universal of moral authority and the exposure and estrangement of the individual are resolved on this middle level, in the synthesis offered in the social science perspective. This perspective, of course, is not entirely the discovery of the modern age. There are strong elements of it in Aristotle and in St Augustine, not to mention Machiavelli who is not without good reason sometimes hailed as the founder of political science. Nevertheless, it is true by and large that the modern era has seen the perspective of social science rising to a position of predominance, pushing traditional political philosophy to the background and relegating the language of morality to the political market-place, dismissed by serious students of the state as mere rhetoric, vulgar propaganda, 'ideology'. Not that a committed ideological purpose is always absent from the political science perspective: it is there, undoubtedly, in Marx as well as in Spencer (no pun intended), in Ferguson, Comte, Durkheim, Pareto and Parsons, Bentley as well as Dahl, and obviously in the writings of present-day neo-Marxist theorists, like Habermas and Poulantzas. What is, however, in fundamental terms, common to all these social scientists is the assumption that the essence of the state is power and that politics is primarily a power-game; furthermore that the power of the state is a direct reflection and expression of the power of groups comprising society; these groups, or the most important of them (classes, ethnic units), stand in a relationship of conflicting interest to one another; and finally that these underlying conflictual relationships, while mitigated and 'adjusted' on the formal state level, nevertheless continue to define the characteristics of the state itself.

Viewed from this perspective, therefore, we are no longer dealing with 'the' state as such and we have no conception of 'the' individual; the latter is resolved into groups of workers, peasants, officials, etc., while the former takes on the shape of a construct which may be dominated by any one or any combination of these substantial groupings, like smallholders, White Anglo-Saxon Protestants, ethnic Russians, the bureaucracy, etc. In all cases what comes to view is a *skewed* edifice, with differential social relationships, asymmetry and unequal distance from the centres of power. Ubiquitous social conflict, the permanent clash of interest between definite groups, does not of course signify open and literal 'war'; on the very contrary, it signifies peace and it is precisely this character of settlement, temporal stability, definite contours in geographical space, unmoving equilibrium, which decisively demonstrates the particular, asymmetrical, structured, ordered nature of the state in question: it contains victors who sit on and jealously guard their spoils, vanquished licking their wounds and temporarily acquiescing in their relative subordination, and groups in between who play for small advantages but usually in accordance with the rules set by the victors. Right through the edifice it is power and interest, rather than authority and obligation, which supply the correct explanatory principles, power in the sense of the successful imposition of the will and ideas of one group on others, and interest in the sense of perceived advantages accruing to individuals in their capacity as members of groups. *This* is reality, hard and naked, and the rest is merely derivative symbolism. Justice is supposed to be universal but in reality it differentiates between the powerful and the powerless, law is said to embody authentic morality but in fact it is the stilted translation of group interest, citizens of states are formally equal but in substance unequal. Government is not of individuals directly but of society, and society is defined in terms of groups, unequal power and conflicting interest.

Now what this perspective further reveals, and of particular interest in the present context, is that personal security in states is directly involved in the group identities and power relationships just described. It stands to reason: if the state is now shown up as the particular reflection of settled group interest, it follows that the good of personal security is also, as it were, unequally distributed. Security is a scarce commodity to which access is differential and unequal. Power and interest play a decisive role here too: those possessing the means required for the display and effective use of power will look at their own protection in the first place, and the protection of others will become in practice a matter of indifference, nominally accepted as a general 'duty' (or even a specific duty, as in the case of the police) but carried out half-heartedly, negligently, or not carried out at all. At best, in the consciousness of members of dominant groupings the interest of the group is simply identified with the wider interest of society, or rather society and state are defined in terms which reflect and presuppose the character of the group in question, taking its legitimacy for granted. For stock-brokers, barristers, judges, civil servants the world would be unintelligible if it did not contain their particular group or if their group did not have its accustomed position of power and privilege; for them it would appear crazy and downright immoral, against the interest of everybody else, to want to eradicate their identity and privileged placing. And at worst, though this kind of cynicism is probably not very common, members of groups holding power may very consciously protect their interest, understanding clearly that this interest is diametrically opposed to the interest of other groups: long live Sunningdale and let Toxteth perish.

It will be convenient to examine this differential distribution of security in society under two headings: within the narrower confines of the state or the 'political system', and in the wider reaches of society itself. As radical (and many other) writers have asserted, authority in the state and the exercise of governing are mediated through particular group interests, semi-consciously perceived or not perceived at all by the people concerned. Government is 'of' the people, obviously, and it may also be 'for' the people in the ideal sense; but first and foremost it is 'for' the government itself, constituting an interest group with its own identity and protected 'by' the people who actually run it. We are not, of course, talking only about monarchs, presidents, cabinet ministers, bishops in the House of Lords or field marshals on active service; government or the political system in this context includes the many hundreds of top- and middle-grade public servants, managers of state enterprises and established politicians. The state is their own, in a very real sense, and in all legislation and special measures involving personal security it is their way of life, their particular circumstances, their strengths and weaknesses, which will receive primary attention and serve as the model to be taken into account when priorities are considered. The judiciary system and the legal profession as a whole, of course, figure prominently here, since within the state they can collectively be seen as the actual authors and producers and proprietors of the good of security in society, and they effectively determine its distribution. By constantly 'interpreting' the law, judges in effect make it – as seen from the ordinary citizen's point of view. Solicitors, barristers, attorneys, writers on jurisprudence also act as virtual creators of the system of security; in a very real sense they *are* the protection (or lack of it) which the state supposedly provides for individuals against the encroachments of other individuals. Any citizen in trouble, with a grievance against officials or a complaint against his neighbour or a desire to escape punishment, must go to the 'law', which means of course the visible embodiments of law, sitting in plush offices and contemplating the amounts of fee to be charged for their services.

It is of course true – but ultimately may not be as significant as radical writers, advocating the alternative of a classless society, appear to believe – that members of the legal profession tend to be drawn from the middle class and thus represent their class point of view, and class interest, on the plenum of the state. Working-class defendants, it has for example been asserted by a British Labour MP recently (as reported in the *Sunday Times*, 22 January 1984), receive 'rough justice' from magistrates who come from the middle class. Sentencing policy thus 'reflects the attitudes to working-class communities of those who live in middle-class areas.' Class is a real issue here, although, as has been suggested above, its significance depends on whether we can realistically conceive of a situation where particular group identities are entirely absent. In order to understand the particular mediation of universal moral relationships through the determinate identity of groups in power, however, we need have no recourse to such large and nebulous entities as 'class'. Office or profession itself is an important and relevant determinant of group consciousness. A judge and a lawyer are particularly determined in their narrow and concrete professional capacity: their interest of *office* is inseparable from the larger interest which the office itself is supposed to serve. Judges will publicly quarrel among themselves over the interpretation and application of statutes but their individual dispute presupposes their collective legitimacy to make authoritative statements. Lawyers fight among themselves like beasts in the jungle – which is their very social function and *raison d'être* – but they don't fight against the group of lawyers as such; indeed their internecine squabbling goes hand in hand with the jealous protection of their group against outsiders, coupled with indifference towards their clients. As a character saw this, in *The Sloane Square Mystery* by Herbert Adams:

> 'I hate these cynical lawyers,' said Joan, almost with a sob. 'It is a kind of a game for them, a sort of chessboard. The man's honour counts for nothing. The

> game is played by the lawyers, and the best player wins. Neither seems to care about the man himself, but only wants to win the game.'

Group interest, of course, plays a large role in the conduct of all 'producers' of goods in society: politicians, officials, judges and lawyers are no different in this respect from greengrocers, professional football players, crime writers and teachers of political science. But nevertheless there is a difference, and a pretty important one, in that the good of security produced and dispensed by this large governmental group is supposed to be for general and equal consumption and moreover it is a good which is constantly consumed by its producers as well.

Here again special mention should be made of the police, the 'retail arm' of the social production of security, if the above terminology be adhered to. Seen from the traditional, idealist perspective the police fulfils a universal function, or as we can put it even more pointedly the police function is *the* universal state function *par excellence*: policing is the ultimate protection of state and society against their most immediate enemies, the guarantee for the upholding of citizenship against individuals whose conduct is deemed to be the negation of citizenship. Marx was certainly right in *On the Jewish Question* in pronouncing the modern state to be essentially a 'police state', though perhaps he was right for the wrong reasons, in that he derived all general state functions from the structural requirements of a particular kind of society. But however that may be, it is quite obvious that the police as a 'force', as a concrete social institution, bears in addition to its universal aspect a particular group identity also. It has a group interest which is not, either in theory or in practice, entirely coterminous and coincidental with the interest of state and society as such. Concerning theory, the brief observations made above in respect of government as such are applicable here, too: as producer and distributor of the good of security the police has a special interest in maintaining itself in a privileged position, logically required for the fulfilment of the policing function. The police as an institution requires a greater degree of security than the rest of society. When it comes to the crunch, the police will always strongly be tempted to look to its own maintenance and protection and even enhancement in preference to a vaguely defined 'public' interest or the 'general' interest of its clients, the citizenry. The law, in most countries, metes out considerably more severe penalities to those who assault the police than to perpetrators of crime against ordinary citizens. There is no reason at all to doubt that the average member of police forces has as much honesty and integrity as the average citizen; indeed, policemen and policewomen may more than marginally excel over their fellows in the virtues of courage and self-sacrifice; after all, exposure to assault and to physical danger in general is as much a professional risk with police personnel as fibrosis is with factory workers and haemorrhoids for those in sedentary occupations, and by and large police recruits willingly accept these hazards when they enrol. They often tend to be lovers of adventure, interestingly sharing this trait with certain classes of law-breakers. But again there is little evidence to suggest that members of police forces excel in the 'ordinary' virtues, in moral goodness idealistically expected from all citizens of the state. The police are human, nothing more and nothing less. Negligence, corruption, bias, partiality, bureaucratism, cliquishness, the use of excessive force do occur, and the structure of the modern state being what it is, these faults and inadequacies affect more centrally the lives and personal security of citizens than the human failings of other professions.

The Bow Street Runners were disbanded in 1834 mainly as it became evident that they were getting rich at the expense of innocent victims of crime. And the creation of the first recognizable modern police force in Britain was treated initially with justified suspicion. 'Not until Sir Robert Peel finally persuaded Parliament in 1829 to authorize creation of the London Metropolitan Police', writes Austin T. Turk, 'was the idea firmly established that the objective of policing is not to terrorize people, but to tranquillize them.'[27] Indeed, as numerous social historians have argued with ample documentation, the police in Britain (and even more so in many other countries) have until comparatively recently been regarded by the poor as an essentially foreign conquering force, a threat to their security, uncomprehending of their way of life and inimical to their interest. Writing about the American police in the twentieth century, Jerome H. Skolnick has asserted that the basic problem is 'not whether police operate under the constraints of the due process of law, but whether they operate within bounds of civilized conduct.'[28] As 'workers in a democratic society', he writes further, the police cannot help but try to fulfil 'production demands' which may well conflict with their role as 'legal actors'; in other words, there is a tension, or even contradiction, between what we have distinguished here as the universal state function of policing and the particular group identity and group interest of the police force. A philosophy of 'professionalism based upon managerial efficiency',[29] in Skolnick's expression, can only serve to make this tension more acute and self-evident. At the best of times, and this has nothing at all to do with what is commonly looked upon as bias or corruption, the police have enormous practical capabilities in interpreting the law themselves, deciding on arrest and prosecution. This usually, as police spokesmen are not slow in pointing out, means less and more selective prosecution rather than more, and is thus as it were in the practical interest of citizens at large. If the police really literally and continually attempted to 'enforce' the law, then arrests would have to be made right, left and centre, within fifty yards of the police station. When interviewed by a reporter for the *Kensington News* (6 August 1984), a Scotland Yard inspector said: 'By and large the gravity of an offence will determine whether caution or prosecution is to be preferred. But offences where an alternative to prosecution will be looked for include, for example, theft, criminal damage, assault, threatening behaviour, possession of offensive weapons or drugs.' This 'velvet glove policy', according to the reporter, could well prove successful in London and elsewhere: 'Judging by the number of court cases . . . any reduction in charges will be welcomed by the whole community – and that doesn't mean only the villains.' But of course this relative leniency and flexibility are often seen to work in the other way. As the *Hull Daily Mail* reported (22 August 1984):

> Ken Baily, the elderly leading supporter of the England football team, today lost his unblemished record when he was fined £5 for riding his bike without a rear light.
>
> Afterwards, the colourful 72-year-old, who has followed his team round the world dressed in his John Bull outfit, said the police should concentrate on muggers and rapists rather than law-abiding pensioners committing trivial offences.

More seriously, one gets to know about policies of 'non-policing' in certain areas where 'public security' is left to the devices of the ordinary individual citizen, effectively living in a 'state of nature'. Parts of the Bronx in New York City have become areas like this. Are there effective (but unpublicized) 'jungle enclaves' in British cities, too? We read in *Private Eye* (No. 619, 6 September 1985):

> With the Toxteth temperature again approaching boiling point, Mr Kenneth Oxford, Murkeyside's [sic] controversial chief constable, is keeping both hands firmly on the lid, for fear of another explosion. His troops, however, are far from happy with current policy, feeling they are being forced to 'non police' the area, and accept insult and injury as a matter of routine. In two recent incidents, prisoners are believed to have been freed and their arresting officers put to flight, by a howling mob of desperadoes, both black and white.

There are other, possibly not so important but still noteworthy, aspects of the problem of policing in modern society as well. In a recent account, for instance, the point is made that police personnel 'on the ground' in Britain, enjoying a fairly large amount of autonomy, are given to the pursuit of 'easing', the avoidance of the boredom of the job through engaging in unauthorized activities. The authors of this account have detected an increase in the range of 'hedonistic pursuits' with the police seizing all opportunities for 'action', like fast-driving and the use of force, 'while other more routine activities tend to be avoided'.[30] The writer Hunter Davies, in his brilliant portrayal of the world of professional football, *The Glory Game*, reports on his conversation with a policeman on duty at a football match. The policeman, having acknowledged the elemental legitimacy of young fans desiring excitement through 'aggro', says: 'I suppose I can understand that. I'm in the police for the excitement. I'm longing for that call in the middle of the night and we'll have to go belting down the street. I suppose I'm lucky. My excitement's legal. Theirs isn't.'[31] And again, while it is probably true in general that the police (institutionally and as individuals) tend to disfavour certain social groups (blacks, male teenagers, tramps, etc.), the flexibility available to them in deciding on policing policy can and is often used to the advantage of minorities. In London, for example, a high-ranking officer has recently proposed a special 'teach-in' for police officers in order to receive education about homosexuality and homosexual life-styles, necessary for combating traditional prejudices. These are all, of course, loosely related snippets which might just faintly indicate the nature of the problems involved here, concerning the particular character of policing and through it the particular skewing of the state's handling of personal security. And we have not even touched on the more explicitly 'political' aspects of policing which are, obviously, to be found in every established state. There is nothing sensational about political policing as such, and nothing necessarily sinister, as long as this part of law-enforcement is confined to the margins and is under proper constitutional control (which, of course, is not invariably the case, even in liberal democracies). But this topic belongs more centrally to the problem of 'illegal politics' within the state, which will receive some comment in the ensuing chapter.

From the state, in the narrower sense, we turn now to society at large. An essential element in the radical and social scientific perspectives on the state is, as has already been mentioned, the view that the power of the state simply endorses and maintains, and indeed expresses, a certain power 'settlement' among various conflicting social groups. As 'authority' is merely the euphemistic translation of dominant group interest, so 'society' is just a misleading short-hand expression for the constant, though suppressed, warfare among antagonistic groups of people. This view was expressed with exceptional force in the 1920s by E. B. Pashukanis, the Soviet legal philosopher:

> One can only grasp the true significance of the penal practice of the class state by starting from its antagonistic nature. The would-be theories of criminal law which derive the principles of penal policy from the interests of society as a whole are conscious or unconscious distortions of reality. 'Society as a whole' does not exist, except in the fantasy of the jurists. In reality, we are faced only with classes, with contradictory, conflicting interests.[32]

Van den Haag, writing from a rather different ideological point of view, nevertheless at least in part accepts the validity of this radical insight: 'However just in applying its rules, retributive justice cannot be ultimately just unless distributive justice is. For retributive justice necessarily defends and sanctions the distributive order in its major political and economic aspects.

Legal justice never can do less, though it can do more. Marxists have been quite correct in pointing this out.' For orthodox Marxists like Pashukanis, we might add here briefly, there could of course be no such thing as a 'just' 'distributive order': if society constitutes an 'order', it stinks (which is not, as we shall see in Chapter 4, necessarily the view of every Marxist or every radical, especially nowadays). But the main point remains: the state apparatus exists to defend dominant interests, therefore members of groups in a position of power and/or privilege can provide for their own personal security much better than their poorer and powerless fellow citizens. In Austin Turk's expression, 'as Jesus, Marx, and many other social analysts have observed, the initially advantaged are better able than the initially disadvantaged to improve and ensure their life chances.'[33] And as radical Labour politician Tony Benn has posed the rhetorical question in his *Arguments for Socialism* (1979), pondering on the effects of growing unemployment and social divisions: 'Are we going to have a small group of white-collar people earning £10,000 a year, on over-time, and 60 per cent of the population living on social security and being kept back by armed guards because they would be so discontented?'[34] Benn's 'argument' as a whole may not be found altogether convincing by everyone but this image of 'armed guards' holding back the resentful mass of the poor is powerful and evocative and it does unfortunately bear some resemblance to the truth, already in existence in so-called 'affluent' societies. The point is indeed perfectly obvious and needs little elaboration: since the power of the state exists to maintain a certain settlement, and since settlement implies some people holding more power, more possessions, more privileges than others, these people will receive a proportionately greater share of the state's provision of personal security. The rich and the established and the well educated and those with 'connections' will be listened to, and their grievances met, while others have to take on the full hazards of civilized urban life, passively enduring or being at the end, in extreme situations, pushed into some form of resistance.

An important point to be noted here is that holders of social power are able to provide for their own personal security, including the security of their property, without direct reference to the institutional power of the state, just by relying on their own private means, continuous with their normal way of life and in consequence of their social position itself. The state defends a whole *system* of power and privileges, and not powerful and privileged individuals in a special way (though that is not uncommon either); this system then tacitly allows, or even encourages, the rich to 'look after themselves' in ways which are unavailable to the poor. In this connection it is quite fascinating to observe the subterranean survival of a kind of social 'feudalism' in modern urban, and nominally individualistic, society: the wealthy are already protected in their social existence, in their private lives, by being able to group together in 'exclusive neighbourhoods', the equivalent of medieval castles, where personal security is so much easier to obtain. In Sunningdale and Tonbridge, and selected suburban areas of all large modern cities, you don't need a patrolling policeman to secure the tranquillity of your siesta; the presence of your similarly privileged neighbours and the natural barriers of walls, locks, spreading lawns, alarm-systems will largely suffice. Crime in these strongholds is of course not unknown; but it is relatively rare and this is why it has such a great news value and is also a constant source of anxiety. The poor, as Conklin remarks, 'have the greatest *fear* of crime because they face the highest risk of victimization and face it every day in their neighbourhoods, but *concern* with crime as a political issue is concentrated in the middle class'.[35] Being privileged, i.e. wealthy, means precisely the social power to withdraw from the bustling frontier of urban life to the security of your home in a quiet area; the state's organized 'fight' against lawlessness and disorder takes place for the most part in the no-man's-land of depopulated city centres and (from the rich person's point of view) the unsavoury jungles of working-class slums and housing estates. The rich are able, furthermore, to duplicate the power of the state by setting up private police forces, like armed security guards and janitors in exclusive apartment buildings. Again, this is not an entirely new phenomenon and it descends ultimately from the custom of feudal retainers (it was rampant in the United States earlier this century, e.g. the Pinkerton guards), but perhaps it is more conspicuous now than ever before, as the present generation, unlike previous ones, has tended to accept the state's claim to provide universal protection at its face-value.

Incidentally, and to some extent paradoxically, the phenomenon of private security guards employed to protect private wealth points to a weakness in the radical perspective: it cannot then be wholly true, as some Marxists would want to assert, that the state is the direct expression and embodiment of ruling-class power; obviously, from the point of view of owners of property the state is too *weak* adequately to protect them, and this surely suggests that the state is something more than a ruling-class defence organization, and that its *universal* character is not just a figment of the political philosopher's imagination. And it seems also relevant briefly to remark here, though the topic belongs more centrally to the next chapter, that the relative security and immunity of the rich from the effects of crime compared to the poor who are more vulnerable, appear to weaken the radical argument that lawlessness is essentially a form of 'protest' against inequality and injustice. It is an undeniable fact that the poor in general (though perhaps excluding the literally destitute) suffer from crime in a degree much higher than their ratio in society would indicate; travelling on the subway exposes you to danger, as driving in your limousine gives you protection; your cheap rented TV set in the front-room of your municipal dwelling-unit is more likely to be stolen than your Persian rug in the lounge of your fortified mansion. It is as though the alleged 'protest' of the poor through crime was an exercise in collective self-destruction, with the great injustice of social inequality being simply and directly translated into piecemeal injustice and heightened individual insecurity among the poor themselves.

Now of course it is true that the wealthy and powerful are also vulnerable to the hostility and malevolent indifference of others in society, though not to the same extent as the poor; as we have observed earlier, perfect security of person and possessions is a myth, wherever we go. And it is also true that in some respects the rich are more exposed to lawlessness and disorder, as they literally stand out among the rest of their fellows, conspicuous for their living conditions and patterns of consumption. The same is true of public figures who might be relatively poor in personal terms but nevertheless symbolize the collective wealth and power of the social structure which they are seen to be representing. It is rich heiresses and millionaire company directors, and not part-time barmaids and junior computer programmers, who stand in constant danger of being kidnapped and held for ransom; it is cabinet ministers and police commanders, rather than refuse collectors and library assistants, who will be the target for the assassin's bullet or the terrorist's bomb. The wealthy and the powerful, as individuals (though not as a group), pay a heavy price for their ease, elevation and privileges, a price mainly in terms of social distancing and estrangement from the rough and tumble of life in modern cities. The 'street' for the middle-class (and especially middle-aged) person is alien and menacing territory, with its smells, noises, sights, atmosphere, and with the poor, sullen and defiant, freely moving and mingling in what is, predominantly, their realm. Social power leads to perceived individual weakness and vulnerability. In Laver's striking observation: 'One of the corruptions of power is that farsighted hard men degenerate into rich hedonists who want their pleasures here and now. That's the time for the patient paupers to take over. There's nothing like a Swiss bank account to make you want to cut and run when the going gets tough.'[36]

But we must get the proportions right and avoid drawing the wrong conclusions from the fact of conspicuous personal exposure. It would be, in the first place, highly misleading to believe that less public exposure means greater security overall; inversely as we descend the social scale insecurity actually increases, though it becomes more diffuse. Respectable poverty is no refuge from hostile attacks from the outside. In the second place we must accept the fact (indeed it is unlikely to be doubted by anybody) that those who face exposure on account of their wealth or public position do this entirely freely, by voluntary decision (with the exception, perhaps, of an hereditary monarch). Whether it be a genuine and exalted sense of duty to society or a convenient means to self-aggrandizement, the danger of being conspicuous and thus insecure in this special sense is not one that any individual will take on and maintain under duress. Elevation and distinction are in fact, as we all know, intensely valued and desired, and the price of relative personal insecurity is willingly – though it may be grudgingly – paid by all concerned. In terms of strict and brutal logic one might be inclined to argue that in society those who have the least to lose are the most secure: tramps, derelicts, vinos, vagabonds, life-patients in mental asylums. But quite apart from the factual incorrectness of this argument, we must remark on the rather obvious truth that *very* few people will ever want to take the option of voluntary social descent, to gain illusory security or for any other reason. The wealthy and powerful always have the option of jettisoning their possessions and positions, and becoming poor; but this is not so the other way round. Society and the state in this very relevant sense are strictly and inescapably asymmetrical. Security as the chief social good is found on balance to lie in wealth, in privilege, in power, in recognition. The state provides primary protection to those who are 'of' it, in a naturally discriminatory manner, to the groups on top whose collective self-identity and self-interest are defined co-terminously with the whole state itself, while others who are merely 'in' the state must remain satisfied with the crumbs. But again, it is in the direct self-interest of those on top to make sure that others *do* get the crumbs, as big ones as are compatible with the terms of the settlement, and that the poor also come to feel that they have a stake in the maintenance of general security. As Charles Gould, mineowner, says in Conrad's *Nostromo*:

> What is wanted here is law, good faith, order, security. Anyone can declaim about these things, but I pin my faith to material interests. Only let the material interests once get a firm footing, and they are bound to impose the conditions on which alone they can continue to exist. That's how your money-making is justified here in the face of lawlessness and disorder. It is justified because the security which it demands must be shared with an oppressed people. A better justice will come afterwards. That's your ray of hope.

This, then, is broadly the picture of the state which the third perspective, the one informed by the social science approach, will place in our view: states are to be essentially understood in terms of their concrete particularity, their differential structures and relations of group identity and interest, and the uneven distribution of power among social groups. It will, it seems to me, be convenient (indeed, rather more than merely convenient) to designate this ever-present particularity of the state as the determinate *order* of the state. The setting up of 'order' as the dialectical opposite of 'law' has here no mere quasi-journalistic purpose; it is a real contradiction and it aptly expresses the internally self-contradictory, plural character of the state. Of course, this disjunctional presentation is not at all new; a favourite polemical device of radical critics of the modern state, it is at least as well known, and almost as platitudinous, as the conjunctional pairing of 'law'n'order', the darling favourite of conservative writers. But our perspective here is neither conservative nor radical, neither philosophical in the traditional metaphysical sense nor hemmed in by social science assumptions. Ours is a *plural* perspective, and thus we shall be arguing right through these reflections that both these designations of the state are valid and that the conjunction of law and order in our understanding of the state is as important as their disjunction. This may not be a very 'neat' conclusion, of the kind beloved by metaphysicians as well as social scientists; but it happens to be the correct one.

The term 'order' is particularly well fitted to epitomize the character of the state as a complex unity of social groupings. The *state as order* represents a profile of the state which is hardly visible, if at all, when the state is viewed purely as law. The relevant and diverging connotations of the two terms bring this basic difference out quite clearly. Law, in the substantive sense as accepted in the mainstream of the Western cultural tradition, properly contrasts to immorality, inhumanity, injustice, unpredictability, arbitrariness, spontaneity, turbulence. Order in this context primarily contrasts to chaos and movement. The seemingly minute but I think crucial difference between the connotative milieu and directional significance of the two concepts is in relation to 'movement'. It is perfectly logical and coherent to conceive of law as 'evolving' (i.e. the principle of constant legislative innovation) but it is odd to see order in this way. While law is as it were up in the air, spiritual and intangible, order is down on earth, it must be *there*, recognizable as having a determinate shape and colouring. In the immediate and colloquial sense, of course, order most often refers to peace, quiet, tranquillity. But behind the colloquialism, and behind the general conservative-inspired demand for 'law'n'order', is the fundamental conviction that peace, quiet and tranquillity are merely the outward symptoms of an on-going, traditional arrangement of group relationships, of an accepted and legitimized pattern of dovetailing identities, of a particular *settlement*. Order is settlement: it connotes an essentially static social and political world, a substantive and structured world where group identities and interests are complementary and proportionate. Peace and tranquillity outside reflect the vigour and viability of this structured settlement inside. The 'law' is observed or broken by individuals; the 'order' of society and state is threatened by the conduct of groups only, that is to say, individuals thinking and acting as members of various groups. And correspondingly, order is observed (or rather 'served') when people accept the overall terms of the settlement in their group conduct.

Order is the peaceful, undisturbed acting out of social relationships, it means playing the game according to the rules, it means people doing in the aggregate what is expected of them. Order prevails when landed aristocrats assemble for the annual hunt and maintain their stately homes in good repair, when civil servants pass on their inter-departmental memos, when stock-brokers do their broking, police constables do their foot patrol, shop assistants serve their customers, miners go down the pits, housewives cook dinners at home, and unemployed teenagers stand in the dole queue. Disorder is not caused by the odd drunk making a nuisance of himself in the pub or in the street outside; it is caused by the non-performance of actions implied in accepted group identities and relations. Law-breaking by individuals acting as individuals and order-defiance by particulars (i.e. individuals acting as group members) are different not only in terms of scale but also in terms of basic principle, even though, admittedly, there are some tricky borderline cases, like rioting football hooligans. We shall make an effort to sort these out in the next chapter. For now the point to emphasize is the close and inextricable intertwining of order and law in the state, which (happily or unhappily) coexists with their disjunction, absolute opposition. The state as order, seen from the latter perspective, certainly appears to encompass and devour the state as law, making the latter completely subservient. The law has substance only as universal, as moral rules derived from the notion of humanity. In the concrete and particular situation, i.e. in the actual legislative, governmental and judicial structures of states, the law is only a *formal* sanction, a device of final legitimation, an empty and abstract shell without its own content or dynamism. The law, in particular cases, directly serves order, puts its distinctive legal stamp on a substantial and pre-existing power settlement. It is order that generates law and it is order that law unself-consciously maintains, unself-consciously, since law on its own has no determinate 'self'. Law, therefore, misleadingly takes on the external shape of order and becomes, for all immediate practical intents and purposes, indistinguishable from it; against its own nature of universality and as evolving, the law in the concrete case itself will appear static, rigid, totally immersed in a determinate structure of social and political order.

Interestingly, this mysterious metamorphosis of law from universality to particularity is precisely matched by the contrary metamorphosis of order into a supposed kind of generality.

'Order' is most frequently employed in political rhetoric as though it was something that could exist in the abstract, as a universal prerequisite of any determinate type of group relations. But of course this is not so. The law does have this character of abstract universality (bound only by the confines of humanity) but order must be particular, a given and definite set of arrangements, assuming a particular configuration of group relations and identities. There is no such thing as 'order in itself', as there definitely is a general concept of 'justice'. As Preston King has convincingly argued in *The Ideology of Order*: 'Probably very few people really desire order quite simply in itself for the elementary reason that (very) few are likely to divorce the demand for it from some more or less explicit conception of the *type* of order under which they would wish to live.'[37] And: 'A political order, a political system, taken as a rank order of norms, does not precede justice; rather, it is an expression of a reasonably, but never a totally, coherent conception of justice.' As there is no abstract, perfect order, there is no total disorder either. 'Ultimately we cannot posit an abstract need for order for the reason that one is never ultimately able to maintain that there is no order.'[38] Thus, King concludes, the view that order, as a general quality of states, precedes justice, amounts only to a 'recommendation' that 'existing injustices should be accepted before they are rejected; or that the existing order should be accepted as a whole, together with its injustices, for fear that otherwise there will be no order at all.'[39] And in a rather similar way A. P. d'Entreves has argued in *The Notion of the State*: 'Order may well be in itself a good thing; but this hardly excuses us from saying what kind of order we have in mind; nor is it enough to say that justice consists in giving each man his due (*suum cuique tribuere*), unless we specify in what exactly the due of each man (the *suum*) consists, that due which is supposed to be guaranteed by the existence of law and order.'[40] Here we have the supreme fascination of our subject, the paradoxical nature of personal security as reflected through the interpenetrating duality of law and order, presented once again in an epitomized form: justice (or law) as a general formula absolutely needs filling by particular contents supplied by order, by the terms of a particular social settlement. Resorting to the analogy used earlier, the soul of law needs to be embodied in order. But let us ask at the same time: doesn't the imperfect, partially incoherent, heterogeneous and finite 'body' of given social and political settlements *also* need the universal, over-arching, humane spirit of the laws in order to exist and survive? This question will be explicitly considered, and firmly answered, in the concluding part of the present chapter.

For now, let us just briefly attempt a schematic summary of the salient features of the perspective which defines the state as order, similarly as we have done earlier, in respect of the state as law. Here it seems to me, the following five underlying clusters of characteristics need separate mention. Firstly, the state as order signifies substantive, concrete arrangements prevailing in any given society, a complex of interlinking structures and group relationships, rather than a codified system of general and formal rules. Secondly, order refers to a situation of settlement, a steady state or equilibrium, with abiding, recognizable contours and colours, a predictable pattern of recurring movement, rather than a constantly evolving entity, finite, not infinite. Thirdly, the state as order is constituted neither by abstract, interchangeable individuals nor by a general, unified body of citizenry but by particulars, i.e. human beings in their objective capacity as well as subjective self-consciousness of determinate group membership and group identity. Fourthly, order assumes a complex of asymmetrical relationships of roles and group identities, the asymmetry being expressed in terms of conflicting group interests and the differential distribution of power. And fifthly (as this point was seen emerging in the foregoing paragraph), the social and political order of the state tends to be something 'given', existing in the 'natural order of things' (or, as the case may be, by virtue of 'objective historical necessity'), in dire need of legitimation through universal moral principles but where these universal principles of 'justice' tend inevitably to be translated into rigid replicas of the prevailing situation.

A brief additional observation concerning the peculiar duality of the *modern* state might be called for at this point. It is not an accident that anybody (including the present author) should find the disjunctive coupling of law and order in the concept of the state so fascinating. Perhaps the thrill (though not, I think, the substance beneath) is a direct consequence of our peculiar modern Western political culture, the way in which we tend to see in one direction only at any given time, while being oblivious of the simultaneous presence and reality of other directions. In the modern state, accordingly, the perspectives of law and of order tend to be oblivious of each other, and indeed this mutual blindness is a positive factor in bringing out in sharp relief the respective fundamental nature of each. Order disregards law and reduces its universality to a more or less vacuous formality; from the point of view of order such universal moral truths as the equal worth of all human beings and the imperative, categorical transcendence of partiality and selfishness just simply don't exist; they are of course formally acknowledged but, in strict terms of substance, entirely irrelevant. And law likewise disregards order and relegates it to the background, perhaps with some degree of embarrassment but nonetheless necessitated by the terms of its coherence and self-recognition: the 'particular' circumstances of people, of their differing and conflicting roles and relationships, their unequal access to power, wealth and recognition, are irrelevant to legal 'guilt' and 'innocence', inconsequential as seen from the heavenly vantage-point of 'justice'. Law legitimates order, *as though* order were the direct embodiment of law itself. And order assumes the character of law, *as though* law were nothing but the formal expression of the prevailing order itself.

Resorting to yet another analogy here, one might liken this situation of mutual oblivion to chemical *fluidity*, to an entity which is both hard and soft, physically bound and recognizable but at the same time tending to overflow its own boundaries, subject to its own direction of gravity but hampered in its course from all sides and at all times. Fluidity refers here to the coexistence (happy or otherwise) of equality and inequality, of individuals and particulars, of universal principles of moral and legal justice and the rigid terms of a power settlement; it usefully contrasts to the *solid* state of traditional societies (including European medieval society), with their congealment of law in order and the full legal sanctioning of unequal social relationships, and to the *gaseous* condition of a putative future 'polity' or perfectly just state where order completely evaporates and really becomes co-terminous with law. This fluid character of our present modern epoch is aptly characterized by Ernest Gellner in *Nations and Nationalism* thus:

> Industrialization engenders a mobile and culturally homogeneous society, which consequently has egalitarian expectations and aspirations, such as had been generally lacking in the previous stable, stratified, dogmatic and absolutist agrarian societies. At the same time, in its early stages, industrial society also engen-

> ders very sharp and painful and conspicuous inequality, all the more painful because accompanied by great disturbance, and because those less advantageously placed, in that period, tend to be not only relatively, but also absolutely miserable. In that situation – egalitarian expectation, non-egalitarian reality, misery and cultural homogeneity already desired but not yet implemented – latent political tension is acute, and becomes actual if it can seize on good symbols, good diacritical marks and separate ruler and ruled, privileged and underprivileged.[41]

Thus fluidity of social relations, the contrary pull of law and order, can at least to some extent explain the way in which in modern society individual law-breaking, through acute 'political tension', can have or display a tendency of approximating order-defiance by definite groups. But is fluidity itself permanent or enduring? Quite a number of people have detected a directional significance in the present relationship between order and law, leading to a future 'synthesis'. As, for example, P. Selznick writes in *Law, Society and Industrial Justice:*

> In its early stages law emerges from and depends upon the assertion of power and the contest of wills; it confirms the outcome of the struggle and, at the same time, provides a moderating framework and a sublimating symbolism. In dialectical imagery, force is the thesis, law the disciplining antithesis. But as a system of discipline law has its own shortcomings. Standing alone, it cannot fulfil its own promise as an affirmative ideal. The latent historical outcome – the renewing synthesis – is the absorption of legal ideals into the political order and, at the same time, the creation of supportive institutions, values, and modes of thought. Law *aufgehoben* is polity achieved.[42]

Law sublated: here we begin to enter the exciting world of radical speculative projection where the tension and incipient contradiction of order and law disappear in a happy, sublime, gaseous social scenario. We won't now follow Selznick and other radical writers in this direction; the radical wisdom of disjoining law and order, and the conservative wisdom of conjoining them, will receive more detailed critical attention at the appropriate place, in Chapter 4.

★ ★ ★ ★ ★ ★ ★ ★

We will instead close this chapter, as already indicated, by reconsidering and to a certain extent reaffirming the truth and relevance of the first perspective on the state, discussed in the foregoing pages. The sequence in which the three fundamental views were presented here was of course neither accidental nor arbitrary. This sequence roughly corresponds to the actual historical unfolding of these perspectives in our civilization, viewed both in its entirety and through the narrower focus of what is conventionally called the modern age. The state as law or moral community is the paradigmatic vision of the ancient Hellenic age. The state as external force confronting the isolated and transcendent individual stems from Christianity. The state as order comes to full view in the modern age only. And within our modern era itself, from Renaissance and Enlightenment right down to post-industrialism, 'crisis-thought' and the 'end of history',[43] the sequence of perspectives as *dominant* (and not, of course, necessarily as emerging) is more or less the same: the modern state is at first viewed positively, defined in terms of moral principles (Hobbes, Rousseau, Kant, Hegel), then approached and criticized from the point of view of the single individual (romantic individualism, philosophical anarchism, utopian socialism, fictional literature), and then finally conceived in terms of power, group interest and group conflict (Marx, Weber, etc.). That this is a somewhat simplified and dramatized picture is of course obvious but there is no need to add here any modification (if we started on that, we would never finish). Nor is there much point in expatiating on the truth that this sequence of perspectives on the state does have a genuine developmental character – the foregoing pages indicated that clearly and forcefully enough. In a very real sense the last perspective discussed, highlighting the nature of the state as order, *is* fuller, more advanced, more circumspect, more coherent and more rational than the other two; here we really do have a sensible story, suitable for adults, as distinguished from the fairy-tale quality of the first perspective and the nightmarish dimension of the second.

But the matter doesn't end here. Against appearances, the view that the state expresses genuine moral community, that it dispenses with authority and embodies justice in society, that it is continuous with the moral will and self of citizens, is not wholly invalidated, and perhaps not even seriously damaged, by the science-inspired critical perspective. In the light of the latter, we have absolutely no choice but to accept that the state is not law only, that it is skewed, marred, blemished, congenitally afflicted by power and conflicting group interests, that it is *imperfect* and *impure* moral community. If, to use the pithy Hegelian expression, the state is seen to have a 'divine' dimension, it has divinity only in a very peculiar Christian sense: incarnated, tempted, faltering, suffering, dying a thousand deaths. And yet in truth it would be just as impossible to conceive of the state without its divine spark as it is to comprehend human beings without *their* divine spark, whether we call this spark the immortal soul, intelligence, self-consciousness, reason, labouring activity or the possession of language. Human beings would not be human beings if they did not have a notion of moral right and wrong, and they would be something else than human (they could be more or they could be less, as Aristotle wrote a long time ago) if their basic sense of morality were not reflected, however dimly, in this the most enduring, most ubiquitous form of human association, the state. The state is truly divine or, expressed in a different idiom, transcendently human; it is basic, eternal, indestructible. States, quite simply, could not exist without their soul or spiritual spark, without their being, at least minimally, concrete embodiments of the universal notions of moral law and justice. As Hegel remarks in the *Science of Logic*, if the state

> . . . were to be wholly inadequate to its Idea . . . if its reality, which is that of the self-conscious individuals, in no way corresponded to the Notion, then its soul and its body would have parted: the former would fly into the regions of thought, the latter would have fallen apart into the single individualities. But the Notion of the State so essentially constitutes their nature [i.e. the nature of actual states], and therefore is so powerful an impulse in them, that they are forced to translate it into reality (even if only in the form of external adequacy to an End), or to submit to it as it is, or else perish. The worst State, whose reality least corresponds to the Notion, is still Idea in so far as it exists; the individuals still obey a ruling Notion.[44]

And if putting it this way should sound too metaphysical and rhetorical to some people, there are I think at least three kinds of plain and commonsensical argument which may also serve to bring the point home. These are, if you like: the empirical and historical argument, the logical argument, and the futuristic, political argument. I shall present them here in a concise manner but they will receive further comment and elaboration at the appropriate place in ensuing chapters.

The first argument: is it not a very remarkable fact that the overwhelming majority of people, always and everywhere (and certainly in the modern age in what we loosely call the Western world), have accepted the moral authority and supremacy of the law as embodied in states? The poor, the oppressed, the disadvantaged, the powerless, all those whose particular 'interest' is supposed to be conflicting with the dominant interest, have nevertheless always displayed in their conduct and in their sentiments a positive and unenforced acceptance (something definitely more than passive endurance) of the state. In spite of discontent and the occasional upheaval, the general rule has been peace and tranquillity, the observance of law and obedience to governments. Revolutions, if we take a really close view, are exceedingly rare occurrences in history, and when they do occur, the presence of compulsion and coercion in them is far easier to demonstrate than the alleged oppression and conflict going on in the state. Just compare the incidence of proper international wars and proper (political, social or 'cultural') revolutions in modern Western history; the former far outnumber the latter; and of course wars are predicated on the acceptance of the state, whereas revolutions at least seem to be predicated on its rejection. People, on the whole, appear to lead the conventional, 'normal' life of subjection to government, without too much concern about inequality and even 'relative deprivation', grumbling about this and that but still law-abiding, conforming, easily 'socialized', adapting and internalizing customary moral codes, and looking to the state for their personal security. Indeed, abiding by the law, in the immediate sense, itself presupposes the presence of positive moral sentiments. As the sociologist Georg Simmel noted a long time ago:

> For political society, the criminal code often indicates the limit beyond which quarrel, revenge, violence, and exploitation are no longer compatible with the

> maintenance of the group. The content of this code has therefore been characterized as the ethical minimum. But this is not quite correct. For a state would break apart if its members rigorously avoided all that is prohibited by the criminal law, while yet engaging in those attacks, damages, and hostilities which are possible under it. Every criminal code expects that most of these destructive energies are prevented from developing by inhibitions to which the code itself does not contribute.[45]

Ordinary citizens might not care too much about the correct definition of the state either, but nevertheless the distinction between state as law and state as government is always habitually, one could almost say instinctively, drawn, and recourse against the latter (as well as against encroachments by individuals) is usually sought with the former, with the visible and concrete universal, rather than with some impersonal and remote 'natural justice'. Richard Clutterbuck writes: 'The public support the police because, even more than economic stability, they want tranquillity, for themselves, their families, their homes and their possessions; because they want protection from fear, coercion and robbery by men of violence, whether motivated by criminal greed or politics – and protection if needed from officials acting in the name of the state. The police act in the name of the law, not of the state nor even of Parliament . . .'[46] And further on he adds: 'The greatest number want industry to prosper and Britain to break out of its agony. They want to recover their pride. The depth of this feeling was demonstrated to a degree which astonished the most euphoric as well as the most cynical in the Jubilee celebrations in 1977.'[47]

Radicals and sophisticated academic commentators will wince at these and similar somewhat naive pronouncements but the facts are undeniable: people want and need the state and they love the state's visible symbols (e.g. the monarchy in Britain, the tricoleur, Uncle Sam, the People's Liberation Army, etc.). In the best sort of radical literature this much is freely admitted, though the facts referred to will not be accepted as anything 'natural'. In one of the most impressive radical texts dealing with the problem of law and order in recent years, Stuart Hall *et al.*, *Policing the Crisis*, for example, an 'apparent *cross-class consensus* on crime'[48] is acknowledged to exist, and the authors face up to the seeming paradox that people seem 'pragmatically' to accept the unequal distribution of wealth while at the same time feeling that 'there is something intrinsically wrong and exploitative about it'.[49] The authors also admit without prevarication that the 'long-term view of the role of the state as a "class-state" is hard to reconcile with the short-term view that the poor should not have what little they possess snatched from them. The ideology of the law exploits and functions within this very gap . . .'[50] It *is* indeed a paradox that our deepest understanding of the state should involve the contradictory notions, and practical experiences, of law and of order, and indeed it is a *very* long-term view, and definitely *not* a conspicuous part of the practical experience of most people, which seeks to conflate them and reduce one to the other. Another writer of radical persuasion has written:

> In a number of ways, various forms of coercion, sometimes exceedingly subtle and insidious, are pillars and allies of the *status quo* – institutionalized norms, symbols, sanctions, and incentives, customs, habits of obedience, sheer inertia, social and economic pressures, intimidation, perceived perils and risks of adventure, and naked police power. A breakthrough is terribly difficult. Advocates of social change labor under the unfair burden of being the easy target of charges of undermining 'law and order' and the peace and stability of the community.[51]

One should pause here for a moment. Why is a 'breakthrough' so terribly difficult? Why can the 'ideology of law' 'exploit' a supposed 'gap' in people's understanding? Why should exploited citizens be so dim as not to be able to perceive the long-term view of the 'class state'? Why should habits of obedience, symbols and sanctions, and other similar 'institutionalized' devices, have such a strong hold on people's minds? The view that is argued here, against the implications of the radical reductionist thesis, is quite simply that people, and especially people who as particulars are not favoured by the order of the state, are not morons. They do see and relate to the state as law also and in doing that they are neither deluding themselves nor being deliberately deluded by others. It is inconceivable that ideological indoctrination or indeed 'naked police power' could function for any length of time and in a sufficiently broad area of experience, were it not for that tiny spark of law, that pale, flickering presence of morality, that has kept all states in being. We are talking about a truly universal phenomenon which could not be adequately explained without reference to universal human morality. The visible body of the state, its particular and differential order, could not survive without its invisible but intelligible heart, the law. People do submit to 'ideologies' of law and order, sometimes quite far-fetched and crude and incoherent ones, but only because these seem nevertheless to manage to connect up with something that is very deep-rooted in human character itself. The 'law' is written in the head and in the heart; all else in the realm of social relations and institutions is secondary, heterogeneous, fleeting and restricted in comparison.

Here we come to the second argument which I have called the 'logical' argument. It proceeds something like this. The reductionist thesis contends, in so many rather laborious formulations, that the only or most essential thing about the state is 'power'. But what, really, is power? Either one defines power broadly, in terms of its visible effects, by reference to the fact of obedience, that is to say, arguing from the self-evident truth that in states people usually obey other people, and the governed accept and execute the 'will' of the governors. In this case, however, a distinct notion of power will at one point disappear and shade into its supposed opposite, the notion of authority. It is obvious that there could be good reasons, perfectly rational and generally satisfactory considerations, for obedience, and it would (for instance) be quite superfluous and misleading to talk about the 'power' of the doctor, the teacher, the bandleader, the mother, the trusted friend, or the railway porter giving directions (as Shaw pointed out in one of his incisive pieces), as distinguished from their 'authority'. Therefore, so the thesis goes, in order to make distinctive sense, power should always be defined narrowly, not in terms of the general *effect* of obedience but in terms of a distinctive *way* in which obedience is gained; in other words, an intelligible understanding of power in the state will have to conceive of power as essentially *force*, a successful assertion of one will against another, and referring to situations where a clash of wills is evident (e.g. a boxing match, a battle, police dispersing demonstrators, etc.). Now this is certainly an intelligible understanding but once confronted its falsity is directly revealed. Of course no sane person would deny for a moment that force in this sense is present in the state and that force *is* used to extract obedience. What else would it be used for? But nevertheless it does not follow from this that force is basic and universal. On the contrary, force in the state presupposes something else, namely authority. In any given, enduring and stable, state formation (as distinguished from temporary, transitional and *ad hoc* configurations, like military occupation or insurrection) force rests on consent and authority (which is very much like the authority of the doctor, teacher, conductor, car-mechanic, etc.), and it rests on consent not merely empirically but *logically*.

This is quite easy to see. The force wielded by the state is an effect of consent and not the other way round. The actual force of the police, for instance, is created by the citizens in the first place, otherwise it would be nothing, wouldn't last for a day, would have no meaning whatsoever. The force of the state is not the physical, natural force of individuals but a created force which results from the union of individuals. Force is not and cannot be simply aggregation, a matter of adding up so many units of muscle, endurance, stamina, athletic prowess, intelligence, technical and weapon skill, it is a product of quantitative aggregation but something else, too, which transforms aggregation into union. My brains and your skill, my brawn and your speed, are as such separated and isolated; there is nothing in these 'natural' qualities *per se* which would make for the possibility of acting together, in harmony, in united pursuit of given objectives, among which must be counted, *par excellence*, the objective of acting out a 'civil' way of life in the state. Individual natural force alone is not productive, not fertile in that way; it is dumb by itself, lifeless, just there. Union must therefore be based on a different principle, and it would be difficult to find as self-evident a principle as that stemming from this basic sense of universal morality or common humanity. This principle *is* fertile and productive and vital, and it demonstrably creates the force of the state; there is nothing else in individual human 'nature' to create it.

And then, furthermore, just as it is wrong to see the state as being merely an expression of power, oppressive and exploitative, it is also wrong to see it as a 'protective agency' whose essential primary function is the maintenance of security, either of person or of material possessions. This merely external and derivative function could never legitimate the universal compulsion of the law, and a truly 'class state' could never survive. If the state merely served the particular 'interest' of *some* individuals, it could not command (and could not obtain) the allegiance of *all* individuals. It would make the law something arbitrary and optional, and that would be nonsense, both in terms of logic and in point of experience. In Hegel's expression:

> If the state is confused with civil society [i.e. the state as order], and if its specific end is laid down as the security and protection of property and personal freedom, then the interest of the individuals as such becomes the ultimate end of their association, and it follows that membership of the state is something optional. But the state's relation to the individual is quite different from this. Since the state is mind objectified, it is only as one of its members that the individual himself has objectivity, genuine individuality, and an ethical life.[52]

Oppression and protection both exist in the state; they are two sides of the same coin, two aspects of the same external 'function'. Both serve to maintain a particular order within the state, and no state is conceivable without a particular order. But neither protection nor oppression is conceivable without there being this universal dimension, logically prior to both, and which is part of the character of all states. And finally on this point I would like to quote an especially felicitous passage from Michael Oakeshott's *On Human Conduct*. What I have been calling here the 'state as law' is described in Oakeshott's terminology as 'respublica':

> . . . *respublica* cannot be authoritative on account of its providing shelter from some of the uncertainties of human life. The civil condition, no doubt, supplies an ingredient of restraint and formality indisputably valuable to human beings who, whatever the magnitude of their generous impulses, remain prone to carelessness in the recognition of the choices of others, who are apt to harm one another deliberately or inadvertently, who are vulnerable to violence, and whose trespasses sometimes receive the encouragement of gratifying rewards, thus providing them with that small amount of compulsory civilization without

> which their transactions would often be distressingly precarious and their lives more irksome and less enjoyable. But this cannot be a reason (let alone the reason) for recognizing the authority of *respublica*: civil association can provide these blessings only on account of this recognition.[53]

The third and last line of argument to be introduced here concerns the way in which radical political movements, fuelled by antinomian and anti-state sentiments and based ideologically on an uncompromising rejection of the state (both as law and as order), themselves appear to fare in the real world. Revolutions often succeed, of course, not only in changing governments and social power settlements but also in radically altering the *kind* of government in a given territory, state boundaries or constitutions, and the actual character of the groups elevated to a position of dominance. It is not to be denied that a changeover from an autocratic empire to a republic, the replacement of aristocratic by bourgeois hegemony, the creation of an Irish Free State, the ending of the regime of the Greek Colonels, or the establishment of an Islamic Republic in Iran, is a very significant event indeed, invariably with grave practical consequences for a lot of individuals and groups. But then how is it possible that momentous changes of this nature are still more or less fully explicable in terms of the same concepts? Both 'law' and 'order', in the sense attributed to them here, are centrally relevant organizing and explanatory concepts of all *status quo antes* and *status quo posts*, applying to the regime of the Shah as well as to the Ayatollah, to the Ancien Régime as well as the Republic of Virtue, to the Tzar and also to Lenin. Continuous communicability, it seems to me, is most easily and straightforwardly explained by hypostatizing a continuous reality: beneath or above or alongside revolutionary changes there runs a continuing thread of the 'state' as law and as order. The state is in this sense really indestructible: no formation has come to pass, after the most radical and most dramatic and most violent revolutions, that would not resemble its predecessor in this fundamental way. All are based on law, i.e. general rules of conduct derived from some interpretation of universal human morality, and all display the features of determinate order, i.e. a complex of differential group identities. We must perceive this underlying reality behind obfuscatory futuristic ideologies, talking about the 'withering away of the state' (when?), and also distinguish the reality from the equally obfuscatory retrogressive ideologies which lament the demise of some traditional and benign 'rule of law'. There is always *some* rule of law and there is always some degree of imperfection in the arrangements sanctified by law. It is of course quite easy to argue that there is no absolute logical necessity for the continuation of the paradox. It is much more difficult to demonstrate this alleged historical contingency in fact. And then a further relevant point to note here is the perceptible tendency of radical ideologies and movements to systematically confuse law in the general sense, and order as manifested in particular political configurations, for the purposes of their future visionary scenarios. As it will be argued at greater length in the last chapter, radicalism is valid in so far as it is directed to the future further (but in principle endless) purification of the law, and the subordination of order to law, and invalid in so far as it is oriented towards the destruction of law itself. Curiously enough, a discussion of the seemingly mundane issue of personal security, of what is tediously seen as the problem of law and order in the modern state, is quite well suited to the clarification of this more intricate subject in political philosophy. As we shall see.

Our reflections, however, will now have to follow the path already cleared by our discussion of various underlying and paradigmatic perspectives on the state. The principal aim here was to explain the state as the paradoxical unity of law and order, through developing the three perspectives of universality, individuality and particularity. The first of these perspectives pictures the state as a set of general, ethically derived and legitimated, rules, as moral association. The second highlights the problematic character of this idealistic picture by approaching the state from the immediate position of the single and isolated individual. And the third resolves (to some extent at any rate) the opposition by explaining the state in terms of group identity and conflicting interest. The argument we have been putting forward is that these three perspectives all contain an element of the truth and are irreducible to one another, and that therefore it is a fundamentally *different* thing to oppose the state (and to be opposed by the state) from the position of individuality and from the position of particularity. It is this difference which renders the problem of security so difficult to resolve, and even to clarify, and this is also why the problem of security is intellectually so fascinating. Our next task then, to be undertaken in the following chapter, is to develop these perspectives even further, with special and pointed reference to the second and the third. The state as universal *versus* the single individual is the opposition which will yield us the concept of 'crime'; the state as particular *versus* given groups within the state is the opposition which is captured in the concept of 'politics'.

3 CRIMINAL AND POLITICAL

We are now face to face with what is the main subject matter of these reflections. The whole endeavour thus centres on this present chapter; hence (I am afraid) its rather unusual length. Our discussion so far has led up to the topics to be explored – and, it is hoped, satisfactorily concluded – here; the final chapter will put further glosses on our argument and enlarge the context somewhat. While our introductory discussion exemplified a discursive and existential approach to the problem of security in society, the second carried us through the somewhat complex but well-trodden paths of political and social theory, until we have reached the present required height. Crime and illegal politics *are* the problem of security in society but before we could embark on an attempt to analyse these concepts and the phenomena defined in terms of them we have had to understand what 'security' signifies in the first place, from a commonsensical and individual point of view, and likewise we have had to become clearer in our minds as to the proper conceptual framework and background to these notions, i.e. we have had to pay some attention to the notions of law, morality, order, power, conflict and the like, since both illegal politics and crime gain their meaning from these. So as to provide a direct link with the content of our previous chapter, and at the same time summarily state the conclusions which we will reach here, we might want to say this much right now: crime concerns the state as law and illegal politics concerns the state as order.

The undertaking before us here is nonetheless a very difficult one and it would not do to conceal the controversial character of some of the arguments, distinctions and definitions that will be advanced. What we are striving after is a clear and conceptually rigorous distinction between crime and illegal politics, and in the process of arriving at this distinction we shall, in all probability, have to blur, demolish or at least cast doubt on some other distinctions, frequently accepted in scholarly literature as well as ordinary discourse without any close questioning. And yet the distinction we are seeking to establish and define in principle is one which is pragmatically endorsed by common sense, a perfectly simple, obvious and 'natural' distinction if you like, and it is subjected to attack and doubt only in committed, ideological literature; extreme conservatism reduces illegal politics to crime, extreme radicalism elevates crime to politics. Both these positions are wrong; the two things are logically, categorially different and must be kept separate in thinking, and above all in deliberations about the problem of law and order. However, ideological and social scientific opinion is certainly right in pointing out that the distinction is difficult, nebulous, fraught with danger on all sides. It is one thing dumbly to feel, as we all do most of the time, that the problem of crime and the problem of political violence (which is the most acute and relevant form of illegal politics) are different problems; it is quite another thing to be able clearly to define them in terms of mutual conceptual exclusion. This can only be done, as we are arguing here, on the philosophical basis of a plural perspective on the state, like the one we outlined in the previous chapter.

We have to begin by noting some of the most obvious obstacles in our way, and by making clear the senses and contexts in which our intended distinction does *not* apply. In the first instance, we ought to admit that this distinction makes little sense considered from the point of view of law understood as positive law, i.e. enacted rules and statutes. From the point of view of law there are only 'actions' which can be either legal or illegal. Of course 'action' in legal understanding (as in any other kind of discourse) does not refer merely to an external, physical, empirical event but includes 'intention' and the awareness of acting. But 'intention' here still refers and is more or less strictly confined to the empirical event itself; the overall human and social context of underlying and substantive intentions and forms of consciousness are and must be excluded. The law itself determines the range of circumstances to be taken into account, and this range must be limited by the presupposition of legality in the given case. Indeed, as we learn from legal historians, the development of modern jurisprudence has been characterized by a broadening, or liberalization, of the notion of intention, as being relevant to guilt or innocence. In medieval courts, as B. Lenman and G. Parker tell us, for example, sows which ate children were solemnly tried and executed. 'What mattered was the evil deed (*actus reus*) not the evil intent (*mens rea*)'.[1] But there is a limit to which this broadening can go, and law cannot very well accept the legality of intentions which imply a questioning of the legitimacy, morality of the law itself as it stands. This is precisely the rigidity which, as we tried to show in the foregoing chapter, the presence of order imposes on law. Order-dominated, concrete law cannot, thus, question the prevailing order; hence it is that 'actions' are abstracted from the political presuppositions of order, and from all concrete group identities and relationships. The law is no respecter of persons, as the hallowed adage goes, but what that really means is that the law is respecter of 'persons' only, i.e. abstract individuals with their isolated, disjointed 'intentions', but not people in their concrete existence and consciousness within the prevailing order. 'Justice', as van den Haag writes, 'requires that offences be punished as such without regard to the offender, that the law differentiate among offenders only in terms of their offences'.[2] More relevantly and pointedly Lord Justice Sachs pronounced in the Appeal Court, in the course of the Cambridge Garden House Hotel trial in the early 1970s: 'When there is wanton and vicious violence of gross degree the court is not concerned whether it originates from gang rivalry or from political motives.'[3] And it says in the Diplock Report:

> Although what distinguishes terrorist activities from other crimes involving acts or threats of violence is the motive that lies behind them, motive does not provide a practical criterion for defining the kinds of crime with which we need to deal.[4]

The Report goes on: 'We are driven therefore to classify the crimes to which our recommendations apply by reference to the legal definition of what constitutes the crime, and not by reference to the motives (which may be mixed) which led the offender to commit it.'[5] Intention, i.e. that you knew what you were doing in the concrete case and actually wanted to commit the act, is relevant; but 'motive' in this understanding, i.e. your ultimate reasons and your encompassing substantive purposes, which would bring in your relationship to the prevailing order, is not. There is, of course, always a great deal of controversy and scholarly debate attaching to this and similar rather stark definitions of relevant and irrelevant motives within the field of jurisprudence; the point we are making, however, is that the issue ultimately takes us out of the realm of law altogether. The law as such is not to be blamed for this one-sidedness and myopia; this is what the law in the concrete (i.e. solidified by order) has to be. But this is precisely the point where we might also see as it were the Achilles-heel of law revealed: this is in the realm of politics.

In the second instance, the distinction between illegal politics and crime should not be seen to obscure the fact that both are attacks on the state, on morality as embodied in the law of the state and the customs of the people. In the state, universal and particular are conjoined and interpenetrating: the state is one body, though with two different persons. And so even in terms of our plural perspective we have to recognize that crime and political violence share this one minimum common denominator; if you like, the two are elementally united in their shared *negative* determination. An assault on the establishment is an assault on the establishment, whichever way you look at it. It might show up the imperfection of the establishment or the imperfection of human character but in all cases it is a blemish, an imperfection, from which society as a whole suffers. Both political illegality and crime signify insecurity in society, and insecurity to boot which affects individual persons in an indiscriminate way, in principle as well as in practice. The distinction we are seeking, therefore, is not in terms of immediate, palpable effect or significance; the starting-point must be a recognition of 'negation' involved in all these attacks, political or criminal. Our distinction will make sense only in terms of deep-lying, ultimate effects and significance, gained in the course of the uncovering of the truth that (as we have already argued in the previous chapter) the state is open to attack and negation in two ways: to the abstract negation issuing from individuals as such and the determinate negation stemming from group identity and group action.

In the third instance, and following from here, the point should be made clear that our distinction is not in terms of recognizable 'action' either. The two things, illegal politics and crime, converge on the empirical level. There is in principle no particular type of action which could be designated as being 'essentially' either criminal or political. All one could say is that there is a vague tendency, well explained by reference to practical considerations, which would make for the typical occurrence of certain kinds of action in a political context, while other kinds of illegal action would be relatively rare here. Child-molesting is not a favoured action among political terrorists, and cat-burglars will not usually storm the Bastille. But by and large it would not be too difficult to find instances of every kind of action in every kind of attack on society, criminal or political. Fraud, forgery, theft, robbery with violence, assault on the person, the causing of bodily harm, the destruction of property and embezzlement appear to be 'criminal' at first glance but they have all figured at one time or another in the activity of illegal political practitioners; on the other hand, the use of explosives with malicious intent, aerial hijacking, wilful attack on the police and on public figures, kidnapping, blackmail and extortion, and many other things often associated with political illegality are also part of the criminal scene. A two-way traffic operates here, with imitations and borrowings. As Bowyer Bell relevantly remarks, with reference to kidnappings in Italy in recent years: 'Indeed, a most important indicator of social decay is the difficulty that both police and perpetrator encounter in distinguishing between criminal and political acts. When revolutionaries began kidnapping symbolic victims and demanding revolutionary ransoms in increasingly large amounts, the attention of the self-interested was instantly aroused.'[6] Thus again, as with the previous point, it is important to go beyond immediate, empirical occurrences and even immediate intentions in the customary legal sense; the direction is beyond and away from actions, and towards an appreciation of deeper contexts and meanings.

Fourthly, the distinction we are endeavouring to formulate is not meant to be a distinction among actual individuals either. We should be able to separate crime and illegal politics in principle, in conceptual terms; it is not thus possible to distinguish between criminals and political actors. Of course there is a rough-and-ready commonsensical difference and it holds up most of the time, but the exceptions are too numerous and the real existential situation so complex that it would be inadvisable to try to look here for a general principle. Quite a number of illegal political actors, including urban guerillas, insurrectionists and terrorists – perhaps the majority – have been people of high moral principles and integrity, and have been innocent of any action or intent which is ordinarily considered criminal. At least political actors, as persons, tend to be idealistic. And correspondingly it may well be that most ordinary criminals as persons tend not to be idealistic in this sense but quite the opposite, immoral right through and seriously lacking in integrity. But this observation should not be pushed too far, and we readily sense that there is a world of difference between this kind of rather simplistic myth and a more complicated reality. There are three points to be borne in mind. Firstly, it is a well-attested fact that, certainly in modern times, the membership of illegal political movements has tended to be contiguous, if not directly continuous and intermingling, with the membership of the criminal 'underworld'. From violent anarchism and nihilism in the nineteenth century (for example, the notorious Ravachol) to the Angry Brigade of the late twentieth, the most appropriate recruiting ground for the rank and file of illegal movements has been the world of petty and violent criminals, already on the fringes of society, antagonistic towards the establishment and antagonized by it, receptive to revolutionary propaganda and the offer of a 'cause' to lift them out of a pointless kind of existence. As Mikhail Bakunin the anarchist is reported to have said: 'We must ally ourselves with the doughty world of brigands who, in Russia, are the only real revolutionaries.'[7] From the point of view of illegal political movements the advantages of this recruitment strategy for the rank and file are quite self-evident: criminals tend not only to be people with a 'grievance' (in fact this is by no means always true) and already in practice rejecting the prevailing norms of state and society, but also usefully practised and skilled in the requisite arts, from forgery to physical violence.

The second point to note is that a prolonged period of illegal political activity can and often does turn individual revolutionaries into criminals, which seems to have been a part of the experience of the IRA in both Southern and Northern Ireland. A Northern Irish resident, pseudonymed 'Pat', had this to say when interviewed by a political scientist: 'The Provos have ruined the ideal of Republicanism. They're gangsters ruling with guns and if you say so you get your knee-caps blown off. You can't rule this district with a gun, you can't protect people like that . . . They're paying now for scraping the bottom of the barrel. The old IRA would never have allowed these hoods into the movement . . .'[8] The point also makes some common sense: frustration, hopelessness, insecurity and the constant exposure to the criminal fringes easily leads to hardening, cynicism, the loss of revolutionary fervour and purity, and the gradual acceptance of the short-change of individual aggrandizement, in the form of personal power or money. As said, the underworld of crime and the netherworld of illegal politics are both volatile, with individuals changing to and fro all the time, often pursuing the two different kinds of activities simultaneously. Which leads to the third and perhaps most telling point here, namely that it is usually difficult, and sometimes impossible, neatly to separate criminal and political 'motives' or 'intentions' in the case of the same individuals. Criminals and political actors are of course not alone in having 'mixed motives' antecedent to their various courses of action, motives the elements of which are often not clear to themselves and which others (such as judges or jurors) can sort out only at the expense of over-simplification. But here especially the extent of ambiguity and mutual interpenetration is acute, and indeed the separate motives of individual advantage and political purpose can be seen to coalesce at one point: after all, the pursuit of politics, illegally or otherwise, is inconceivable without a certain degree of aggression, intolerance and personal power-seeking, and equally the criminal pursuit of self-advantage is in reality never total. Self-advantage and political purpose seem certainly to have nicely coincided in the activities of the Angry Brigade. As G. Carr writes: 'To people whose definitions of legality and illegality were their own, stealing cheque books and credit cards, mostly from students at the universities they visited, provided a lucrative and politically acceptable solution to the financial problems of full-time revolutionary involvement.'[9] We shall have further occasions to consider 'coincidences' and 'border-line' instances later, and at the end of this chapter there will be more extended comment concerning the Angry Brigade.

★ ★ ★ ★ ★ ★ ★ ★

As we have remarked earlier, clarity and simplicity must be looked for where they properly belong, viz. the world of ideas, and not where these qualities themselves are alien and have a distorting effect, i.e. concrete individual persons. Principles are, or at least they ought to be, clear and simple; people are irreducibly complex. Now what is certainly incumbent on us, in the light of what has been discussed up to this point, is the isolation and clear definition of a relevant concept of *crime*. To this we shall accede by first making the all-important point that any coherent understanding of crime must conceive of crime as.

belonging to the category of morality, i.e. to put it simply at first, crime is to be defined as basic immorality or moral wrongdoing. It is the contravention of the basic moral law, nothing more and nothing less. As we have argued in the previous chapter, for us in the Western tradition human life, consciousness and experience are inseparable from the awareness of a fundamental and universal moral law, defining right and wrong, good and evil. It follows, therefore, that we must also have a conception, as a fundamental and integral aspect of our conscious make-up, of those human actions, motives, intentions, opinions and forms of consciousness which directly contradict morality. It is proposed here that we call this direct contradiction of morality 'crime', but of course it is not denied that many other terms and concepts have been and can be used to denote the same phenomenon, such as the terms 'sin', 'wrong', 'evil' or 'wickedness'. 'Crime' will be used here for the definitely polemical but (in the light of our overall conceptual framework) quite respectable intention of highlighting the very close connection, and indeed conceptual meeting-point, between the underlying 'moral law' and the 'law' *in general* as embodied in the state. As the moral law and the 'state as law' are closely connected, indeed continuous, so there is a line of unbroken continuity linking acts of immorality and (certain) acts of illegality. At least ordinary usage (as distinguished from criminological usage) seems to bear this out, as in common parlance 'crime' and 'criminal' are habitually equated with the morally reprehensible, the absolutely evil, the condemnable, the unspeakable, the inhuman and anti-human. Crime is the most glowing stigma signifying acts and intentions against humanity. It is interesting to note that in the many varieties of penumbral usage (from which the term 'crime', as any other general term, is obviously not exempt), which shade into the sense of foolishness or absurdity, there is yet a faint suggestion of moral reprehension remaining, e.g. in the colloquial expression, 'crime against good taste', or in the legal expression, 'criminal negligence'. It is as though it were generally felt that a really serious deficiency of humanity can best be characterized by the tag 'crime' to indicate its magnitude; bad taste in itself, and even negligence up to a point, are not as a rule regarded as instances of immorality but they become immoral and by the same token 'criminal' on reaching a certain limit.

I am of course perfectly aware of the fact that this moral approach to crime is not one that would be accepted by everybody, or certainly not without further argument and clarification, and least of all by influential sections of scholarly opinion within the fields of legal science and criminology. The assertion is often heard that 'crime is not a behavioural but a legal phenomenon' and that 'by definition all forms of human conduct are natural';[10] or that 'crime is a sociopolitical artifact, not a natural phenomenon.'[11] There is certainly some truth in these views and, although in danger of exaggerated emphasis, they at least serve to call our attention to this important question of magnitude. That is to say, the assertion that crime is a 'legal category' is meant to point out two things: that there are immoral actions which are not criminal, and criminal (i.e. illegal) actions which are not immoral. It is the first of these which we have sought to explain by reference to 'magnitude'. Some immoral actions are certainly not serious enough to be called criminal and, I would like to argue, it is this relative lack of gravity which *both* prevents us in ordinary usage from attaching to them the criminal label *and* renders these actions also legally indifferent and irrelevant. Such actions or modes of conduct would include, for example, neglect, malice, selfishness, untrustworthiness, infidelity, mendacity, lack of mercy and civility, rudeness, pettiness, jealousy, arrogance, etc. – all these and many other morally deficient forms of conduct could become 'criminal' in certain circumstances which, however, always tend to signify an increased magnitude and corresponding seriousness. The metamorphosis of lesser immorality into criminality is *more or less* (an important qualification but it ought not to be overemphasized) at the point where legal indifference becomes illegality.

Very roughly, but certainly not without some claim to truthfulness, it could be argued that the actual legislation of states in history has followed the line of development taken by general opinion as to what are and what are not serious cases of immorality, and further it could perhaps be also asserted that there seems to have been a kind of historical 'natural selection' tending to confirm quite consistently in legislation what moral opinion has *consistently* held to be seriously immoral. It is highly unlikely to be either accidental or conspiratorially contrived, for example, that the wanton or malicious taking of human life, bodily injury to persons, the spontaneous and arbitrary taking of material possessions or their destruction should usually have been held seriously immoral and at the same time made illegal. Illegal criminality is the highest peak of criminal immorality: it is that form of conduct which makes social existence – civil relations among individuals – itself problematic and precarious. As James Q. Wilson has put the point: 'To steal, to rape, to rob, to assault – these acts are destructive of the very possibility of society and affronts to the humanity of their victims.'[12] People definitely expect the 'law', i.e. the state's security apparatus, to protect them against the effects of serious immorality, against actions which 'revolt' their moral sense. 'There are offences', as J. Raz says in *The Authority of Law*, 'which when committed by certain people or in certain circumstances do actually revolt people and strengthen the law-abiding inclinations of the public.'[13] And in Patricia Morgan's view:

> The most serious crimes, such as murder, violence against the person, cruelty, theft, or destructive acts such as arson, do reflect violation of deeply held norms, which are expressed in informal techniques of social control: disapproval, ostracism, even spontaneous reprisals. Here, the community is not doing the job of law, so much as crudely asserting the values which it expects the law to uphold on its behalf.[14]

On one side therefore, it seems, the rather stark assertion that crime is a 'legal category' can be reasonably countered by pointing out the quite consistent correspondence between popular conceptions of serious immorality and crime as expressed in legal terms. Crime is a legal category but it is that *because* it is also, antecedently and in most cases simultaneously, a moral category. There is no serious form of immorality which does not at least *tend* to fall under the rubric of illegality.

The other side of this same assertion, however, would appear to be more of a stumbling-block. Almost everybody, from expert legal scholars to the least academically minded citizens, would immediately feel, and say, that there is a significant discrepancy between the categories of immorality and illegality, once we approach the issue from the side of actual legislation, e.g. the myriad kinds of actions, big and small, frequently or infrequently encountered, which the varying and sundry laws and regulations of states, provinces, regions, cities or sometimes even semi-private institutions pronounce 'illegal' and a 'contravention' of their rules. There are and have been, technically and formally, innumerable instances of legal contravention which it would seem to be entirely absurd to call immoral. It will, it seems to me, be useful to distinguish between four quite different sorts of issues here. In the first place, there could be such a thing as a morally blemished, wicked state, with 'laws' that are not proper laws in the moral sense. Secondly, there may be situations where an overriding moral concern validly supersedes legislation which is otherwise accepted as perfectly moral. Thirdly, we have the problem of petty laws and petty law-breaking, like the contravention of traffic regulations, sanitary bye-laws, taxation laws or property laws. And fourthly there is the issue of so-called 'victimless crimes'.

Now I would contend that against appearances the question of morality and immorality is by no means clear-cut with *any* of these four kinds of cases, i.e. it could still be argued that illegality in all four cases amounts to, or at least borders on, immorality. Concerning the first two, I shall make only a couple of very brief observations, as they will be touched on again later, when we are discussing politics. As regards the first: clearly in a state like Nazi Germany or South Africa, with legalized racialism (and there is hardly any doubt that racial discrimination *eo ipso* contravenes the fundamental moral law, as defined in the previous chapter) and racial persecution, there is no obvious and clear-cut moral obligation to observe these laws, and hence their contravention, though technically 'criminal', does not by itself constitute immorality. But from this, as far as I can see at any rate, it still does not follow that there is a blanket moral exemption from the observance of *all* laws in states of this kind, and least of all laws which we have earlier identified as coinciding with consistently held popular views about serious crimes. Murder (as distinguished from political assassination), rape, violence against persons and wanton theft are still immoral and criminal, irrespective of the fact that they are also pronounced illegal by the legislation of a state which itself bears some 'criminal' blemishes. There are bad laws and consequently states which are much more obviously imperfect from the moral point of view than others; but these are still 'states', bearing at least a minimal moral quality and this quality lies precisely in their legislation's pronouncing *also* on what are generally regarded as serious criminal offences. And as regards the second case: an overriding moral concern can be claimed on behalf of particular groups, e.g. stealing bread from the supermarket in order to feed the destitute, or on behalf of a single individual, e.g. helping my convicted (validly convicted) brother to escape from prison. The former situation clearly takes us to the threshold of politics where different moral rules apply (as was already fleetingly observed in the previous chapter, in connection with moral 'duties' *against* the state). The latter situation seems to me unproblematic: personal affection and subjective feeling in general will sometimes cause us to contravene laws which we otherwise accept as morally valid; this can well be considered 'humanly' understandable and perhaps even exonerable but it is still a case of immorality, again coinciding with criminality.

Let us then take a look at petty and technical offences. Am I 'immoral' when committing the punishable legal offence of parking my car in a restricted zone, leaving my dustbin on the pavement, allowing my dog to foul the kerb, pocketing the bank note which I have found lying on the floor of a restaurant, drinking in a pub after hours, failing to pay my bus fare or rounding-up the expenditure in my annual income tax return? It is deceptively easy to dismiss all these and similar cases, of which undoubtedly we are all 'guilty' some of the time, as being morally indifferent, even though strictly against the law. As D. Lyons writes in his excellent book, *Ethics and the Rule of Law*: 'Traffic regulations, for example, are somewhat arbitrary. They do not mirror moral principles. No Kantian argument is available to show that driving on an arbitrarily determined side of the road or stopping at a light of a certain color is a breach of moral duty and thus subject to punishment.'[15] There may not, indeed, be 'Kantian' arguments available, couched in strictly universal terms of moral rights and duties but surely some aspects of the 'Hegelian' development of Kantian morality may have relevance here. That is to say, we ought not to look for morality directly and immediately expressed in legislation of this sort (or indeed in any sort). Yet morality must be presumed to lie behind them all, and I think that both logic and sentiment do lead us eventually to the acceptance that there *is* a moral duty incumbent on us as individual citizens to observe all rules and regulations, however petty, pointless and seemingly arbitrary, and consequently that their contravention is 'criminal' as well as immoral. The universal moral law itself appoints and sanctions the state as its concrete embodiment, and it is through this embodiment only that we become moral beings and citizens. And if once the state is accepted as the expression of morality, it must follow that all its legal emanations reflect the same morality, albeit indirectly. The rule to drive on the one side of the road is *in itself* arbitrary, contingent, morally meaningless. But it is wrong to take these minor rules in isolation; their very character as rules or laws stems from the moral authority of the state, and if the rules are discarded in principle as not being morally obligatory (which is of course not the same thing as their contingent breach in practice), then the logical implication is that we deny and defy the authority of the state. But if we do this, then once again we reach the threshold of politics, i.e. now confronting the state on the basis of a conception of moral duty *opposed* to the prevailing law, and in terms of which this law itself is pronounced 'wrong'. But obviously this is a very different kettle of fish altogether from looking upon certain rules and regulations as morally indifferent, i.e. petty, arbitrary, inconsequential, iniquitous, and expendable on that account. This attitude, it seems to me, is not rationally open to us as moral beings. Either we reject the overall authority of the state or we accept it, and accept the implications in both cases. I may be perfectly correct in regarding some laws as silly, confused, unpleasant, but I cannot logically regard them as unimportant and I cannot claim exemption on this subjective (and of course similarly 'arbitrary') basis alone. Now further it seems to me that this logic is, generally speaking, endorsed by popular sentiment and that popular sentiment is absolutely correct in this regard: there is, palpably, at least a faint tinge of immorality and irresponsibility, felt by most people most of the time, an uncertain, subtle feeling of unease and inner tension, the hardly audible voice of a deep conscience, accompanying these minor contraventions of the law. We do exceed the speed limit and we do cheat on our tax returns but these are not very comfortable things to do.

By and large, it seems to me, so-called 'victimless crimes' fall under the same consideration, i.e. can validly be regarded as immoral as well as illegal. Victimless crimes, as for example listed by Golding, would probably include such things as consensual homosexuality and prostitution, bigamy, polygamy, incest, adultery, fornication, contraception, abortion, obscenity, pornography, and also suicide, euthanasia, gambling and the use of drugs and alcohol.[16] This issue opens a veritable hornets' nest, as every student of political philosophy knows. What are the proper and precise limits of 'authority' and individual 'liberty'? What indeed? We obviously cannot, and hopefully need not, follow here in any depth or detail the raging argument between the paternalists and libertarians, from Mill and Stephen to Hart and Devlin. From the point of view of the overall direction of these reflections we shall need to advance only a few general considerations, so as to clear the way. Some of these will be enlarged on later. The first consideration is that whereas from the point of view of actual legislation it might make perfect sense to talk about 'victimless' offences, from the moral (i.e. 'legal' in the deeper sense) angle this division itself appears highly problematic from the very start, if not invalid altogether. As there is no 'action' without outward – public and social – consequences, there can be no offence, if it should be regarded as an offence, without victims. This is true of suicide as well as gambling as well as alcohol-consumption as well as consensual prostitution. *Somebody* will always be affected and in a great many cases it would not be to difficult to argue that somebody, or some bodies, will be *adversely* affected, e.g. the gambler's family, the alcoholic's colleagues, the prostitute and her customer who are both 'degraded' in their humanity through the transaction. No individual *qua citizen* is an island and moral obligations in principle always reach further than legal injunctions and prohibitions; in some cases the law is 'silent' only on practical-technical grounds (e.g. the impossibility of enforcement) and in some other cases, as we have observed earlier, by virtue of a societal judgment differentiating between more and less serious forms of immorality.

The second consideration, which follows on from this, is that the foregoing argument notwithstanding there is undoubtedly some sense in distinguishing between actions, or offences, which as it were directly, immediately and measurably involve personal victims and those whose adverse affect is more remote and diffuse. Mill could not perhaps make his distinction between 'self-regarding' actions and 'other-regarding' actions entirely watertight but he was scarcely a fool in drawing the distinction. There is an important moral difference between self-inflicted harm and violence against others, between gambling and stealing, between being drunk and disorderly in public and being an inconspicuous alcoholic, between rape and consensual prostitution. Again, very roughly, one may detect a remarkable parallel between what civilized opinion has over the centuries regarded as really serious crimes and those that involve direct victims. Moral feeling concerning 'victimless' crimes is by no means as strong and consistent as it is where there are obvious victims; it is volatile, heterogeneous, susceptible to change and development, more tolerant of diverse tastes and customs. There is clearly, though we might find it exceptionally difficult to define this in precise terms, a difference between the minimum and absolute needs of a civilized kind of existence to maintain itself (i.e. for the 'state' to exist) and the particular needs of a particular kind of order. The latter are obviously not so central and basic, and this seems clearly reflected in popular attitudes' being markedly less confident here in their condemnation. Pertinent examples may be the differential attitude taken towards drug-use which is as such victimless and drug-pushing which has very definite victims, and towards consensual homosexuality among adults and 'consensual' paedophilia. It is one thing to dislike or be disgusted by a certain kind of practice (sexual or otherwise), it is quite another to detect in it direct personal threats to those who, like children, are not or not yet in a position adequately to care for themselves. The degree of the immorality of victimless crimes is always problematic, and this quantitative uncertainty itself will always put a question mark to their quality as being 'immoral' in the first place; here then at least we must accept the validity of change and an evolution of attitudes.

Our third observation, however, will amount to a definite criticism of the libertarian standpoint which our foregoing remarks in the paragraph above may appear to have favoured. Just as the notion of a perfect moral and legal order, implied by the paternalist position, is a myth, so too is the libertarian vision of a situation where individuals are totally 'free' to indulge in all kinds of victimless pursuits, where there is perfect tolerance and the complete absence of discrimination and societal 'persecution'. Individuals can never be free literally to pursue their own thing without socially defined moral limits, since 'individuals' become moral beings, with rational freedom and rights, only by virtue of living in a state, and no state can exist without its embodying a particular order; and every order, however tolerant and internally diverse it may be, necessarily excludes its contradictory. We can always expect some people some of the time to grumble and feel resentful at being discriminated against: if it is not prejudice against homosexuality or alcohol, it might be pornography, marijuana or tobacco smoking. It seems to follow, therefore, that being thus socially disadvantaged in one's individual capacity does not by itself give anyone the moral right to do *more* than 'grumble'. Moral opinion, and thus actual legislation, might well be constantly changing but they still have – at any given time – moral superiority. People who claim to be 'in advance' of the general moral consensus have to accept the consequences and pay the price of being out of step. Victimless crime therefore is still, in principle, crime and therefore immoral. The crucial question is of course the dividing line between those pursuits and complaints which are capable of *politicization*, i.e. presented as legitimate group interest and pitted against the interest of the prevailing order, and those which are really no more than individual grumbling, and therefore morally ineffectual and meaningless. We shall not shun this question: it will come up relevantly later, in the course of our discussion of the nature of the 'political'.

After this lengthy but unavoidable digression we have to continue elaborating further on the first of the two main themes of this chapter, i.e. the nature of crime. However, yet another brief remark is called for, arising out of the discussion above of minor law-breaking and victimless crimes. While, I think, the principle that these contraventions of the law are properly to be considered acts of immorality must be upheld, one cannot but observe the very real existential difficulty confronting the upright and law-abiding citizen in most recent times. I am referring to the general and increasing sense of frustration, confusion and moral unease consequent upon the huge proliferation of laws and regulations which, together with the underlying social and economic stress and political conflicts of contemporary communities (especially in the West), makes it very difficult for us not to become 'criminals', albeit in a minor way. The more laws and regulations there are, the more our everyday activities are circumscribed by legal injunctions and prohibitions, the more the thin dividing line between law-abidingness and law-breaking tends to be blurred. This line is never in practice very clear at the best of times and probably most people, while upholding morality in a big way and genuinely recoiling from serious crimes, are not overly squeamish when it comes to minor irregularities, marginal dishonesty, cheating, lying, cutting corners, a little malice and bloody-mindedness towards the other fellow. If crime is some kind of a moral/mental/psychological defect, then we all have it, potentially at any rate. As van den Haag: 'For the most part, offenders are not sick. They are like us. Worse, we are like them. Potentially, we could all be or become criminals.'[17] Pamela Hansford Johnson: 'We must never think that *we* are safe, and that therefore everyone else is. None of us is safe.'[18] And a telling dialogue between two detectives in Edgar Wallace's *The Missing Million*:

> 'It's these amateurs that baffle, because there's no starting place when you come to look for them. And the vast majority of people are criminal-minded; there are not five thousand truly honest men in the whole country.'
>
> 'That's a sweeping statement,' remarked Jimmy.
>
> 'It's true,' said Bill Dicker seriously, 'Suppose it was known tomorrow that there was a horse running on one of the racetracks that had been doped up to his eyes, or had been substituted – that is to say, some better-class horse had been run to impersonate the poorer type of animal. Suppose, I say, that every man in the country knew this, and thought that the secret was peculiarly his own. Why, they'd suffocate the bookmakers!'

Assuming that this is a general tendency, probably present at all times in organized societies, more or less civilized and prosperous, then it is only reasonable to expect a marked increase in minor and diffused criminality in modern conditions, when individuals are more atomized and institutions become more markedly impersonal. It is less difficult to experience a bad conscience when we short-change a neighbour, a customer, an employee or a boss personally known than when we fiddle the motor insurance company over some repair charges – the company is remote, nameless, characterless, vastly superior in terms of wealth and power. It is in some way felt to be 'just' to behave in this way, though at the same time the deep and residual immorality of actions of this kind continues to be dimly perceived. The result, as has been suggested above, is a blurring of distinctions and a gradual loss of confidence in telling what are and what are not real crimes, where morality ends and immorality begins. Thus today we are facing the highly paradoxical situation of people becoming exceedingly anxious about the erosion of personal security, and the visible malfunctioning of law and order, while at the same time they themselves, in minor and diffused but nonetheless relevant ways, participate in and materially contribute to the process. Intolerance and vindictiveness go hand in hand with a climate of leniency fed on a feeling of shared general guilt. The 'law' is supported and contravened at the same time, offenders shunned and loathed while there is also considerable sympathy and 'humane' understanding shown towards them. Crime continues to be equated with immorality but simultaneously we are becoming less and less certain as to what crime actually is. Though the point ought not to be exaggerated. It seems to be true, on the one hand, that a sizable majority of people in modern cities, when questioned in confidence, admit to having committed a variety of indictable offences (which are, of course, never officially handled and thus do not get into criminal statistics); in the early 1970s, for example, a survey based on 'self-reporting' in London found that 63 per cent of the sample admitted to various offences involving property, motoring, public order and acts 'against the person'.[19] Also, according to a recent report by the Policy Studies Institute, one in ten among Londoners has 'a complete lack of confidence' in the Metropolitan Police and about half the city have 'serious doubts about the standards of police conduct' (*Sunday Times*, 6 February 1983). On the other hand, however, as an independent inquiry commissioned by the Humberside Police found (with a sample of 1,633), 63 per cent had had no 'hard' contact with the police in the last two years, and a remarkably high percentage (59) had had no 'soft' contact either.[20]

But back to our main argument: it is not really possible to grasp the nature of crime unless we take as our departure the nature of morality. As morality has been defined as the conscious and active identification with general humanity, crime must be defined now as the direct and active denial of humanity. In moral conduct we act as 'universals', assuming our interchangeability with other human beings, acting on their behalf, and willing that our mode of action be granted the status of a general and categorical law. In direct opposition to this, in criminal conduct we act as 'individuals' in the strict sense, oblivious of our own universality and in defiance of it, acting (directly or indirectly) against other human beings, and willing that our action be taken as a *unique exception* from the general moral law. Crime is thus to be seen as the assertion of sheer, pure, abstract and 'natural' individuality, the divorcing of the single person from the moral community of the species, the elevating of a dominant self-will over against the moral will. In criminal conduct I act solely and literally for myself as a unique, unrepeatable, self-conscious person, in furtherance of my immediate, understood, unshareable and indivisible advantage. I intend and act so as to gain personal elevation, an achievement of a kind of personal divinity, a unique position for myself among my fellows. Crime is the repudiation of moral barriers to the attainment of individual purposes, the conscious disregard of the universal limits of a shared humanity binding on me. In criminal conduct I am and feel unbound; the ultimate limit of my own individual 'moral' authority and my freedom is equivalent to the limits of my personal power: my intelligence and physical prowess. The pursuit of personal gain, furthermore, here necessarily implies acting at one point against other people who are not recognized as people at all; they are transformed into mere means to the accomplishment of my own ends. They can be positive means to be used or negative means, i.e. obstacles in the way, in which case they will be trampled on, shifted away, annihilated. I am the only 'human' being and the rest, without exception, are dehumanized. The outward expression of criminal conduct towards other individuals and society in general is thus malevolent indifference, in varying shades, ranging from unfeeling, playful disregard to black hatred, total personal hostility. I am against the whole universe, and indeed here I become the whole universe for myself, heaven is my personal satisfaction, hell is others endeavouring to stop me.

In the perspective of criminality therefore there is no such thing as a human community or human society. Any kind of unity, sharing, common purpose and action are totally meaningless. There are no groups, group interests or identities. The criminal universe is a completely atomized universe, a chaotic and orderless universe inhabited by essentially unrelated and self-enclosed individuals. It is a world of entropy, a colourless void of clashing wills, conflicting purposes, zig-zagging units pursuing their own lonely paths and continually passing one another, with friction a-plenty. The criminal world is in many essential respects like the popular image of the 'jungle', with its menacing noises, unsavoury odour, dark hues, moisture, thick undergrowth, trees encroaching on trees, impenetrability. Perhaps, it might be surmised, this popular image of the jungle is itself an original projection of criminality, as experienced potentially within ourselves as individuals and actually as we perceive it as an aspect and layer of human societies; in the same way indeed, as a number of thoughtful writers have recently reminded us, that so-called 'animal' characteristics (like ferocity, ruthlessness, indiscriminate violence) have in reality nothing to do with animals but quite a lot with humans. The criminal universe is also similar to the Hobbesian 'state of nature' but *without* any 'laws of nature'. The criminal in the performance of criminal conduct is strictly, literally, unconditionally *alone*, and everybody is an enemy, potentially or in the actual situation. Once on the path, you must accept this loneliness, be on constant guard and act for yourself; there is no choice. As 'young Alf' in Clarence Rook's *The Hooligan Nights*:

> 'Look 'ere,' he said, 'if you see a fing you want, you just go and take it wivout any 'anging abart.'. . . 'See? You got to look after yourself, and it ain't your graft to look after anyone else, nor it ain't likely that anybody else'd look after you – only the cops. See?'[21]

Criminal conduct is concentrated on and guided by one single source of light: personal gain in disregard of the interests of others and directed against them, and the rest of the world is covered in darkness. This concentration is also present in other dimensions. Personal gain is imploded, centred on itself: it is abstract, indeterminate, not tied to any particular kind of achievement or satisfaction; it can be readily translated into terms of money, power, recognition or an exclusive kind of personal 'security'. There is also temporal concentration: criminal action focuses on the present, has an immediate significance, and for it both past and future are irrelevant, non-existent. Crime as basic, elemental immorality is just there, it is self-generating and self-perpetuating; it emerges out of human life and society in general, and has no determinable past antecedents, no discoverable 'causes'. (Particular types of offence in particular situations might, of course, have partially discoverable causes but we are not here concerned with this 'scientific' level of investigation.) As long as there is individual self-consciousness, acting on this solely or essentially is always a permanent general possibility and a partial actuality, and while various kinds of legally defined 'crime' might emerge and submerge as societies change, crime as such remains and all crimes converge on this fundamental conceptual level of present-oriented, self-concentrated, individually-focused, chaos-generating immoral conduct. Criminality is thus irreducibly unpredictable; it has no past. Neither has it as such any future: the meaning of a criminal action is exhausted, absorbed by that action itself. As there are no definite social antecedents, there are no definite consequences either, no further implications, no significance for society or for other individuals or even for the individual who has engaged in this particular instance of criminal conduct in the first place. Crime comes and goes, it is in principle pre-social and anti-social in general terms; without 'causes' in the sense of antecedents, likewise devoid of a 'cause' in the sense of an outlying, overall purpose.

Now it is not to be denied that this basic characterization of criminality has again a certain feeling of the fairy-tale about it, a quality of remote, stark, angular, sublime pontification – possibly even more so than in our depiction of the 'universal' nature of the state in the previous chapter. But I trust that the purpose of the exercise is not lost from view and, to reiterate once again, I believe it is perfectly reasonable to argue that fundamental *conceptual* clarification and isolation (a kind of 'ideal-typing' or phenomenological 'bracketing' if you like) should proceed before analysis of what many people regard as the 'real' world, i.e. the world of empirical events and processes. Of course this real empirical world does not look *exactly* like the world of pure concepts, but could we really make sense of the former without attempting to achieve the latter? Could we make any headway with our effort adequately to understand the problem of security in modern society, the very practical and 'empirical' problem of law and order, without isolating as it were a pure concept of crime, an extreme terminus or polar opposite ('moral conduct', including politics, being the other pole), and working our way back from it? These reflections, of course, assume that this kind of conceptual clarification is indeed necessary, and further that the above characterization of crime as a pure notion is correct and relevant to the purpose in view. That is, what we will be arguing is that the empirical world, though not exactly like the pure concept just defined, is not entirely different from it either. Some modifications are needed though.

For one thing, it ought to be made clear that the foregoing definition of criminality is meant to apply to criminal action as such, and to actual people only to the extent that their conduct, whether occasional or habitual, is organized essentially around the pure individualist principle. But it is certainly not meant to characterize even exemplary instances of 'criminal' persons *in toto*. Criminals in this definition are those whose main and socially relevant activity is crime, the exclusive pursuit of individual advantage and corresponding attitude of malevolent indifference towards others; but nobody is or can be a criminal only, with all actions and all relationships completely subordinated to this end. Inwardly, this would be logically impossible: while criminal actions are isolated and unpredictable, without a pattern, individuals pursuing crime still think and plan consistently, with a life-pattern and habits, convictions, beliefs, longer-term perspectives. Total criminality would define an insane person. Yet the distinction, I think, would apply in relative and quantitative terms: other things being equal, a predominantly criminal pursuit does mean a comparative lack of overall consistency, the absence or uncertainty of a settled life-pattern. It is scarcely an accident that in ordinary circumstances abiding by the law is from the personal point of view unproblematic, while the pursuit of criminality is a problem in itself. Morality is capable of being pursued by the whole person and right through life; immorality, precisely by virtue of being what it is – *lack* of universality, lack of overall organization, lack of community – is not. And outwardly the same consideration applies, though here I suspect one ought not to postulate any kind of logical necessity or impossibility. That is, it is perfectly possible and rational to conceive of a criminal person whose only 'link' to society outside is his criminality and who therefore has no 'relationship', properly and humanly speaking, to anyone around him, pure hunter and pure hunted. But I doubt if anyone like that, any 'rogue male', has ever existed, outside the pages of fiction. Criminals, too, accept some sort of moral law binding on them, alongside their criminality, and their overall jungle milieu is mitigated by strong personal and group relationships: they love their parents, keep marital faith with their spouses, dote on their children, contribute to charity, make sacrifices on behalf of their friends, support the local football team, and (like the 'Dirty Dozen') can show themselves ready to die for a patriotic or ideological cause.

It is, however, misleading and strictly speaking incorrect to entertain and accept the validity of a notion of 'criminal association'. Such a thing cannot exist. There is no 'honour among thieves' or rather in so far as thieves (robbers, killers, toughs, bullies, con-men) are honourably associated, the honour is irrelevant to their thieving and indeed logically (and existentially) contradicts it. What is commonly referred to as 'criminal association' is either purely instrumental association or pre-existing tangential association. The former is not 'human' association in the required moral sense, while the latter is logically irrelevant to criminal conduct. Instrumental links, like the forming of a gang of pickpockets for the Derby, is ephemeral and inherently unstable; it is wholly subordinated to individual ends which are thus aggregated rather than united, resembling a standing conference of ambassadors representing the interests of sovereign states rather than a parliamentary assembly or a political party congress. Atomization and entropy are implied in this kind of link; the association evaporates as soon as its limited practical objective is attained, or when its pursuit is externally thwarted or if the parties to it envisage some kind of personal danger accruing to them from the outside or from their partners. And even while in existence, instrumental association is and must be suffering from constant mutual suspicion of motives and chronic distrust of intentions, in planning and execution and the sharing out of profit. By definition the individual interests of criminal associates remain conflicting during the association: it was exclusive individual interest which brought it into being in the first place, dominates it during its life-span, and in fact causes its demise, while the same individual interest goes on surviving it. Criminals are and remain strangers *in crime*, and the criminal world is not a proper world but atoms in the void. The activities, and even the pleasures, which are seemingly shared are just aggregated unitary instances which are always liable to fall asunder, like the shared joy of watching a public execution in Coventry Patmore's famous poem, 'A London Fete':

> The dangling corpse hung straight and still,
> The show complete, the pleasure past,
> The solid masses loosened fast:
> A thief slunk off, with ample spoil,
> To ply elsewhere his daily toil.

Here, and *not* in the state, power dominates and interest rules: authority and community are absent. This it seems is why, if we may be permitted yet another sweeping statement, crime has rarely presented a serious social and political problem to established states, *pace* the rhetoric of 'law'n'order' advocates. Governments have vastly more important and potentially dangerous things to worry about and (though this might seem unfair to the individual law-abiding citizen who happens to be statistically unlucky) police forces are not unduly anxious to eradicate crime as long as it is confined to an accustomed level; what they do worry about is precisely the scale of criminal association. As N. Lucas puts it in *Britain's Gangland*: 'Law enforcement agencies realize that crime can never wholly be obliterated. The lone crook is invariably picked up sooner or later and even the existence of small gangs can, to a large extent, be controlled. They often fight among themselves and, ultimately, cancel out each other, but the unexpected growth of a gang is a menace that can lead to such formidable organizations as those set up by the Richardsons and the Krays.'[22] Ultimately, of course, even gangs on this scale are as a rule too weak, scattered and disorganized to pose anything like a political threat or a threat to 'order'. And in this connection we may also briefly note that it is this relative weakness of criminal organization, the literally 'underworldly' character of crime, that probably accounts for the overwhelming lack of interest shown by political philosophers in this subject. As treason is no longer treason if successful, so association, even though subversive and menacing, is no longer criminal if it does reach the level of the state; it is then political. Still, I think that this relative neglect of the notion of the 'criminal' by political theorists is highly regrettable, since determination of the limits of the political realm requires a clear understanding of what falls on the other side.

The other kind of association which plays a role – and without doubt a very important role – in the actual world of crime is what I have called tangential pre-existing association. It is tangential since, logically speaking, it is independent of and irrelevant to criminal activity. But without its existing in modern societies the crime problem would assuredly be very different. The reference here is primarily to family and extended kinship groups, particular localities with their 'criminal' traditions, socially defined groups, peer-groups, ethnic minorities living on the fringes of society, impoverished and estranged sections of the urban and rural working class, and the like. No 'Mafia' would be conceivable without such pre-existing (and continuing) links; without Puerto Rican ethnic consciousness 'crime' in places like New York would be rather different from what it is; and even Britain's 'gangland' in localities like the East End of London, Glasgow and Liverpool flourishes to a large extent on old kinship traditions of certain forms of law-breaking. Here of course we touch upon an extremely important point, seemingly somewhat at odds with our conceptual presentation of criminality so far, and not to be overlooked for that very reason. The point is that although (as it seems to me) it is perfectly reasonable to define the 'state' as the embodiment of morality, and correspondingly 'crime' as the concrete expression of immorality, one must not gloss over the *historical* character of modern states and the correspondingly historical modification of the actual borderline between law-abiding and criminal conduct. As modern states and societies established themselves by (more or less) forcibly breaking up traditional communities, these communities' protracted (and in the event doomed) resistance has often manifested itself in what the state has regarded as crime, but what from the point of view of these communities has continued to appear legitimate forms of activity. As B. Lenman and G. Parker argue, in the symposium already cited: 'It is clear that, previously, the community did not necessarily regard as "crimes" every act declared by the state to be illegal; and some communities – pirates, gypsies, bandits – were entirely outside the law. Only gradually did the values of government and the governed come to coincide . . .'[23] In the same volume Jennifer Davis says: 'While it may be an exaggeration to suggest that London's casual labour market only survived through its recourse to crime, further research may well show that law-breaking activity provided an important source of outdoor relief in an age when legal charity was so difficult to come by.'[24] And V. A. C. Gatrell, pointing to another aspect of the same phenomenon: 'Despite efforts to present them as an impartial body above politics and sectional interest, the English police have never been able to divorce themselves from the class structure which they uphold; so that many working-class communities, then as now, were deeply alienated from the police and the law, and resistant to both.'[25]

It is obvious then that here, in the area of pre-existing association involved in criminal activity, we reach one of many of these fascinating *twilight-zones* between crime and politics, and we shall have more to say later about embryonically 'political' groupings whose 'resistance' to the state *looks* like crime but really isn't; it takes the form of law-breaking but in substance it is order-defiance. Nevertheless it seems to me that the general principle adumbrated above is still applicable and to be reaffirmed: clearly not every kind of 'resistance' to the state is political, and not every kind of seemingly 'social' grievance is legitimate. Acting against the state from the individual point of view and in the individual interest is still crime and still immoral, whoever does so and whatever the historical background. The modern state, notwithstanding its paradoxical duality, is still to be seen as the actualized, more developed expression of the same universal moral principle which the broken-up traditional communities represented in a less advanced form (i.e. based on kinship and status rather than citizenship); and scattered and possibly oppressed remnants of traditional groups, as well as new underclasses emerging, always have had in principle the choice between following the paths of politics or the path of criminality.

This may seem to be a convenient place to advance a few more observations concerning the alleged 'social' causation of crime which was dismissed perhaps in a too cavalier fashion earlier in this chapter. While it should be conceded that in some cases the particular antecedents of particular types of offences are capable of being isolated and identified with some success (e.g. as Geoffrey Pearson cogently argues in *Hooligan: a History of Respectable Fears*, so-called 'street crime' is definitely connected with the material conditions and cultural background of an 'underclass'),[26] the general proposition often put forward by (mainly) radical writers concerning the causes of criminality is open to serious questioning. We ought I think to take it as read that 'statistical' information concerning either the varying quantitative incidence of crime or the social correlates of crime is inconclusive and subject to arbitrary interpretation. Conservative writers make a great show of statistically demonstrating the horrendous increase of crime in recent years, only to be knocked down by radical criminologists who point out the 'definitional' element in this increase.[27] In their turn, radicals go to great lengths in correlating criminality with poverty, estrangement, deprivation, frustration and the like, only to be corrected by their conservative critics who show (and in my view quite convincingly) that no such correlations can be established: crime can issue out of affluence and poverty does not uniformly lead to criminality. As Wilson: 'If economic want were the cause of crime, one would predict that delinquency for gain would be more common among those less well-off, and delinquency for "fun" more common among the better-off, but the opposite seems to be the case.'[28] And as Robert Nisbet has argued in *Twilight of Authority*, 'hard-core poverty' is if anything a preventive of crime: 'Precisely as the impulse to rebellion is muted in such conditions, so is the desire for crime.'[29] At most what could be asserted with reasonable assurance is that certain types of criminal conduct have identifiable 'necessary conditions', antecedents without which the conduct could not take place; but no antecedent in this sense could be called a 'sufficient condition', something that necessarily and invariably leads to the conduct in question. This is not only belied by empirical evidence (such evidence as appears available); it also entails a degree of determinism which flies in the face of ordinary common sense.

What is perhaps more interesting from our point of view is the general argument put forward by some eminent authors concerning the causes of the underlying attitude or disposition leading (among other things) to criminal activity – here of course reliance on mundane day-to-day crime statistics is not to be had, either by advocates or by critics. This underlying disposition is usually defined in terms of 'aggression' – resembling what I have earlier described in terms of the 'pure individualist' standpoint and 'malevolent indifference' towards others – and the presence of 'aggression' in modern society in turn is accounted for by reference to 'frustration' and 'relative deprivation'. Among writers who achieved some renown for their forceful advocacy of this view is Ashley Montagu who has argued in *The Nature of Human Aggression*: 'What we can legitimately conclude when the full range of human behaviour is considered, from the most loving to the most murderous, is that humans are creatures potentially capable of any form of behaviour, depending largely upon the socialization, the conditioning, which they have undergone from infancy.'[30] And: 'No child who was ever adequately loved ever became a delinquent or a murderer.'[31] In a more circumspect manner T. R. Gurr contended in *Why Men Rebel* that it is 'relative deprivation' that causes 'frustration' which in turn leads to 'aggression': 'The disposition to respond aggressively when frustrated is part of man's biological make-up; there is a biologically inherent tendency, in men and animals, to attack the frustrating agent.'[32]

One obvious problem with this and similar views is their somewhat too eager reliance on a naive environmentalist thesis which, once immensely popular in scientific circles (deriving from the Enlightenment conviction in the 'original goodness' of the human species), has today come in for a great deal of well-deserved criticism, relying in turn on Freudian depth-psychology, Lorenzian ethology, bio-psychology and various more recent departures in comparative anthropology. There are, it seems, too many and too diverse kinds of 'environment' which go hand in hand with a rather restricted range of conduct among humans, and what is usually called 'aggression' is well-nigh universal. This is convincingly shown, for example, by I. Eibl-Eibesfeldt in *Love and Hate* who sums up his argument: 'For all the incompleteness of our knowledge, one thing is already proven: the assertion of the environmental theory that man is shaped by his environment alone does not hold good.'[33] Another questionable point in the environmentalist view and arguments based on it is the ill-defined, open-ended nature of the concepts that often tend to be employed. It is not easy, for instance, to understand what 'adequate loving' or 'frustration' means, without recourse to *petitio principii.* Where does loving end and at what point does frustration begin? It could be argued quite cogently, it seems to me, that nobody can ever be loved 'adequately' and that nobody can ever completely escape from some frustration in life. Again, as Eibl-Eibesfeldt says: 'One can always assume some kind of frustration, if need be that of being weaned, or even an experience at the time of birth, and thus explain every instance of aggression. But in the process the frustration hypothesis loses its scientific value.'[34] We are down to basics once again: humans are *individuals* and as individuals they do not melt smoothly in their social milieu, they are never perfectly satisfied, never feel completely secure and never provide complete security to others. Distance, friction, suspicion, ignorance of the future and unpredictability of intentions are just as much a part of the scene as solidarity, peace and co-operation. And if individuals are thus existentially dissatisfied, 'frustrated', 'unloved', is it entirely unreasonable for them to display 'aggressive' conduct from time to time?

Here we reach what to my mind is really one of the most important points in the whole argument, and here we will be contending against both conservatives and radicals who often seem systematically to overlook the truth that there is something elementally, existentially, primordially *good* and *human* involved in aggressive conduct in general and criminally aggressive conduct in particular (Chapter 4 will go into greater detail concerning this shared blindspot in the literature). Conservatives rightly perceive the basic immorality of crime but tend to miss its general spread in society. Radicals correctly point to this general spread but fail to note the basic immorality involved. Both tend to regard criminality as 'evil' (whether socially caused or part of an eternal 'human condition') and therefore to be eliminated or strictly controlled and isolated from law-abiding society. As practical endeavours these are of course valid and to be endorsed (even though one might be doubtful of their success). But on the plane of theory one must note the all-important human element even in what is taken to be evil and immorality. The individual and abstract negation of state, law, society and morality – which is what crime essentially is – has also as it were a *positive* aspect, to be recognized. Ultimately crime, aggression, violence, intentionally immoral conduct is the only way open to the individual to assert perhaps an insubstantial but nonetheless deeply experienced natural self against humanity in general, against the universal moral law, against moral goodness, against the individual's own moral self and own humdrum 'security'. It may be tragic, deplorable, condemnable but nevertheless immorality, and especially its climatic conclusion in criminal immorality, contains an element of the sublime, the resistance of the void, the dark pride of Lucifer. There is a pre-moral goodness involved here, disturbingly paradoxical, absurd and irrational, a profound aspect of freedom and escape (or attempted escape) from the normal world. Criminality is utter insecurity yet it is chosen, in preference to boring poverty; criminal rebellion against society takes, in most cases, a kind of audacity, hardness, courage and confidence which law-abiding conduct does not require and indeed does not tolerate. The point to note here, making use again of some of the external evidence provided, is that although most crime (especially petty crime) remains undetected and unsolved, most habitual criminals do get caught and punished eventually. Society is too powerful for the individual. As Clarence Rook: 'it must, indeed, require a certain amount of courage to earn your living by taking things that do not belong to you, with the whole of society, backed by the police force, against you.' In introducing the story of 'young Alf', the hooligan, Rook makes the following interesting point:

> Poetic justice demands that young Alf should be very unhappy; as a matter of fact, he is nothing of the sort. And when you come to think of it, he has had a livelier time than the average clerk on a limited number of shillings a week. He does not know what it is to be bored. Every day has its interests, and every day has its possibility of the unexpected, which is just what the steady honest worker misses.[35]

The point is of special interest, as Rook himself only a few pages later admits: 'And it came upon me with something of a shock that I had never, so far as I could remember, seen him laugh. His face was grave, tense, eager, as always.'[36] This, then, gives us a more balanced and at the same time deeply contradictory picture which is also borne out by most professional accounts of the psychology of criminals: having 'fun' but worried and uncertain at the same time, carefree and irresponsible but worn out and prematurely old, constantly trying to escape tedium yet finding life on the whole empty, gloomy, tragic, devoid of real and lasting excitement. Perhaps one might say that it is the very contradiction, the very absurdity, the existential negation and 'nothingness' which lends immorality its disturbing attraction, experienced by its active practitioners as well as uninvolved spectators outside. Pointless and that is its very point; meaningless and insignificant yet real, living and inescapably human. It is movement and turbulence and unpredictability and drama, as opposed to the steady course, calm direction and prose of life as it is lived in accordance with the norms.

> Macavity, Macavity, there's no one like Macavity,
> He's broken every human law, he breaks the law of gravity.
> His powers of levitation would make a fakir stare,
> And when you reach the scene of crime – *Macavity's*
> *not there!*

We are these days warned, sometimes rather sanctimoniously, by radical and conservative commentators alike not to 'romanticize' criminality; yet without a recognition of this strange 'romantic' element we could not satisfactorily comprehend the phenomenon.

Special emphasis should be placed on the element of personal aggression and violence as they occur in conduct, by no means confined to criminality but here perhaps most conspicuous and revealing. Again, it seems to me to be mistaken to regard crime as a kind of 'business', as simply instrumental activity undertaken for personal profit in the material sense. Most crime *is* business in this sense, no doubt, but it is also something more than that (as ordinary 'competitive' business conduct is, though in many ways definitely similar, yet something less than crime): it involves a particular *way* in which to seek and secure individual advantage. Personal aggression and violence against others are often the best means to achieve an outlying end; but at bottom they are also ends in themselves and thus irreplaceable. They are the purest expression of rebellious individuality, of immediate palpable, exclusive, concentrated and intolerant self-assertion. Aggression is the will to dominate as an individual, and violence is the realization of this will, its self-proof as it were. The meaning of aggression is subduing other persons, not annihilating them (unless this is technically warranted). 'The satisfying experience', as Lorenz says in *On Aggression*, 'consists . . . in administering a good beating, but certainly not in shooting or disembowelling; and the desired objective is not that my opponent should lie dead but that he should be soundly thrashed and humbly accept my physical and, if I am to be considered as good as a baboon, my mental superiority.'[37] The causing of actual pain is incidental. As Marsh: 'Rather aggression might be viewed as the intentional process of subduing or achieving dominance over a rival.'[38] Again, in Macfarlane's very apt expression: 'Coercion is seen not just as a legitimate means for each party to use against the other, but as part of the end itself – not simply to beat one's opponents, but to beat them by beating them up.'[39] Aggression and violence signify the suspension of civility and civil relations, and they are more often than not, whether in crime or elsewhere, accompanied by emotions of dark hatred, anger, contempt of the opponent. Victims of street-crime often give shocked and thoroughly disturbing reports of being struck, jostled, kicked 'without any good reason', since they were anxious to hand over their possessions to the attackers; burglars vandalize the homes which they rob; arsonists want to see and enjoy the spectacle of the destructive flames; football hooligans are disappointed if their rivals run away too soon. Hunter Davies reports his meeting with Tony, a 'gang leader' of Tottenham Hotspur supporters, in the train *en route* to an away match.

> Of all the fifty or so in his gang, he was the only one who said he actually looked for fights.
>
> 'It's more exciting if you hit someone,' said Tony, 'especially some Northern bastard. I hate all Northerners. You've got to show them the cockneys are best. It's satisfying to hit someone. It feels good. Now get lost. I'm going back to sleep.'[40]

There is a deceptively 'political' character defining, at first glance, the conflict: 'Cockneys' against 'Northerners', a division which is predicated on definite group identity and solidarity. But in reality this does not go very deep and very far: the logic of Tony's aggression turns him, at a second remove, against his own group as well, over which he wants to reign and rule as undisputed master. The leader in this situation, whether we talk about a gang of bootleggers or of street rowdies, is a 'political' leader in appearance only; in truth he is a 'natural individual' writ large who succeeds in extracting obedience from his followers, and their loyalty, by the power of his personality (muscle, brains, audacity, aggression). Football hooliganism straddles the three interlocking worlds of youthful turbulence, criminality and embryonic politics, and it embraces instrumental as well as pre-existing tangential association. It falls short of 'politics', of course, in that the personal violence displayed (as distinguished from committed – and possibly very turbulent – support for the team) has no 'end' beyond itself. Ordinary law-abiding citizens, as distinguished from the habitual 'men of violence', need special circumstances which might force them into the committing of aggressive and violent actions but their actual experience of these actions, to their surprise and against their anxious anticipation, might in fact be quite similar to that of Tony. As Lionel Davidson imaginatively described the experience of his main character, Nicholas Whistler, an unwitting 'secret agent' trying to escape from Prague in *The Night of Wenceslas*:

> There is something about coshing a man for the first time that inspires a certain wild but unstable confidence. One moment you are faced with a powerful and unnerving obstacle; the next, without thought or subtlety, you have overcome it. By disengaging from the habits of a lifetime you have slipped into a new effortless gear in which all things seem possible. Minutes afterwards the adrenalin aftertaste still tickles the roots of the tongue, nauseous, exultant, the unique flavour of rewarded violence.

Here again we might want to take brief notice, already remarked on in other contexts, of the enormous and unabating interest taken by the law-abiding public in all aspects of criminality and above all in criminal aggression and violence. Especially when we know ourselves to be individually unaggressive and non-violent might we find these manifestations of human conduct strangely fascinating. I am boringly honest, disappointingly meek, pedestrian in my cowardice and conformity; daring and dishonesty and the irrational display of raw force, as being on the other side and inconceivable in my own accustomed life-style, will thrill me all the more. 'We are', as Marsh says, 'outraged and appalled. But we are also vicariously aroused. For when the effects are indirect, violence is fun.'[41] Pamela Hansford Johnson: 'Violence excites me when I see it, as it excites most people . . .'[42] Nobody in their right mind wants to be a victim, nobody wants any injury to come to their loved ones, and we can and do identify with victims whom we recognize as being similar to ourselves; we also (most of us, probably) genuinely abhor aggression and violence meted out to the weak and manifestly innocent, like children. But the matter doesn't end here and it is by no means sure if there being 'victims' in the abstract, and innocent victims at that, is not somehow strangely and disgustingly an integral part of a wide and complex human experience and consciousness which also contain the awareness of universal and binding moral rules. As revenge is the marginal limit of morality, so the excitement felt at contemplating (or viewing) the legitimate causes of revenge – actions which call for and evoke revenge – is what makes this margin itself intelligible. Unreservedly sharing in the triumph of the hero in the forcible destruction of evil – St George slaying the dragon, Sherlock Holmes grabbing Moriarty in the death-fall, James Bond shoving Blofeld into the acid-bath – yet our feelings towards the personal ized symbols of evil and criminality are not entirely unmixed. We sense that St George needs the dragon to be St George and the dragon needs innocent victims in order to be the dragon. Are peaceable and respectable spinsters who couldn't hurt a fly yet secretly support the Great Train Robbers against the police, and old ladies who go into ecstasies in the front-row of the wrestling arena, really 'sick'? If so, then we are being confronted with a sickness that has very deep and tenacious roots indeed and which social change and medical treatment have so far done precious little to eradicate. It may be then that individuals are not just 'maladjusted' or 'paranoid' or 'sado-masochistic' but simply *individuals* – or we might say that scientifically identified and labelled deviations are just so many and varied manifestations of what we have here collectively termed natural individual self-assertion, with aggression and violence, actively or vicariously experienced, as its corollaries. Natural individuality is not morally justifiable or legitimate – that would be a contradiction in terms – it is just *there*, to be recognized in human life and society.

This leads to another, possibly rather romantically inspired (and again by no means original), observation: criminality as raw immorality has a close connection to *youth*. I am not sure if statistics would help at all here, and we must certainly heed criminologists and social historians who point out that young people are by no means predominant in certain types of offences, like fraud. However, it can scarcely be an insignificant coincidence that precisely in that kind of paradigmatic criminality which connotes an extra high level of aggression and physical violence the young are and always have been prominent. It seems that the 'social' explanation for this, as for criminality in general, can go only part of the way; certain conditions (like those prevailing in the 1980s) – widespread unemployment, deteriorating educational and welfare services, material pressures, broken families, etc. – will undoubtedly swell the number of young offenders and contribute to a climate of increasing chaos and violence. But this is merely a quantitative change and in any case it presupposes an already existing tendency on the part of young people to react to pressures in this particular way. And most importantly, gloomy paternalistic descriptions of the 'sub-culture of despair' in which the young unemployed and unattached apparently find themselves tend to gloss lightly over the fact that turbulent young offenders, from shoplifters through street rowdies and city-centre wreckers to football hooligans, are no more disconcerted about their conduct than 'young Alf' was at the turn of the century. 'Where they have been asked,' Patricia Morgan reports, 'delinquents put the pursuit of fun high in their list in a substantial number of cases. Far from being miserable, they are enjoying themselves.'[43] We shall be struck by answers of this kind, and find them baffling, only if we go in oblivion of a concept of natural individuality or if we assume, against weighty evidence (empirical as well as introspective), that human individuals naturally, smoothly, harmoniously melt in with their social environment and take on the general morality of society without friction. It is so much easier, commonsensical and economical (in Occam's sense) to assume individuals to conduct themselves as individuals – as so many actually *do*, especially when young.

Thus one ought always to expect a constant undercurrent of

turbulence and seething discontent and primordial anti-nomianism, and it is only reasonable to expect these on the part of human beings who have a more abundant flow of adrenalin in their bodies and a quicker rate of hormone reproduction or whatever (as the 'biological' explanation would have it, again begging the question), and who have not yet been cowed into routine activities and responsibilities. If anything, young people are more natural precisely in this sense, more spontaneous and instinctive in their conduct than their elders, and thus youth and turbulence go together; turbulence in itself, of course, is not criminality but it is a usual precondition of crime. Indeed, the widespread 'fear of crime' which afflicts the respectable and well-to-do so much these days often turns out to be nothing but the 'fear of youth', apprehension and anxiety in the face of quick-tempo movement, shrill voices, unself-conscious intolerance, vivid colours, excess of energy. As reported by Rhodes, an opinion poll in Webster City, Iowa, showed that the main concern of the citizenry was 'crime in the streets'. However, the *actual* complaints were only 'of youngsters drinking beer, driving too fast, and breaking an occasional window.' In Garnett, Kansas, too, citizens were up in arms over crime. Yet they had not had a single case of rape in ten years, not a murder for twenty-one years, and the only person in jail was a seventeen-year-old hot-rodder.[44] These polls took place in 1968; the result could have been the same in 1868 and 1768. As Geoffrey Pearson shows brilliantly in *Hooligan: a History of Respectable Fears*, fear of youth, fear of the streets and fear of crime have been with us, all connected, for a very long time indeed.[45] Youthful turbulence – pure aggro, looking for trouble and making trouble for its own sake – are and have been the seedbed of habitually immoral conduct. And perhaps one might add here that, conversely, criminality could be presented as petrified, arrested adolescence, the lamentable (but understandable) extension of turbulence into areas where, we feel, orderly norms and moral conduct should prevail; instead of settlement, in the criminal life-style we see an indefinite continuation of upheaval. It has been noted, and the point is certainly relevant here, that a 'life of crime' usually signifies a life-style of chaos, excitement, insecurity and turbulence not only on the 'productive' side (in criminal activity itself) but also on the side of 'consumption': criminals and criminally oriented elements tend to be more conspicuous than the rest in gambling, brawling, drug-taking, alcoholism, promiscuity and other, socially unorthodox, pursuits.

We are slowly approaching the end of our reflections concerning the nature of criminality. An interim conclusion here might be that criminality to all commonsensical intents and purposes represents a well-nigh intractable problem from the point of view of personal security. Most people do want and need security most of the time, and the average human being in our modern societies does tend to accept and follow the dictates of morality, at least in serious matters; but as long as and in so far as *insecurity* (with all that involves) holds even a marginal attraction, to some people most of the time and to most of them some of the time, even if experienced vicariously as thrilled spectators, crime is here to stay. It has basically very little to do with particular social problems; it stems from and is an expression of the problem *of* society. It most definitely 'ought' to be controlled, as immorality has absolutely no right against morality, and by and large it *is* controlled, naturally kept low and on the margins (our remarks above regarding criminal association should suggest at least some reasons why this should be so). But at the end of the day, there is an inescapable, gruelling feeling of pointlessness about the whole issue: the meaninglessness of criminality is almost exactly matched by the *hubris* of constantly renewed and rhetorically asserted efforts to win the 'battle' against crime, a battle which state and society – judges, police, prisons, social workers – cannot ever conclusively win. 'It would be folly', as a cognoscent observer has argued recently, 'for the police to accept the romantic image of the television scene and to allow the public to regard them as responsible, almost unaided, for combating crime. That is a struggle they could never win.'[46] The matching pointlessness is graphically expressed in Howard Brenton's scintillating tragicomedy, *Revenge*, in which the role of the villain and the role of the police chief are played by the same actor. Both end their career in frustration. Adam Hepple, the villain, downcast in the country:

> All my efforts come to nothing. All my efforts to brighten up criminal life, sweet nothing. All I wanted to do was entertain the general public, and make a bit on the side, naturally. And look at their gratitude – forced out into the country like a leper. You bleeders,

> don't you want your streets full of spectacle and danger?

And MacLeish the police chief:

> I fought the good fight. Aye, and lost. Lost, Adam . . .
>
> It's the 1980s now. Rapes every night. No citizen abroad after dark. The coppers armed. Gangs roaming at will, burning down police stations. The country's gone to the devil. You lived before your time, Adam.

Just before turning to our second main concern in this chapter, which is politics, however, a few more observations will have to be made about crime, and these might then serve as a convenient transition to the next topic. The first point is that, as so many commentators have noted, in spite of its being an onslaught on the establishment, crime in political terms has usually tended to be 'functional', i.e. objectively strengthening, affirming state and society. Crime is by its very nature *conservative*. There are at least two good reasons accounting for this apparent paradox, both already touched upon in the foregoing pages. On the one hand, the criminal as we have argued is essentially 'alone' facing society, out in the cold, hunted. The more conspicuous he becomes, the more he will be hunted; 'crime', as one of Durkheim's more famous pithy observations goes, 'brings together honest men and concentrates them'; and: 'everybody is attacked; consequently everybody opposes the attack'.[47] Thus crime, by evoking an anti-crime atmosphere (what is sometimes called a 'moral panic') around it, keeps itself as it were in check and thereby reinforces prevailing law and order; though, we hasten to add, this is not invariably the case, and certainly not, as J. E. Conklin notes, in the recent wave of urban violence and lawlessness in cities like New York, Detroit and Philadelphia.[48] On the other hand, and I think more pointedly, emphasis should fall on a further implication of criminal 'loneliness' and individuality: the existential logic of criminal conduct requires that the order of society should remain the same after the performance of crime as it was before. The point of criminal action is personal advantage and aggrandizement, and these would be rendered meaningless if the same action were to change the overall social context also. A general upheaval contradicts the rationale of the individual upheaval intended in the first place. Macfarlane notes: 'Those who rob for a living do so because it suits and pays them to. They are unlikely to have any objection to the existing distribution of property rights, or to the principle of such rights being protected by law.'[49] And Morgan: 'The professional criminal is out to rub shoulders with the legitimately rich and famous, not to publicize the evils of society.'[50] To this we might also add the attendant observations that criminals as consumers in the normal course of affairs do go on expecting and demanding that others should behave 'morally' towards them (giving the right change for the champagne in the night-club where the loot is spent) and that – as a matter of sociological fact – the criminal underworld as well as the twilight world of young tearaways have always been a useful recruiting ground for extreme right-wing political movements (e.g. the National Front in Britain).

Many an influential and learned author has extended and generalized this point about the functionality of criminal law-breaking and deviance, seeing crime indeed as a 'normal' aspect of social life, deviance as an 'evolutionary' device of human societies, and an exceptionally *low* level of crime as a thing to worry about. We might like to listen briefly to three opinions, as these proceed more or less in the same direction as the present reflections (and no doubt influenced them in the first place). Thus Durkheim writes in *The Rules of Sociological Method*:

> [to accept crime as normal]. . . is to affirm that it is a factor in public health, an integral part of all healthy societies.[51]
>
> To make progress, individual originality must be able to express itself. In order that the originality of the idealist whose dreams transcend his century may find expression, it is necessary that the originality of the criminal, who is below the level of his time, shall also be possible. One does not occur without the other.[52]
>
> Crime, for its part, must no longer be conceived as an evil that cannot be too much suppressed. There is no occasion for self-gratulation when the crime rate drops noticeably below the average level, for we may be certain that this apparent progress is associated with some social disorder.[53]

Kai T. Erikson in *Wayward Puritans: a Study in the Sociology of Deviance* comments on the curious implications of recidivism and the recurrence of deviance:

> For if our culture has supported a steady flow of deviation throughout long periods of historical change, the rules which apply to any kind of evolutionary thinking would suggest that strong forces must be at work to keep the flow intact – and this because it contributes in some important way to the survival of the culture as a whole.[54]

> [we should then be wary of] . . . the assumption so often made in sociological circles that any well-structured society is somehow designed to prevent deviant behaviour from occurring.[55]

Finally we read the following in R. F. Sparks *et al., Surveying Victims*:

> It does not follow from this [i.e. recent increases in crime], moreover, that for *societies in general*, relatively high crime rates can be unambiguously regarded as being in some sense 'bad'; conversely, a relatively low crime rate is not necessarily an indicator of 'social health'. Crime is usually connected, in ways far from being understood, with many other aspects of social life; and it is at least conceivable that, for example, in developed industrial societies a certain amount of property crime is a necessary consequence of an otherwise healthy socio-economic system, so that a relatively crime-free society would also be an economically or culturally stagnant one.[56]

Our second observation concerns significant quantitative increases in criminality, as regards both the secular volume of crime and its degree of seriousness, like the one which has *ex hypothesi* occurred in recent decades in the Western world. Now whether or not this has really been the case today, in our midst (and as we have noted above, some radical criminologists would seriously question the evidence on which such assertions of a crime 'explosion' are based), it is undeniable that there are over-time and place pretty big fluctuations in criminality, and it is not entirely idle and arbitrary to identify relatively tranquil periods and places, and relatively turbulent and insecure ones. It is one thing to accept the point made by Durkheim, Erikson and Sparks concerning the ambiguity – and indeed undesirability in the longer perspective – of exceptionally low crime rates. From this it does not follow, however, that an unusual and dramatic increase in criminality ought necessarily to be welcomed as a sign of 'social health'. This too might indicate some sort of impending social disorder, however remote and seemingly unconnected. Two points need to be made. Firstly, a significant increase in the level of crime can no longer be regarded as a pure symptom of criminality, in the sense in which 'criminality' was defined in these pages. Logically cannot, since the existence of the state as (imperfect) moral community presupposes that the majority of citizens are law-abiding most of the time. Immorality must be confined to the fringes: to a relatively isolated and small criminal underworld, to the turbulent young, to petty law-breaking. If there is a change in this balance, then the change relates no longer to individual conduct but to state and society as a whole. Criminality as such *can* be derived from human character or the human predicament but here quantity does change into quality and large-scale immorality can only be derived from actual conditions existing in the state; we are now again on the threshold of politics. Note that this is not a 'radical' argument and not based on a belief in the pure 'social' causation of crime and in the real possibility of a crime-free, perfectly moral community. The argument follows directly from the principles of traditional political philosophy. As Spinoza put the point, with exceptional clarity and unassailable logic:

> The best condition of a commonwealth is easily discovered from the purpose of political order: which is simply peace and security of life. Accordingly, the best commonwealth is one in which men live in harmony, and the laws are kept unbroken. Rebellions, wars, and contemptuous disregard for law must certainly be attributed to the corrupt condition of the commonwealth rather than to the wickedness of its subjects. For citizens are not born, but made. Besides, men's natural passions are the same everywhere; hence if wickedness is more dominant and crime more preva-

> lent in one commonwealth than in another, this is certainly due to the fact that the first has not done enough to promote harmony, has not framed its laws with sufficient foresight, and so has failed to acquire its absolute right as a commonwealth.[57]

The second point, however, is to insist that large-scale criminality is not yet, as such, a political phenomenon. What Spinoza calls 'rebellions' and 'wars' must still be sharply distinguished from the 'contemptuous disregard for law'. Crime on a significant scale, like rioting, is indicative of discontent, social malaise, serious political problems facing the state; it connects up with the particular position of groups in society, calls attention to power and the conflict of interests, begins dramatically to turn the limelight on the state *as order*. But crime, as a phenomenon explicable in terms of the nature of natural individuality, is still negative in principle, and thus pointless, abstract, indeterminate; however large and widespread, it still does not 'add up' to anything beyond itself, aggregative rather than unificatory. Its political significance is indirect; we are on the threshold but we have still not arrived. A thousand burglars or muggers are still only burglars and muggers, individuals in isolation and not a political entity; a criminal 'locality' is still only a geographical expression.

Our third and final observation relating to crime concerns 'criminal politics'. The fact that pure crime enters the world of politics has to be squarely recognized. The exclusive and immoral pursuit of individual advantage can take place on any level and in any occupational area, and indeed since politics is, among (many) other things, the pursuit of power, it has not only some surface resemblance to criminal conduct but has obvious attractions to those who are engaged in crime; also, politics as power does tend to corrupt, as the old platitude has it. There is a two-way connection here, as we have already noted in brief at the beginning of the chapter: it is by no means unheard of for criminals to rise in the world and become the occupants of legitimate power positions and still use these positions for the pursuit of pure criminal ends, and likewise many a political activist, through frustration, corruption, temptation, flaw of character or whatever, can and does sink into criminality. There are Al Capones, Dutch Schultzes and Papa Docs to be found in many places. However, I think that these phenomena are still relatively rare, and 'criminal politics' in this sense should on no account be confused with what is *commonly* referred to as 'political crime'. This is precisely the kind of confusion which these reflections are endeavouring to dispel. When the 'monsters' of the political world are denounced as 'criminals' (the Himmlers, Mengeles, Berias, Stalins, Idi Amins) the primary and intended reference is to their politics, the public character of their conduct and principles, and not to their conduct as individuals acting for their own individual end. That the two things can empirically coincide is beside the point. No good purpose is served by conflating them into one mass.

★ ★ ★ ★ ★ ★ ★ ★

This is where we begin our reflective journey into the world of politics, our primary and central purpose being the drawing of a telling distinction between criminal illegality and immorality on the one hand, and illegal and (supposedly) 'immoral' political principles and conduct on the other. The main argument to be advanced here, to put it first in stark terms, is that illegal politics, however horrendous and repugnant, however violent and uncivilized, however seemingly absurd and pointless, must still be recognized as a sub-species of politics, deriving from the world of politics and bearing political characteristics, and that it is not to be confused with crime, from which it is categorially different. The essential feature of illegal politics is its opposition to the *particularity* of the state, of society and the establishment, its intended and determinate negation of *order*. Formally against the 'law' – as of course it must be – illegal politics is yet in substance no more and no less than the defiance of a given, concrete order. It is no less: political conduct is meaningful and significant, with a definite group context, a past and a future, in a way in which criminal conduct is not. And it is no more than the defiance of order: politics of all kinds is predicated on the recognition of the validity of the moral law, however faint, mistaken or pernicious this recognition might be in different cases. Illegal politics, therefore, in as much as it expresses determinate negation of the determinate character of the state, also shares a dimension of universality with the state; morally speaking, the legal politics of the state and the illegal politics of given groups opposed to the state can be in principle (and often manifestly are in practice) equivalent. But we shall have to begin, as we have done earlier with crime, by identifying the essential character of political conduct in general.

The approach taken to politics in these reflections is similar to the one adopted in the case of crime, in that what we are seeking to define in conceptual and schematic terms is probably no more than the popular, commonsense view, clarified and as far as possible divested of its ambiguities and incoherencies. The commonly shared *sense* of the concept of the 'criminal' was the pursuit of individual advantage, in defiance of the moral law. The sense of politics to be grasped at first is the pursuit of group interest, not in defiance of the moral law but through an endeavour to interpret it so as to endorse a particular group interest. Political conduct (subsuming both principles and practice) then will be defined here as conduct undertaken to formulate, seek, discuss, implement or forestall alternative particular arrangements to those existing in a given state, conduct which has to do with the substantive nature of the state. These substantive arrangements might range from fundamental institutional and constitutional matters like the drawing or re-drawing of state boundaries, the gaining or forfeiting of legal state sovereignty, or the form of governmental offices (deciding, for instance, between republic and monarchy, universal and restricted franchise, common and private ownership of the means of production, etc.), to small-scale and mundane matters like local governmental elections, changing the statutes, the level and form of taxation, the extent of welfare services, the impeachment of representatives, educational or environmental policies, etc. In every instance though, minutely or drastically as the case may be, politics is intended to interfere with *order*, defending the prevailing order or assailing it. It is through order that political conduct becomes involved with the law but this is only *positive* law, i.e. law as sanctioning, legitimating the prevailing order. As the positive law in states can be described in terms of an ongoing mediation between the demands of particular, settled order and the dictates of universal morality, so politics would appear as attempts to rewrite the terms of this mediation, pushing positive law away from order and towards (what is assumed to be) a more faithful approximation, reflection of the universal moral law, institutionally expressed.

But order in the state, as we saw in Chapter 2, inevitably connects up with the outlook, identity, position and relations of particular groups within the state (and indeed outside it); order is formally expressed in law but in substance has to do with group interest, group conflict and the distribution of power. Thus politics, to employ yet another well-worn platitude, is basically 'about power', about arrangements which are expressive of a particular power settlement. Politics is conducted on behalf of certain groups and in opposition to certain other groups, playing out conflicts of interest and pitting power against power. Politics is group activity: it is carried on, obviously, by 'individuals' but individuals acting now as particulars, assuming social roles which are intelligible only in terms of group identity and group interest, such as the roles of 'representative', 'leader', 'voter', 'activist', 'spokesperson', 'agitator', 'demonstrator', 'vigilante' or 'urban guerilla'. As the universal character of the 'citizen', matching the universal dimension of the state as concrete moral law, is in practice diffused and differentiated into group identities, so the particular roles played out in the arena of politics represent no more and no less than a conscious, intentional rearranging of the kaleidoscope; it is in and through politics that citizens become aware of order and of their own particular position within it. Order is the static expression of group relationships while politics is their activation, mobilization, the unsettling of order, the coming into life of a particular, determinate, differentially self-conscious citizenship. In an adaptation of the Hegelian-Marxist expression: order is a set of group relationships 'in itself', while in politics this becomes a situation 'for itself', recognized for what it is and consciously attended to.

One very important point follows from this understanding of politics, and this in our present context needs to be spelt out clearly and with emphasis: politics can never be entirely 'immoral', it can never go totally against the universal moral law. A critic will of course immediately point out that this statement might not amount to more than a definitional conjuring trick, merely shifting the problem of what is moral and what is immoral to what is properly to be called 'political' and what is not. The objection will be met, however, in due course, in our discussion below of the borderline between politics in the proper sense and politics as it shades into criminality (which is still a very different thing from crime taking on a political colouring). But first things first, and as it was with crime, our primary task here is to isolate a pure and relevant concept of the 'political'. Now the assertion that politics can never be entirely immoral, or in other words that its departure as such is moral conduct, can I think be argued for on the basis of the following considerations. In the first place, politics *eo ipso* signifies the transcending of the pure, natural, immediate individual point of view. Politics starts with community, with association, with a public dimension, however small and insignificant in practical terms this dimension might be – otherwise, I would contend, the concept would be entirely devoid of a distinct meaning. Crime remains crime, individual and essentially 'private', whatever its scale and effect; politics is always public, always particular and never private and individual, though it may be effectively concentrated on one single person (like a prophet in the wilderness) and might have no visible, measurable external influence at all (like obscure academic monographs on politics, pulped or remaindered). Political conduct logically assumes at the very minimum a particular group, on whose behalf politics is engaged in, an entity which is 'us' and with which I, as a single person, identify in and for my political action. Furthermore, this elemental association is never, in principle, 'instrumental' association, entered into for finite purposes but rather a pre-given associational framework which itself defines the range of purposes to which political action is directed. Criminality effectively stops at association, whereas politics is spawned, generated out of it. With crime, association is incidental, purely practical, ephemeral, irrelevant and ultimately contradicts individual ends; with politics, association is absolutely essential, logically required, encompassing particular ends (carried out by individuals), preceding as well as surviving them. Crime is immediate and concentrated on itself, in the individual act. Politics has no absolute beginning and no (logically) foreseeable termination; single actions, instances of conduct, like a particular campaign, an election or a revolution, take place in an unbroken continuum, in an infinity of historical backgrounds, cultural and social contexts, and envisioning durable outcomes. A single political action has no 'political' meaning unless understood in this deeper and wider context; an action gains its 'criminal' meaning precisely by thus falling out of all contexts. The meaning and effect of crime are atomization, individuation, both inwardly in consciousness and outwardly in human relations; the meaning and effect of politics is *particularization*.

Political action is certainly 'caused', in that it always has discoverable antecedents which constitute part of its meaning, and it is also determinately future-oriented, typically (though not invariably) explained and justified in terms of an overall 'cause', an end to be reached. This end justifies the means, and it is, in categorial terms, *moral* justification – criminal action, as we have seen, has no 'end' in this sense, nothing beyond the individual, and is thus not capable of moral justification. In politics individuals seek power and self-aggrandizement but they do this as particulars: the cause, the end to be reached, might imply the necessity of doing harm to other people, of using them as 'means', but it also implies the conscious sacrifice, jeopardy of the individual who is acting. Universality, the hallmark of moral conduct, is reached therefore at least in this hard and uncomfortable sense: there are no individual exceptions when it comes to promoting the 'cause'. Patriotism (and similar political causes) might well be 'the last refuge of the scoundrel', as Samuel Johnson contemptuously remarked, but it is by no means an imaginary, fictitious or arbitrary refuge; political identity and commitment are not gratuitously chosen by individuals but, as they feel, 'imposed' on them, and politics *per se* moralizes individual conduct. I might have to kill you, I have a 'moral' right to do so, but this implies, or certainly should imply, also a moral *duty* on my part to expose myself to harm and violent death. Note that this elemental logic of political conduct has not always the further implication that you, as my opponent in the conflict played out, have the moral right to harm or kill me – perhaps this latter could be regarded as the hallmark of a more advanced, more 'civilized', more humane kind of politics. But the point is that a bare symmetry, a stark and maybe frightening, negative and inhumane, universal standpoint is reached even before advancing to this higher level: everybody can be reduced to a means, *including* myself. The political cause which justifies certain actions is (or can be) self-enclosed, concentrated on itself, oblivious of the outside world, of other views and other interests, composing a moral universe on its own, exclusive and intolerant, and in this it does bear some resemblance to the universe of criminal conduct but with one crucial difference. Criminal conduct centres around me as an individual: I *must*, logically, be exempted from the world of means around me. In direct contrast, in political conduct I submerge myself in this world and cannot, logically, be exempted; I am myself just a part of the cause; I am a 'weapon' that harms or kills and which, by the same token, can also suffer the same calamities.

Surely this fundamental categorial distinction is amply borne out by what we see around us in actual experience. The self-sacrifice of the political actors in acting for the cause – and of course illegal political actors *par excellence* – is quite common but we do not find this normally in the world of criminality. For criminals to sacrifice themselves in crime and for crime is very rare (I myself am not conscious of ever having read or heard about any instances) and in any case this would contradict the very rationale of criminal action. With politics, however, self-sacrifice is always consistent with action: the cause, the group on whose behalf I am acting, will survive me. It may well be that from the point of view of general security in society this attitude makes illegal political actors more 'dangerous' than criminals, but that (for the moment) is beside the point: their being dangerous to others is matched by their being dangerous to themselves. The conduct of a Bobby Sands or a Leila Khaled has a moral symmetry to it which the conduct of a Dillinger or a Reggie Kray has not. Political actors of all varieties, whether we like it or not, belong to a different category, and political logic does in most cases tend to be accompanied by the appropriate political psychology: you ought to be ready to sacrifice yourself for the cause and, in most cases, you *are* ready. As Laver in *The Crime Game* describes the 'just hijacker' as a kind of 'altruist': 'An altruist is someone who is not solely concerned with his own payoffs. It is clear that some altruists, like Captain Martyr Mahmud, will be prepared to die for others.'[58] And: 'The sudden termination of his life, even if he does not believe in Heaven, is no problem. His enhanced credibility can be bequeathed to his comrades. Such people are not masochists; they are willing martyrs.'[59] Ted Honderich in *Violence for Equality*: 'Something for which sane and admirable men have always been willing to risk and to accept death, torture, punishment, and also self-accusation and the experience of guilt, is something worth having if anything is. There is no alternative to this conclusion.'[60] (Honderich, let us note, draws a qualitative distinction between 'causes', a point which we have not yet reached in these reflections.) Concerning the psychology of illegal political action, Bowyer Bell in *A Time for Terror* reports a priest's description of the character of Zvonko Busic, hijacker: '. . . an honest and good man, very strong in his beliefs, a quiet man who felt that life was not worth living without justice and freedom for Croatia.'[61] The general point is well expressed by Hannah Arendt in *On Violence*:

> As far as human experience is concerned, death indicates an extreme of loneliness and impotence. But faced collectively and in action, death changes its countenance; now nothing seems more likely to intensify our vitality than its proximity. Something we are usually hardly aware of, namely, that our own death is accompanied by the potential immortality of the group we belong to and, in the final analysis, of the species, moves into the center of our experiences.[62]

Arendt's analysis is not specifically concerned with the distinction between 'criminal' and 'political' but I think that this passage captures at least one aspect of the distinction with stark force and clarity: loneliness and impotence on one side, vitality on the other. The immorality of one is philosophically as well as existentially expressed in mortality; immortality is the element which supplies morality to the other.

Another point made in passing by Arendt in the same passage leads conveniently to our next observation. The basic, minimal morality of political conduct consists in acting for and on behalf of a group; politics necessarily implies a minimal acceptance of *some* moral duty to *some* other people; it thus transcends the standpoint of the single individual. Indeed, we have to reverse Niebuhr's dictum: 'immoral' men become 'moral' in society and only in society. In other words, in politics there is always some incipient, potential, embryonic recognition of 'humanity' as the proper and ultimate recipient, and beneficiary of the cause, even though general humanity will be immediately represented by a determinate group. Now the point here is that in 'genuine' political conduct (and the qualification will be explained in the next but one paragraph) the group on whose behalf action is performed is not *sharply* distinguished from the rest of humanity. There is a close and crucial connection, as Arendt says, between the group to which I belong, and whose immortality I share, and the 'species' of which this group itself constitutes a part. It is a mistake to suppose, as it is often enough done in academic and ideological literature, that politics necessarily implies 'enemies' or 'conflict' in the sense of there being *irreconcilable* clashes of interest between determinate groups. Conflict there is, to be sure, and it would be rather difficult to imagine politics without it, but conflict in this hard and basic sense is, logically, superfluous. You can very well do without enemies; it is *friends* who are absolutely needed, friends or perhaps rather 'comrades' associated through and for the cause. It is the criminal who has enemies only.

Politics, as well as being about power, is also about comradeship, about doing things together, engaging in common action, one for all and all for one. You do fight but you don't necessarily fight foes determined as identifiable groups with interests that are directly, incorrigibly, eternally opposed to yours. As well as comradeship, politics in the third instance is also about persuasion, debate, argument, the winning over of erstwhile opponents which could not be done unless one started out from a conception of an overriding 'human' interest. Your enemy need not be people ultimately: it could be ignorance, superstition, misunderstanding, the prevalence of false beliefs, a psychological condition. That is, and here we come to the point suggested by Arendt, in politics it is (almost) universally assumed that the interest of *your* group, on behalf of which you are acting, is at bottom the same as the real interest of *all* groups. The particular in political conduct is constantly being elevated to the level of universality and identified with it. Your group as it were concretely represents humanity and universal moral justice, it acts immediately in its own interest but *mediately* in the interests of all others as well. The country 'needs' its miners, the nation itself is 'better off' if old-age pensioners are adequately looked after, the interest of General Motors is the same as the interest of the United States of America. In the words of the Manifesto of the 'Fighters for Free Croatia', terrorist hijackers of the 1970s: 'National self-determination is a basic human right, universal and fundamental, recognized by all members of the United Nations. . . We fight for Croatia, which will be, for all people, either a cherished presence or a beloved homeland.'[63] Note the reference here to a 'universal' right and the assumed interest 'for all people', and compare the *logic* of this mode of thinking and action with the underlying 'logic' of young Alf, the Capones, the Krays, the Richardsons. Nothing could provide a more striking contrast. Even further, and no doubt controversially, it should be pointed out that this tendency to universalization is to a large extent present also in the case of *really* extreme political movements. Perhaps with radical left-wing doctrines, like Marxism, this is not too difficult to show: the proletariat in Marxist terms represents humanity and fights for humanity, and the 'enemy' is capital or even the capitalist 'class', to be liquidated *as a class* but not necessarily as 'individuals'. After all, as it is unambiguously said in Marx's *Paris Manuscripts*, capitalists are also 'alienated' and thus the proletarian revolution will be beneficial to them, too, liberating them as human beings. But universalization is not entirely absent from extreme right-wing doctrines, like Fascism and Nazism, either, and this unpalatable fact, elevating these movements to at least the borderline of 'politics' proper, must be clearly faced: Nazi propaganda often enough asserted that it would be in the 'real interest' of Slavs, Jews and other sub-humans to live tranquilly under Aryan leadership. (The very bottom line, it seems to me, is to be drawn not with racialism but with intended genocide; by no stretch of ideological ingenuity can it be argued that it is in the interest of Jews to be dead.)

This leads us then to the rather difficult issue of attempting to decide the proper conceptual limits of what we have above labelled 'genuine' politics. It is quite clear that not everything and not everybody could be accepted at their face-value as 'political', however strident the claim might be. Any gangster can declare himself to be an urban guerilla, any collection of faded and scattered émigré stalwarts can appoint themselves a government in exile. (In actual fact, let us hasten to add, this happens relatively rarely and almost all political movements and groupings that *we hear about*, those that do manage to make a splash, seem to have at least a minimal valid claim to act politically, i.e. for and on behalf of a pre-existing association, exhibiting the elemental features of comradeship, fighting to gain power, effectively achieving the particularization of society, presenting their cause in universal moral terms, etc.). Now there is, inevitably, an external criterion for politics, just as there is an external criterion for the state, viz. *success*. In terms of this criterion the state proves its character, its essence, simply by existing as a state, i.e. holding effective power within a given territory and performing minimal governmental functions (as argued by St Augustine and Max Weber). But this external criterion is inadequate and unsatisfactory in itself, either with the state (as we endeavoured to show in Chapter 2) or with political conduct. Just as the state requires moral authority to be recognized as a proper state (i.e. acting out the moral law, acknowledging common humanity, formally guaranteeing equal citizenship and equal rights, etc.), so, to be deserving of the label, political conduct requires, at the very least, moral *aspirations*, potential and *bona fide* universality, an ascertainable intention and ability to act on the state level. This means, in principle and also in practical terms, that the clearest case of genuine political action is undertaken on behalf either of state-forming groups, like nations, or state-dominating groups, like classes. State, nation and class together constitute, as it were, the fundamental ontology of politics (certainly in modern times), the perfect triangular form of political conduct.

But here it might be more useful to set out the more important internal, i.e. moral, criteria of political action in negative terms. Let us say that the genuinely 'political' quality of conduct undertaken on behalf of groups becomes more problematic the more *narrowly* the actor's own group is defined, the more this group is defined in *objective* terms, the more that conflicting group interests are regarded as *irreconcilable* and incapable of compromise solutions, and the more the prevailing conflict situation is taken to be *unalterable*. Thus fringe and minuscule politics falls on the threshold; racialist politics, postulating eternal, objective barriers between human beings, is imperfect and morally highly ambiguous politics; the politics of pure violence is bad politics, as it leaves no room for persuasion, discussion and compromise; and war as such is the terminal point of politics (which does not, of course, exclude war being correctly seen as the pursuit of political objectives by 'other means'). At one extreme end of the spectrum, as exemplified mainly in the conduct and ideology of Fascism, politics ceases to be politics in the genuine sense once the opponent is considered *literally* non-human or sub-human, a beast to be permanently subjugated or, if need be, exterminated without any compunction. This 'pseudo-speciation', in Lorenz's term, is more common among primitive tribes which employ the same word to denote their own group and the species; those outside are not considered 'human' at all. When aggression and the 'hunting instinct' come together, as Marsh considers, there are 'quite horrific consequences. And they come together when the rival one is seeking to subdue is no longer a man – he is a special kind of animal. Unlike other animals, however, he still poses a threat. He is a dangerous animal and he is also a rival . . .'[64] Clearly this politics is on the borderline of the criminal. Still, I think (as already hinted at above) it would be misleading to characterize conduct and principles like Fascism simply in terms of crime. Nazi and Fascist politics undoubtedly had a criminal element – in dehumanizing some opponents, for example – but it was still, categorially speaking, politics, displaying the basic distinguishing features of political conduct. Immorality here was externally projected, as the dehumanized opponent was reduced to a pure means, a pure obstacle to be trampled on (exactly as it happens in criminal conduct). Nevertheless inwardly Fascist politics still postulated a minimal element of morality, in aspiring to be a state and, once in power, to act like a state, in claiming to represent a determinate, pre-existing group in society, in transcending in principle the standpoint of natural individuality, in at least attempting to connect the cause to the putative interests of universal humanity. It might be useful to compare a real, and partially criminal, Nazi or Fascist empire with a fictitious, and purely criminal, empire of an evil 'master-mind', like Blofeld of SPECTOR. The former is a state, albeit with very ugly blemishes, still embodying and expressing the values and culture of a particular *society*, on-going ordinary human relationships. The latter is not a state at all, does not proceed from any kind of society or pre-existing group identities, but a pure creation, emanation of an individual mind, with all its gadgets just a criminal gang writ large. (Of course, SPECTOR is pure fantasy, childish escapism, whereas Fascism is not and has to be taken seriously – for this very reason.) I shall return later in this chapter to consider the more interesting case, at the opposite end of the spectrum, of left-wing extreme 'humanism' which can also reach the borderline of politics and crime.

But on with our main story. Though undoubtedly we have to recognize marginal and penumbral instances of political conduct, these do not and cannot cancel out the truth that politics is *sui generis*, to be distinguished from criminal conduct. With most mainstream politics, of course, with legal and constitutional politics, this is no problem. Politics of this moderate and circumscribed nature is self-evidently moral (it might be more or less stupid, misguided, wrong-headed, divisive or whatever), in that it accepts the law of the state as it stands and acts strictly within its terms. But politics cannot entirely be defined in terms of positive law, for the simple and obvious reason that positive law itself derives from and is dependent for its legitimacy on the universal moral law. Positive law, since it embodies and sanctions a particular order, cannot be a *perfect* replica of the moral law. The state is imperfect moral community and its imperfection may find its exact (more or less) moral equivalent in politics which is, in the particular definition of positive law, illegal and unconstitutional. Just as crime is not wholly intelligible as a 'legal definition', nor is the meaning of politics exhausted if we try to define it exclusively on the basis of the *existing* state, within any given constitutional framework. As the state falls short of the moral ideal, so anti-state politics expresses in principle an endeavour to reach beyond the state and, *ex hypothesi*, move towards this same ideal by taking another route. The morality of anti-state politics is not therefore principally dependent on its legality formulated in positive terms but on 'legality' in the more remote and deeper, but nonetheless directly present, perspective of the moral law which bestows on positive law *its* legitimacy also. Either of the two can be, in given cases, a more creditable expression of the inherent end and rationale of political conduct: the formation and maintenance of moral community. Thus anti-state politics, violent, subversive, terrorist politics, cannot properly be understood in isolation from ends which this politics, in principle, shares with the established state. It is, as Anthony Arblaster well expressed the point, 'an insuperable obstacle to intelligent discussion of these and other cases of terrorism to begin by assuming that the legitimacy of the state or states in question can be taken for granted. Quite clearly it cannot, and whether or not the terrorists' challenge is thought to have any justification, the least that must be done is to understand why and for what reasons they are making such a challenge.'[65]

The point to grasp then, and here we gain further illumination concerning the difference between crime and the 'challenge' presented by illegal politics, is that illegal political conduct always has determinate *reasons* behind it. Criminality cannot be derived from any definite antecedents, causes or reasons, and this is why ultimately crime is not a serious challenge to the state. Illegal politics, on the other hand, presupposes a condition of dissatisfaction, a definite, identifiable set of 'grievances' suffered by a pre-existing group, and not by individuals as such, and by a group which is not defined in terms of these grievances alone. This is a crucially important point, not to be missed: groups figuring in politics are not constituted by politics but on the contrary politics grows out of their experience and consciousness. Neither are these groups created by the 'wrongs' they might have to endure. Intellectuals and messianic, fanatical political leaders, *pace* some well-established and influential academic opinions abroad these days, cannot create groups like nations or classes, nor can they invent suffering. Their impact (and it is of course considerable) is directed to the awakening of popular consciousness, to making suffering feel more like suffering, to generating a literary and political culture expressive of group identity. But groups do, and in terms of pure logic must, exist before they become conscious of suffering wrongs and before political purposes and movements can be fashioned out of their objective social position. It would be clearly absurd – not to invent various groups or grievances, which any crank or any fanatic can do quite easily – but to engage in any kind of political activity that can really rise to the level of a 'challenge' on the basis of fanciful groupings and fictitious or merely 'imputed' wrongs. It just wouldn't work, from the point of view of the political actors, the challengers themselves, that is; from the point of view of the state and established society outside it could still of course constitute a certain amount of nuisance (and of course it might bear tragic consequences for random individual victims). If it came from nowhere, anti-state politics would obviously be crime, pure and simple, with no consequences for the state. If it proceeded nowhere, had no definite purposes to carry out, it would be crime and in addition it would be utter folly. But we can be assured that the most dangerous anti-state movements are not like that at all; as their origins and background are easily ascertainable, so their courses of action are, in general terms, predictable. Talking about the Provisional IRA, E. Moxon-Browne says: 'The image of a small band of ruthless criminals holding a cowering population to ransom is a comforting illusion, but it has little to do with reality.'[66] And concerning the alleged unpredictability and arbitrariness of illegal politics, Paul Furlong makes the telling point, with reference to the Italian 'Brigate Rosse': 'But though terrorist violence may be unacceptable and abnormal, and indeed often does occur in environments not normally associated with violence, nevertheless it may not be unpredictable in its general selection of targets nor is it indiscriminate. If it were indiscriminate or arbitrary, the symbolic value or representativeness of its victims would be undermined.'[67] Anti-state political activists, e.g. the German 'Red Army Faction', which engage in pure violence run the danger of cutting themselves away from the mainstream politics of the groups which they claim to 'represent', as the point is made in David Miller's excellent article, 'The Use and Abuse of Political Violence'; however, where there is a 'symbiotic relationship' between activists and given pre-existing groups, as in Northern Ireland, then violence can and does have some genuinely political effect.[68] Illegal politics is thus predicated on two things which make it 'valid': on the internal, moral side it assumes and requires 'authorization' by pre-existing and identifiable groups within society (and this lifts it out of the world of criminality), and on the external, practical side it needs the actual support of the groups concerned (which makes it effective and noticeable, a real 'challenge').

So far we have been considering illegal, anti-state politics in highly abstract and as it were celestial terms only (apart from some illustrations and quotes), which is clearly inadequate. We ought not to be seen wanting to avoid the really pressing, really controversial issues. Everybody (I suspect) is quite happy to endorse the general principle – and quite vacuous because so general – that some illegal and even violent politics, in a very carefully defined set of conditions, might be condoned, accepted as morally legitimate, and perhaps even encouraged. Few people, outside a small band of devotees, would condemn von Stauffenberg for wanting to assassinate Hitler in 1944, and probably no qualms would have been caused to civilized conscience if Stalin had been forcibly, and illegally, put out of the way in the 1950s (perhaps he was, for all we know). But, it is said, what may be morally permissible in 'dictatorships' is definitely forbidden in 'democracies' where citizens' moral obligation to abide by the law is absolute, goes all the way and is that upon which the survival of these systems of government depends. Democracies, as paradigmatically represented by the mainstream 'liberal-democratic' polities of the Western world, are pluralistic, tolerant, flexible, benign, receptive to the grievances of groups which might feel disadvantaged, and exemplifying the 'rule of law' which precludes governmental arbitrariness. Liberal-democratic states are recognized precisely in terms of their constitutionality, which provides protection against naked political and social power, and in terms of their legislative mobility, which ensures that changes can be peacefully effected. Everybody can be heard, everything can be discussed, majorities can be freely and peacefully formed, and minorities can claim special rights. And therefore if the 'state' in these polities can be seen exclusively in terms of 'state as law', it follows that anti-state politics here does not deserve the name of politics at all; it becomes crime: terrorism, subversion, fanaticism, sheer irresponsibility and immorality. Here proper politics and legality are co-terminous. Indeed, political violence in these conditions is said to carry a special kind of blemish, worse than criminal violence, since it will affect more people, more 'innocents', and since it undermines the foundations and destroys the fabric of morality itself. Thus Clutterbuck: 'Political violence should be treated more seriously than criminal violence, not only because it has a more arrogant motivation, but also because it affects the lives of more of the community.'[69] And similarly Sir Robert Mark asserts in his autobiography, *In the Office of Constable*, that 'the worst of all crimes is the furtherance of political or industrial aims by violence . . .'[70]

Let us say at once: there undoubtedly is and (logically speaking) must be a very important distinction between polities where there is *some* chance of altering the power structure within the framework of the law and those where, as in autocratic traditional state forms, the law of the state and the order of the state are completely identified. The relationship between law and order in liberal-democratic states, as we pointed out in Chapter 2, is highly ambiguous, and this fact itself indicates, with special reference to the present context, that there is a leeway, a hiatus, a kind of political no-man's-land, some room for manoeuvre, a possibility to *use* the law as against order. Pragmatically, as any sane revolutionary knows (and as Miller points out in the article already referred to), if there is any possibility to resort to legal politics in the furtherance of particular causes, it always pays to do so; illegality and violence are a burden, highly uncomfortable and personally dangerous to those actively involved, and their success is by no means assured. And morally also, there could scarcely be any doubt as to an absolute moral obligation to have first recourse to the law, if there is any law in the real and relevant sense to resort to. To obey the law and to observe peace and civility in social and political relationships is a primary obligation, incumbent on any human being as a human being. However, having said all this, regrettably it still does not follow that liberal-democratic states can be totally exempted from *moral* liability – and of course empirical vulnerability – to suffer anti-state politics, and oppositional political violence, in their midst. In the first instance, this can I think be shown quite convincingly by resorting to *reductio ad absurdum*: to claim total moral exemption from political violence against the state means to declare the *full* divinity, absolute moral superiority of the state, not only *vis à vis* individuals (where the claim is reasonable, to say the least) but also *vis à vis* particular group identities and interests. In other words, exemption means the square denial that liberal-democratic states also constitute a particular *order*, a particular power settlement, and such a denial, I believe, once revealed in this stark form, defies all logic and common sense. Order is an absolute presupposition of the state (without it the state would be inconceivable) and order means asymmetry, rigidity and finitude, in group terms. However flexible and tolerant, the law as it exists cannot tolerate its own contradiction, however broad and benign, the 'constitution' is still in the last analysis reflective and expressive of one settlement as against alternatives, however mobile and evolving, the legal, political and social structure of the state is *always* burdened with its own relatively petrified identity. At one point, in principle, any constitution becomes morally inadequate to itself, and so at one point, in principle, anti-state politics becomes a genuine moral option. It is interesting to note (and more will be said about this in the next chapter) that conservative defenders of 'law and order' in liberal-democratic states are indeed set on course towards a special kind of self-contradiction, on the one hand asserting the imperfection of the state, its inherent mobility, flexibility and pluralism (the traditional 'liberal' view), while on the other hand maintaining its absolute superiority where this really counts, at the frayed edges.

But of course there is no need to follow the high road of logic, of philosophical reflection, to appreciate the moral liability of liberal-democratic states to generate and suffer anti-state politics. The point made above could perhaps be more congenially expressed by calling attention to the discrepancy between the self-appointed rhetoric of liberal democracy and the *reality* of the liberal-democratic world, in the domestic as well as the global context. Whatever the rhetoric might say, alas there *are* groups oppressed, disadvantaged, distanced from power in democratic states, too, and it is not easy to concede that their 'moral' obligation to observe the law is of the same magnitude, or indeed the same kind, as that of the members of more fortunate groups, or that they have any real alternative to illegal political conduct. Democratic obligation assumes the possibility of 'fair compromise' as between groups, and this possibility does not always exist. As Peter Singer points out in *Democracy and Disobedience*: '. . . groups may be denied the opportunity of being heard effectively because violence, intimidation or law prevent them from being active, or because their activity, for some reason or other, is not accepted as right and proper by the active majority. It is clear that no justification, in terms of fair compromise, can be given for such exclusions.'[71] And: 'The poor, for example, cannot organize properly as a pressure group, and are not numerous enough to have national electoral significance. These defects mean that the political system is permanently, or for long periods, biased against certain sections of the community.'[72] His conclusion, though forceful, is by no means unreasonable:

> But those people who are deprived of the share of influence on decisions they would have had under a fair compromise do not have this basic reason for obedience. In respect of this particular reason for obedience, these people are in the same position as they would be if they were living under a dictatorship.[73]

And indeed, though this might sound at first as an exaggerated sleight of hand, we must accept the unpalatable truth that the sheer *existence* of anti-state politics, on a scale and with a duration that make it a veritable challenge to the state, goes a very long way towards suggesting its putative moral legitimacy. Here *de facto* comes almost as close to *de jure* as it does with established and outwardly pacific state forms which, in more instances than one would care to enumerate, themselves came into being as a direct result of anti-state political conduct and violence. The past is no more exempt from moral judgment than the present, and the present is no less amenable to an understanding in terms of an historical continuum than the past. Black extremists in America, as Angela Davis *et al.* put the point in *If They Come in the Morning: Voices of Resistance*, 'killed and were consequently tried for murder. But did they commit murder? This raises the question of whether American revolutionaries had *murdered* the British in their struggle for liberation.'[74] Questions like this should be regarded as more or less entirely open: history, if not exactly the 'judge', is certainly the most important 'material witness' to the moral verdicts passed by a succession of generations. As established states have all come out of politics, so illegal political conduct at present ought to be seen, at least in principle, as leading towards new settlements, new establishments. Thus a challenge, worthy of its name in terms of sheer magnitude and effect, must be distinguished from the isolated action of cranks; the latter, like crime in general, is always unpredictable, whereas the former leads back to definite causes. As Hyams again rather forcefully expresses it, the 'true anarchist' or pure destroyer 'is a rare animal. I can find no single case in which recourse to terrorism was not forced on the organization in question by denial of all other means of fighting against social injustice. Whenever I have seemed to come upon such a case, it has turned out that although other means exist in theory – they have been found useless in practice – a common case in the great oligarchies called parliamentary democracies, and the invariable case in the great bureaucracies called Communist or People's republics.'[75] The condemnation of 'terrorism' therefore is ultimately the condemnation of conditions which have evoked it in the first place; who could seriously and credibly maintain that the IRA, the PPLF or Brigate Rosse for that matter would constitute a grave 'problem' if there had not been a *pre-existing* 'problem' of institutionalized religious and national discrimination, wars involving the large-scale dislocation of populations, protracted and rigid social differences leading to the disaffection and alienation of sections of the people? This much, to me at any rate, does stand to reason – if anything ever stands to reason – stands to attention before the measured gaze of the academic observer, in the crazy, messy, topsy-turvy whirlpool world of politics.

Here it might be appropriate to enlarge a little bit on the vexed issue of political 'violence'. Illegal politics in many forms might be readily condoned even in liberal-democratic societies: it is all right, morally acceptable even though illegal, to engage in acts of passive disobedience, to refuse to pay taxes or to serve in the army, to chain oneself to the railings of Buckingham Palace, to camp on Greenham Common, or even to immolate oneself as a form of political protest, as did Jan Palach in Prague and Buddhist monks in Saigon. But 'violence' – the active causing of harm to others in the course of illegal political conduct – is *taboo*, repellent to public opinion and the civilized conscience. Why? What is so special about violence? What is violence, how to fill with intelligible content this highly emotive term? Where does violence really begin?

Starting from basics, it is scarcely open to serious doubt that the intentional causing of harm to others, as such, is an act of immorality, absolutely to be condemned (and for that reason often found absolutely fascinating, as we saw above, in the course of our discussion of crime). But then, moving away from this abstract and celestial plane, it is quite commonly felt that in the concrete context of politics a satisfactory definition and understanding of violence might not be so easy to hit upon. In political rhetoric, both left and right, 'violence' like 'terrorism' (or like 'oppression' and 'exploitation') is emotionally charged, deliberately defined in such a way as to favour one particular settlement as against others; violence is what the other fellow does, against you. As a word and as a concept it is not merely descriptive of certain kinds of action in politics, it is also an active *part* of politics, a verbal weapon in conflict, drawing on the repugnance which all political actors and movements share towards the absolutely immoral and from which they all seek to dissociate themselves. Violence, if anything, is one of the most essentially contested concepts in political discourse, and contestability is really its innermost essence. It cannot thus be unitarily, unproblematically defined: instead of a clear, generally agreed understanding (that would reach beyond mere tautologies like defining violence in terms of 'harm') what we have is a field or expanse of ideologically oriented definitions. Radicals who envisage a community drastically different from the existing 'state' and which realizes the ideals of love, co-operation, equality and personal freedom, will define violence broadly: for them it is present now, in a diffused form, in the general 'harm' that asymmetrical power relations themselves inflict on individuals; the state itself, and society itself, exemplify political violence. As in one of the Angry Brigade Manifestos: 'What violence is, is the fact people end up in a situation where they are so freaked about the way they live, that they beat up the people they love.'[76] At the other extreme, conservatives for whom the existing situation is essentially good and satisfactory, the best of all possible worlds, a truly moral situation, will define violence narrowly: it is something that occurs outside and contrary to orderly actions and relations, immediate and palpable physical injury, unauthorized by the law. Here, as J. Harris says, 'preoccupation is with law and order, and violence is contrasted with this to yield a narrow definition designed to capture the twin monsters of civil disorder and criminal assault.'[77] We have, throughout these reflections, been arguing against any hasty and unwarranted 'coupling' of the two 'monsters' of crime and illegal politics; but the disjunction is significant in both directions. That is to say, the line maintained here is that a broad 'conservative' view (with a small 'c') is the correct one, concerning criminal violence. However it seems to me that the radical perspective (also with a small 'r') goes considerably nearer the mark concerning political violence, i.e. conduct which, though involving the causing of physical harm to others, truly belongs to the political category in the sense in which we have defined the concept of the 'political' earlier. In principle, it cannot be said that the state, including liberal-democratic states and the *world* as arranged and maintained by the great powers, bestows equal or equitable benefits on all identifiable groups, many of which have legitimate grievances not remediable within the confines of the law and within orderly relations. Therefore in principle it cannot be said that 'violent' action in politics is not justified.

The moral law, which we attempted to define in its bare outlines in Chapter 2, might be clear and unambiguous in respect of causing harm to others: the deliberate, intentional, gratuitous killing, maiming, injuring, wounding, maltreatment of other human beings is prohibited – full stop. Violence in the abstract is immoral, there can be no doubt about that. But while moral philosophy and the moral consciousness might be clear and straightforward, life unfortunately is not. We are *never* dealing with an abstract, ideal situation but always confronted with a concrete world where the moral touchstone of an ideal 'humanity' is mediated, refracted, projected and where morality is only *imperfectly* realized in the state and under positive law. Human life should always be preserved and protected, and the general health, happiness and freedom of all human beings should everywhere be promoted – fair enough but how can these moral injunctions be genuinely observed and followed in the real world? What does morality involve *in practice*? Whether we like it or not, it does involve, certainly on the level of political conduct and maybe elsewhere as well, the occasional recourse to 'violence', to killing and harming. Morality means responsibility: if I hold that life is sacred and if I see that life is in danger, I must make a particular interpretive *judgment* of the situation, and if I see that life (e.g. the life of an innocent by-stander walking down Knightsbridge near the barracks) can only be protected by physically harming or even killing those who threaten it (e.g. a political terrorist about to deposit his explosive charge in a paper bag), then I hardly have a moral choice which *ab ovo* excludes the resort to violence. Politics can never totally function with an absolute, categorical rejection of forcible and physical means, and this is primarily the case with the state, which can never completely renounce the physical sanction, and secondarily also the case (but in a restricted sense) with political movements which aspire to become states and which, if successful, will face the same responsibilities as established states face now. Moral perfectionism has no place in politics. Here we deal only with varying 'quantities' (without having necessarily to accept a form of utilitarianism) of probable harm, with relative entities and in the last resort particular, and uncertain, interpretive judgments.

The issue of the death penalty, as administered by the state, might be a good case in point. The abolition of the death penalty is not *necessarily* an act expressive of a greater valuation of human life in general. As van den Haag has put the point: 'No matter what can be said for the abolition of the death penalty, it will be perceived symbolically as a loss of nerve: social authority no longer is willing to pass an irrevocable judgment on anyone.' And: 'Life becomes cheaper as we become kinder to those who wantonly take it. The responsibility we avoid is indeed hard to bear. Can we sit in judgment and find that anyone is so irredeemably wicked that he does not deserve to live? Many of us no longer believe in evil, only in error or accident.'[78] Roy Hattersley, in the course of his speech in the House of Commons, opposing the restoration of the death penalty, called attention to the general 'loathing' in which violence is held in a 'decent society': 'That loathing must be directed against all violence – by the state as well as by individuals. By killing murderers we become too like the murderers themselves. The whole community is lowered to their standards.'[79] Now quite irrespectively of the pros and cons of the proposal which evoked the speaker's opposition (in fact the motion debated, in July 1983, was significantly that of the Tory Home Secretary's amendment to bring back capital punishment for 'terrorist' – and not for criminal – murders), this view, if taken literally, is one that would lead us away from the political world altogether. 'Killing' and 'murder' are different things and the 'community' cannot, logically, lower itself to the level of individuals. The absolute rejection of killing signifies a preference for inward moral purity over the protection of life and security in practice; it is, without doubt, an admirable and eminent moral stand but its coherence in the practical context of politics is questionable. For moral absolutism, as Harris aptly expresses the point, it is 'good *states of mind* that matter, not life itself. . . .'[80]

But to go a step further: the ubiquitous presence of power in the state and the presence of the physical sanction and violence, do not by themselves necessarily elevate anti-state politics to the level of legal politics. There is definitely one ultimate point, or one thin line, at which the two would be revealed as moral equivalents: one represents power in a settled state, the other emerging power. In actual practice, however, this thin line is by no means always reached and invariably it is difficult to reach; the road to it is beset by enormous obstacles of a pragmatic as well as moral nature. That is to say, in by far the greater proportion of actual violent encounters between the established state and illegal political movements the former still has the edge, a relative and troubled but still serious moral *presumption* in its favour. (There is no need to expatiate on the sheer technical superiority of states as against anti-state groups; this is self-evident and amply borne out by events everywhere, with very few and special exceptions.) Ultimately the state may not possess a moral authority which is entirely different *in kind* from the presumptive authority justifying illegal political action on behalf of determinate groups but the state nonetheless does possess this superior moral authority as seen in *immediate* terms. This is a point not at all difficult to comprehend or appreciate; the truth of the matter is that the state, by its sheer existence as a state, by its durability, territoriality, settled legality, has *already* proven and demonstrated its minimal moral content and character. Towards anti-state movements the state represents pure war, a veritable state of nature, no doubt, and anti-state groups represent war towards the state and towards society outside. But the state *also* represents peace, represents regularity, orderliness, tranquillity, predictability, protection of personal security – however imperfectly, tenuously, asymmetrically and inequitably these *universal* moral state-functions might be carried out in practice. Miller is again right:

> The incidence of violence is unpredictable and its use is not controlled by any formal set of rules. The use of force [i.e. the physical sanction by the state], on the other hand, is rule-governed, so that people are able to predict when and in what quantities it will be applied to them, and they should in theory be able to avoid it entirely. Since most of us attach a considerable value to regularity – because it affords us to plan our future lives and projects – we properly draw a morally-laden distinction between legal force and violence.[81]

History is hard on us all and it is especially hard on emerging groups who inevitably have to wage an uphill struggle. This cannot be helped. Anti-state movements might be equipped with superior moral ideas, a more advanced conception of political and social justice, but this is of course not quite enough: in addition they have to demonstrate in their conduct that they can really stand up to, and match, the substantial historicity, real as well as ideal existence, of the state. From this follows a point of enormous importance which cannot be overemphasized. It is that the onus, the weight of moral responsibility, always falls on anti-state political movements – and certainly not on the state against which they are fighting – to show that they are *really* in the business of politics, and not just a bunch of disguised, individually self-oriented criminals, other-worldly fanatics, messianic and childish cranks. They have to project, already in the oppositional, illegal situation, their future putative state-forming or state-dominating quality, and this means acting with moral restraint, circumspection, patience and tolerance. In one succinct expression, responsible political action in an illegal context must signify the conscious recognition of one's *weakness*, one's relative political immaturity, one's having, as it were, constantly to underwrite a futuristic guarantee that things, if the movement succeeds, won't become worse than in the existing situation; indeed, that they will become appreciably better. Moral credit must be preserved at all costs. Even if we concede the point (and from a traditional 'liberal-democratic' angle this concession would be highly suspect itself) that illegal political conduct is justified in principle, and that from an ultimate and universal moral perspective the established state has no absolute moral superiority *vis à vis* oppositional groups, we must at the same time stress that anti-state conduct is *no more* exempt from general moral rules than the state. This would really be absurd: to cashier the state for being partial, unjust, oppressive, cruel, violent, and then to go on cheerfully proclaiming that your own illegal movement is morally permitted to display the same features, and actually practice cruelty and partiality. It is morally permitted to fight against order, if really necessary by illegal and even violent means. But it is never permitted to breach the moral law. A limit must be recognized *outwardly* beyond which you cannot and will not go. It may be 'just' to fight for Free Croatia, Palestine, United Ireland, the complete emancipation of black people in America or the rights of mineworkers, but it is unjust and immoral to want to sacrifice the whole world, people indiscriminately outside, for the cause. The line must be drawn at large-scale, indiscriminate, terroristic killing, the taking of life merely for effect, acts of deliberate cruelty, individual revenge, retaliation – not because these contravene the law of the state but because this kind of restraint is demanded by the inherent morality of political movements themselves.

To conclude then on this issue, on illegal political conduct and political violence: what is the situation here with regard to the problem of personal security? It seems to me that, in line with our overall argument in this chapter endeavouring to distinguish between criminal and political conduct on the level of basic philosophical principle, here too a distinction ought to be drawn and maintained. Concerning crime our conclusion was, roughly, that the state ought to provide personal protection, ought to endeavour to maintain our personal safety but that, since criminality arises unpredictably in all kinds of social contexts (and for many other reasons as well), it was not reasonable and realistic to expect total protection. In society we – the uninvolved, unpolitical, law-abiding citizen, rich or poor – are always vulnerable to a modicum of insecurity and neither ourselves nor the state can be held completely responsible for this. Personal insecurity as a result of random criminality is in the nature of things. The state fulfils its duty if it contains crime (by whatever means: education, prevention, punishment), keeps it at a low level, and provides, as it were, 'statistical' protection. And the citizen fulfils his or her duty by remaining law-abiding and by showing a certain amount of 'public responsibility', e.g. helping victims, reporting on crime, providing information, etc. But the point is that this general citizenly responsibility, involving threats which do not affect the individual citizen directly, (although important), does not go very far, either in theory or in practice. As an individual citizen I am not, in the last resort, responsible for the occurrence of crime in my own broader society, and I am not 'guilty' for the criminal law-breaking of others, whatever their particular reasons might be in given cases. In regard to crime the citizen's role is essentially *passive*; here the existence of state power and state authority does mean that, in Hobbesian terms, we have relinquished our 'natural right' and have shifted general responsibility on to the appropriate societal organs. In this realm and on this level we are truly primarily 'consumers' of security.

As far as I can see, however, the same does not apply in the case of personal insecurity caused by the presence of illegal politics. On the one hand, since illegal politics calls into question the legitimacy of the state itself – i.e. the state *as order* – it cannot be unambiguously asserted that the state 'ought' to control and suppress illegal politics, that it ought to provide me, an individual, with security against anti-state political conduct. This would logically presuppose the absolute moral superiority of the state as it exists now, and of course it is this very superiority which the presence of illegal politics renders questionable in the first place; it is precisely this attack, this questioning, which defines illegal politics, distinguishing it from crime. The state, obviously, has to take cognizance of illegal politics and it is, undoubtedly, the state's moral duty to deal with illegal politics, so as to maintain or restore peace and tranquillity in society and to promote the general interest of the citizen body. But this 'dealing' is definitely not the same as the controlling and containing of crime. While the state confronts illegal politics as the repository of authority, as 'the law' *vis à vis* illegality, it also confronts illegal politics as *politics*, and on this level the two may well become moral equivalents. In other words, at one point or in a certain respect in this situation the sublime elevation of 'the state' itself disappears, becomes dissolved, vaporized, gaseous, and instead of a clear confrontation between moral 'right' and moral 'wrong' we have a conflict now between a right which is also wrong and a wrong which is also right, a 'law' whose character as order becomes now more pronounced and thus its moral imperfection revealed, and illegality which involves claims to proceed towards the creation of an alternative order and which thus itself makes an entry into the realm of universality. The (logical and existential) culmination of this conflict is civil war, a situation where legitimacy and authority are suspended, where power becomes dominant and where the provision of personal security is the *diffused* moral duty of the contending parties. What I am suggesting is that the state's proper attitude towards illegal politics, as sharply contrasted to the attitude towards crime, should always be defined in terms of a *potential* civil war situation, should represent thinking and action from, as it were, the logic of a civil war projected backwards, and should therefore concentrate on prevention, not retaliation and punishment. That is, in confronting illegal politics the state should accept full moral responsibility for the former's appearance in the first place, should consciously recognize its own weakness and imperfection as directly reflected in the anti-state movement, and should seek to deal with the challenge of order-defiance by appropriately changing *itself*, altering its own character as order: the very opposite of rigid resistance and the deliberate criminalization of opponents. And perhaps it is superfluous to add that in the contemporary scene, states have this primary moral responsibility extended also on a global scale: the potential civil war situation is worldwide.

On the other hand, I believe it follows from the above considerations that the peaceful and law-abiding individual citizen cannot claim *complete* moral irresponsibility and indifference, complete aloofness, complete innocence, complete passivity, and a complete 'consumer' status *vis à vis* illegal politics. Abiding by the law means that we are not guilty of criminality but this, unfortunately, does not mean that we are living in a moral ivory tower. As citizens we are consumers of the law but we are also, at least minimally, the producers of order and therefore we become, at one point, actively and morally responsible for the continuation of this order. We are benefiting from *this* order, existentially involved in it, we affirm it in every action we perform and every thought we formulate and every opinion we communicate. This order, in the last resort, could not exist without my (in the aggregate) active participation, and without this order I would not be me, in terms of my particular group identity and interest. I am in a teeny-weeny, tenuous, wispy but nonetheless morally relevant way responsible for what is going on around me; in a minimal sense I have a moral share in the maintenance, and perhaps also production, of an overall global situation which can generate such things as the conflict in Northern Ireland, large-scale insecurity and confrontation in the Middle East, urban guerillas in Italy, the plight of intellectuals in the Soviet Union, racial violence in Southall, rioting in Toxteth, the mineworkers' 'insurrection' in South Yorkshire. We may not want wholly to accept the radical argument as put forward in Stuart Hall *et al.*, *Policing the Crisis*, but there is definitely a large dose of truth in the statement:

> Politics is a harder task-master than is dreamt of in the *Sunday Times* editorial rooms. The 'imperfections of the system' look slightly less like a *vademecum* for extremism from the west bank of the Jordan. Only in the abstract world of classical liberalism can the world

> be so easily split as this into the public self, which has rights and duties, and the private, unpolitical self, which is wholly 'uninvolved'. The 'politics' of violence comes up out of nowhere and hits us between the eyes, not in spite of the fact that we are 'uninvolved', but *because* the links of exploitation which connect us, collectively, through the imperialist chain to another, far-off, forgotten and abandoned section of humanity have been allowed to pass for so long, behind everybody's back.[82]

It should be made clear here that I am not advancing a maximalist moral argument, like those put forward, among many other writers, by Harris and Honderich. That is, I am not saying that as ordinary citizens we have a standing moral duty to *act* so as to wind up the 'imperialist chain' of exploitation, to end worldwide poverty and starvation, to stand up and be counted in struggles against domestic and global inequality and injustice. I think this maximalist argument is somewhat nebulous, precisely because it is so general and tails off into infinity; at least *some* radical ends and scenarios can be shown to be utopian and unrealistic, and therefore there can be no moral 'duty' attaching to endeavours directed to their promotion. But this is beside the point here: in the next chapter we shall discuss these scenarios in greater detail. The relevant point to note is that the argument advanced here, in the context of citizens' responsibility for the continuation of order, does connect up with a *minimalist* moral position. That is to say, irrespective of whether or not I have a moral 'duty' to be actively involved in certain political causes, I certainly do *not* have the moral right to expect to remain wholly unaffected by the consequences of the social and political order which I am maintaining and of which I am a beneficiary. I can reasonably feel aggrieved, hurt, resentful at being exposed to political violence, by my plane being hijacked, by getting inadvertently involved in a pitched battle between police and secondary pickets in Scunthorpe, by coming uncomfortably close to exploding bombs in Beirut or Brighton – and of course if I or my loved ones should become direct victims of political violence, this is nothing less than unmitigated, unrelieved, untranscendable personal and human tragedy. Yet nevertheless I cannot claim to have a moral right to complete security and protection; my exposure to politics, all kinds of politics, is integrally related to my being a citizen and a partaker of order in the state. If I remain passive, I have to pay the price. I think that it is in this minimal sense only that the oft-heard radical argument about our general 'guilt' for trouble and injustice in the world can be entertained; in politics I am certainly the part-maker of my own security and thus have to accept part of the blame if my own personal security is threatened.

★ ★ ★ ★ ★ ★ ★ ★

I shall wind up this chapter by returning to an issue mentioned in passing earlier, viz. the borderline between crime and politics as revealed in an examination of the ideology and conduct of extremist radical movements on the left. This is an issue that deserves to be tackled on its own, and besides it connects up with some of the things said in the foregoing paragraph, and also conveniently leads to the main topics to be discussed in our next chapter. Our reflections have already touched upon the tricky problem of distinguishing between the criminal and the political in two contexts: in the personal to-ing and fro-ing of criminal and political actors (gangsters becoming political power-holders and *vice versa*) and in extreme right-wing politics. The former, as we argued, has relatively little practical importance and even less theoretical interest. The latter can also, in principle, be relatively easily dealt with. Just to recall the main point here: political extremism, as typified in the modern era in Fascist-oriented and racialist movements and governments, ceases to be political in the proper sense and becomes contiguous (and even more) with criminality, the more narrowly and objectively it defines its own group and the more it tends to push opponents into the sub-human category, logically culminating in deliberate genocide. The incipient immorality/criminality of this 'politics' lies in its restrictiveness, in the extent to which the outside world, other groups in society, are reduced to a mere means. Again, in point of principle, there is little difficulty in showing this (which is also proven by the tendency of the ideologies in question to play down their racialist exclusiveness and emphasize instead a nebulous kind of universality) and correspondingly the theoretical interest aroused by this topic is not exactly overwhelming. It is very different with left-wing extremism. Here the points which are of greatest momentum from our point of view must be threshed out analytically, slogans and well-sounding phrases must be interpreted in the light of unstated assumptions, actual and relevant meanings must be isolated from an abundance of confusing verbiage. But correspondingly on this side the imperceptible shading of the political into the criminal, their mutual interpenetration, can be shown much more dramatically.

In a nutshell: the criminal danger in left-wing extremism, as opposed to the restrictive character of extreme right-wing politics, lies in its spurious and misleading claim to *universality*, to a representation of the widest, general interests of 'humanity' (or even a more embracive category: sentient beings, nature, the environment, etc.). Whatever this extreme humanism or humanitarianism is taken to signify, it is clearly not politics, it goes beyond politics. At best, if it is confined to sloganizing, passive and peaceful disobedience, opting out of the system, doing one's own thing, living out a 'counter-culture', effecting the 'great refusal', meditating, singing, dancing, love-making, it can be defined in terms of a new *religion* – and I am using the term 'religion' here in a descriptive sense, with neither a recommendatory nor a denigratory connotation intended. (I have argued this elsewhere, in connection with the 'New Left' in the 1960s.[83]) At its worst, I think, extremism of this sort can easily become the equivalent of criminality, in the basic moral sense of criminality employed earlier in the present chapter: the pursuit of individual advantage and the corresponding repudiation of humanity. This is the case, pointedly, when left-wing extremism involves actions which are generally regarded as serious crimes, i.e. the taking of human life. Thus left-wing extremism is in truth the direct opposite of what it claims to be: anti-human as opposed to its self-professed humanism, individual-oriented in spite of its *soi-disant* representation of universal humanity, immoral rather than, as it claims, the bearer of a more advanced morality. Now politics, as we argued earlier, does properly fall into the category of moral conduct, and this includes illegal politics. However, illegal politics has at least to fulfil three relevant criteria in order to qualify for the label of genuinely political conduct: firstly, it must clearly be directed against the prevailing *order* of the state, contravening positive law but not rejecting the universal moral law – this excludes antinomian individualism. Secondly, its departure must be the existing grievances of one or another determinate group in society, acting on its behalf – this excludes universal humanism and the essentially religious quest to 'save our souls' if necessary against our own present wishes. And thirdly, genuine politics proceeds by way of particularization, heightening a consciousness of 'them' and 'us', looking for active and increasing support among the political actor's own group but also attempting to widen the base by persuasion and discussion – and this appears to exclude the politics of avant-garde fanaticism, pure conspiratorial politics, the politics of pure drama and pure violence. In order to show that left-wing extremism *can* (to say the least) fall short of these criteria and thus signify a descent into criminality, I shall employ some illustrative material relating to the self-professed political philosophy of the 'Angry Brigade' in Britain and the 'Red Army Faction' in West Germany – while not for a moment asserting either that these groups represent paradigmatic 'terrorism' or that the people involved in the activities referred to were not, personally, high-minded and, in their own eyes, pursuing genuine political objectives. Here what we have is conduct which is *objectively* the equivalent of criminality, as distinguished from intentional and pure criminality. There is *still* an important moral difference between the Meinhofs, Baumanns, Barkers, Prescotts (and Himmlers, Eichmanns, Mengeles) on the one hand, and the Capones, Dillingers, Krays and Richardsons on the other.

I shall begin by quoting a few very interesting passages from a remarkable book by Alan Burns, *The Angry Brigade: a Documentary Novel*, which claims to be an accurate 'press report' by the author who interviewed six members of the Brigade in 1973, young people living as outlaws in London and (as the public will remember) responsible for some bombings and violent encounters with the police. In the book pseudonyms are used. 'Barry' speaking:

> I am both a political and a mystical person. My sense of moral outrage which is political is also a mystical experience arising from identification with another human being, with a pantheistic view of humanity, with a sense of oneness with the human race.[84]

'Jean':

> I often thought the whole thing was completely hopeless, but you had to fight, one way or the other. The new year would bring new things, because whatever the leaders were doing, however much they messed things up, there was always the mass of kids who were getting more and more dissatisfied, and of that

mass there would always be some who were activists.[85]

'Barry' again:

It happened on a trip. I'd known it all my life but never realized it until I'd taken acid. It was reality because I saw it. Vision is essential to reality; you understand it as a thought, but as reality you have to see it. That's what acid is about.

That's where the battle is at: the acid level and the reality level. Reality level is fascist, elitist. Acid level is the revolution level, disposing of all concepts. Acid says we all have potential, we all have incredible gifts.[86]

'Suzanne':

I was a little bit sick of the way I had to live, paying an exorbitant rent for a tiny room, and that was why I felt depressed. I wanted to take a positive stand against that kind of sordid oppression. If that was so, if I really did believe that, then I was going to commit myself to a violent act and I would either go to the whole extreme and do something that would kill everyone in Central London and rase every building for ten miles, or else not do anything at all.[87]

'Barry':

What we want is a fantastic leap of the imagination, something that will make people jump right out of their skins, like King Kong walking down Oxford Street or a space-ship landing on St Paul's.[88]

My aim was achieved when I was changed. When you change yourself, you change the universe.[89]

The Angry Brigade is about actual concepts rather than intellectual concepts. It's about the fundamental fantasies, dreams, madnesses of mankind. *That*'s what it's about . . . The intellectual knows nothing. The intellect is a wonderfully subtle and flexible structure of pretence, something for everybody except the person who wants to abandon pretence and find the Thing Itself.[90]

In Bommi Baumann, *Terror or Love? The Personal Account of a West German Urban Guerilla*, we read about a very similar subjective background of indeterminate, general, diffused dissatisfaction with life that led to the author's becoming in turn a terrorist and then an advocate of universal 'love', and a similar ethereal vision of life and reality:

> In my case, at the beginning in Berlin, it was like this: if you had long hair, things were suddenly like they are for the Blacks. Do you understand? They threw us out of joints, they cursed at us and ran after us – all you had was trouble.[91]
>
> The first day of my apprenticeship, on the ride to the construction site, it suddenly hit me: you're gonna be doing this for fifty years, there's no escaping it. The scare of that just stuck in my bones. I had to look for ways to get out.[92]

About his vision:

> For me, the whole time it was a question of creating human values which did not exist in capitalism, in all of Europe, in all of Western culture – they'd been cleared away by the machine. That's what it's about: to discover them anew, to unfold them anew, and to create them anew.[93]
>
> You lead a life without a past, living without a personal history. That's exactly the situation for you. You're exactly the person you are at that moment. No history follows you any more. That's when it first gets interesting, when you live in illegality, because it has advantages. You can't be integrated into the bourgeois system any more, you're always outside, you're not burdened with a thousand prejudices, you've stepped into a completely new interim zone; of course very few people are doing that at this time. I can only say, it's really a good thing.[94]

The emerging picture is undoubtedly a fascinating one. The philosophy of left-wing extremism as it is glimpsed in these revelatory passages is not without its attractions, as criminal immorality also thrills. Here we have the sublime, the high-minded, the desperately crazy and the crassly selfish blended all together; in a way one might say, with reference to an observation of Durkheim's quoted earlier, that in this kind of extremism the 'originality of the idealist' who is ahead of his time and the 'originality of the criminal' who is behind his time are coalesced in one amorphous whole. Inwardly, in terms of pure intention, it is the most sublime idealism, while outwardly, in its effects, it amounts to criminality pure and simple, and of course this glaring discrepancy can arise only if there is something faulty, something incoherent about the original intention itself. And so there is: this intention is not what it appears at first sight. That the 'acidic vision of reality' has nothing at all to do with the reality of human society and that 'life without a personal history' has nothing to do with human life go, I think, without saying: these are momentary and unstable figments of the imagination, artistic fancies, intoxication, incapable of generalization and realization. We *all* have 'existentialist' moments and *some* people experience *some* of the time the pleasures of imaginary transcendence caused by intoxicating or hallucinatory substances. But no life and no society can be based on these moments and these experiences. In futuristic terms, this stance then certainly amounts to a repudiation of reality: the vision is not about a future, not about a temporal expanse at all but instead concentrated entirely on the *moment*. Like criminal conduct and criminal action, it goes nowhere, its meaning is exhausted in the act, in the unique experience. And as repudiation of reality, it is also rejection of the moral law of humanity, its injunctions of personal restraint and the acceptance of the moral limitations on the individual's natural 'freedom'.

Looking at it in terms of past antecedents, past background, we are led to much the same conclusion. This kind of left-wing extremism only purports to start out from definite grievances of definite groups of people, but in reality it does not. The dissatisfaction with having to live in a tiny room and with working on a construction site has to do with a particular *order*, with 'capitalism' or the 'machine', only on the surface; really it is a much deeper dissatisfaction, a dissatisfaction with life itself. Tedium, regularity, limited economic means are a part of human experience in any society that we know and we can maintain; we do rebel against these deficiencies but only as natural individuals, not as moral beings with a determinate political purpose. Individual dissatisfaction is diffused, indeterminate, it comes from personal choice, accident, luck, it arises and goes unpredictably and does not connect up with a particular order and with differential group relationships. Having long hair does *not* put you in the same position as the Blacks. It is relevant to note here that left-wing extremists of this idealistic persuasion, with some notable exceptions of course, tend to be recruited from well-to-do social groups and not from the poor: they are larger-than-life individuals, clever and articulate intellectuals, rebelling against their own social power, their own comfort and privileges;[95] they claim to represent the 'kids' in general, which is not an identifiable social group anyway, but nobody in particular. Natural individuality does lead to rebelliousness, it *means* rebelliousness, turbulence, antinomian effervescence, spontaneity, the impulse constantly to kick against the rails – what it does not and cannot involve, and which political action does, is authorization to *act* intentionally against other people, trampling on their conscious wishes and interests, putting them out of the way. There is a frightening, shivering kind of absurdity in the connection between dissatisfaction with living in a tiny room and wanting to blow up Central London, and even more with claiming to have a *moral right* to perpetrate such indiscriminate acts of killing. There is of course no moral right here at all; it all comes from individuals as individuals, and perish humanity. The language of politics is employed but in truth it is the denial of politics; universal humanity is claimed as the source of authorization but in truth it is revealed as individual fancy, inflated out of itself. In their self-professed theory extremists identify with and represent the widest social group imaginable: the totality of the human species (and even beyond); in actual fact, actual experience, the extremist is desperately alone.

Politics presupposes and heightens the particularization of society; you act on behalf of a certain group whose actual and pre-existing grievances give you the right to act, with whom you identify in your conduct and whom you expect to identify with you, and on whose increasing and active support you base your activity. With the Angry Brigade, the Red Army Faction and similar clandestine organizations (like the more recent 'Peace Conquerors', responsible for an explosion at Frankfurt Airport in June 1985), this logic and this strategy do not seem to be present. On the contrary, the attitude appears to be indiscriminate hostility and even arrogance, coupled with an intention *not* to identify, not even with those in whose interest you claim to be struggling, but instead to shock, scandalize your surroundings. This leads away from politics and towards either ineffectual posturing or criminality – like in the case of crime, as Durkheim noted, it results in antagonizing the rest of society, causing others to turn actively against you. But extremists do not seem to be too much bothered by this. The Peace Conquerors, as recently reported on BBC News (24 June 1985), seem to believe that it is 'no matter if women and children are killed' because 'there is no innocence'. 'Barry' of the Angry Brigade makes it quite clear whom he regards as the ultimate enemy: it is not the system, not the government, not capitalists but you and me, ordinary mortals who are so benighted as to accept humdrum reality.

> I will annihilate Enoch Powell. I will assassinate Heath. I will applaud. Good. He's dead. One more, drag him away. If there's a million Powells, a million Heaths, I will kill the lot. But it doesn't end there because a reason for them exists. One has to get at that reason. The reason lies in the people of this country, a mass of people have a reality in their heads which to me is total fantasy though they call it reality. It's that you've got to get at. You have to change it.[96]

Baumann also gives open expression to a view of his young contemporaries, which is not exactly flattering:

> When they don't know what to do, they go back to the factory to work – they can't handle this new-won freedom which for them has really come overnight; they don't know what to do any more. They let themselves be persuaded, and go back to the factory again, instead of finding creative forms of life, through which they could find a common ground.[97]

In G. Carr's dispassionate and by no means unsympathetic account of the life and conduct of members of the Angry Brigade we find some revealing illustrations of the gap between the 'outlaws' and the world outside. The Angry Brigade protested against housing shortages in Britain and the abysmal standard of working-class housing – and to this extent, without a doubt, their stand was 'political' in the genuine sense. But at the same time, apparently, for themselves they did not think that 'decent housing' – what most poor people will probably regard as decent housing – was desirable. What in others they saw as a state of deprivation, a mark of dehumanization, they desired and acquired for themselves: for the people it was wrong to have inadequate sanitation, insufficient privacy and personal space but they themselves wanted to live like that. Their rejection of society did not stop at capitalism or the system; it went as far as the repudiation of the accustomed and sought-after lifestyle of the vast majority, the repudiation of hygiene, privacy, personal modesty and family-type relationships. When the police raided the Angry Brigade 'Commune' at 29 Grosvenor Avenue, the young men and women constables, mostly from lower-class backgrounds, were astounded and repelled. 'Most of them, even those who had been on the drug-squad, were dealing with a life-style they had never come across before. They were shocked by the conditions they saw in the communes they raided. They could not begin to understand how people could live that way by choice.'[98] This is of course no more than an illuminating footnote to the story: subsisting in derelict housing in Stoke Newington is no more a mark of immorality than luxuriating in a penthouse on the Costa del Sol is a mark of morality. This kind of detail is relevant only in so far as it further accentuates the question mark concerning the presumptive 'political' character of extremist groups like the ones discussed. Isolation, whether splendid or sordid, precludes the process of particularization, pre-empts support from the relevant social groups outside, and thus further negates any possible claim to authorization. People who are bent on saving the world against itself are not in the business of politics; if their repudiation of the world is purely self-sacrificial they are mystics, prophets, missionaries, venerable or laughable seers; if their 'self' that is sacrificed for the cause includes other people, an indiscriminate quantity and quality of them, then regrettably they also partake of criminality.

There is an air of gloom, despair, sadness and pointlessness surrounding the beliefs, life-style and conduct of political extremist groups with a universal, religiously oriented aspiration, and this again is a feature negatively shared with the world of crime. These two underworlds are united in their lack of hope, in being relentlessly pushed down and kept on the fringes of society, on the margins of the political world which they cannot change, and of the wider moral world of ordinary, everyday, humdrum conduct which continues to ignore them and reject them. They are no threat to order but of course, like crime, a permanent and unpredictable source of discomfort, definitely a threat to personal security. Their malevolent indifference to the actual wishes and desires of people outside – resulting tragically from their overwhelming benevolent concern for justice and humanity in the abstract – is in effect indistinguishable from the conduct of ordinary outlaws. Fanaticism and extremism can arise anywhere, at any time, in any circumstances; the law-abiding citizen is no more responsible for their appearance than for the ubiquitous presence of criminality. And thus again, as with crime, their control and suppression, and the provision of personal security against the threat posed by them, lies inescapably and continually with the state.

4 CONVENTIONAL WISDOMS

The overall conclusions of the foregoing chapter can be stated under two main headings. Firstly we made an attempt to separate out two distinct sources of personal insecurity in society, crime and politics, drawing their conceptual boundaries and also commenting on their various meeting-points at the margins and their possible interpenetration. Secondly we argued that the state, the 'law' and organized society in general, can provide only very limited protection against threats to personal security stemming from either of these two sources: the state, by its very nature, is incapable of stamping out crime which it can only contain and control, crime being a basic manifestation of human individuality, whereas illegal politics rising to a 'challenge' reveals the state's own ambiguity and corresponding weakness and vulnerability as order.

In the present chapter our reflections will continue and be concluded with our attention primarily focused, again, on two things. The bulk of the discussion will be concerned with certain aspects of the recent academic literature on law, order, crime, punishment and related issues, or what are being called here the 'conventional wisdoms' of the political right and the political left. Already we have made numerous references to these in the foregoing: indeed, the 'reality' cannot be separated from its perception and interpretation from various angles. It seems to me, however, that a further, separate and at least a little bit more systematic comment on characteristic conservative and radical stances on law and order is warranted, partly on account of the intrinsic interest of these stances, partly because it will give us an opportunity further to develop the distinctive standpoint of our reflections, and partly because the literature concerned deserves more 'justice' and recognition than it has hitherto been afforded in these pages. Alas, it will not be possible to do anything like full justice to the writers concerned, from whose knowledge and insight the present author drew great benefits but who, somewhat unfairly, will be used here as illustrations of certain themes. And in the second part of the chapter we shall conclude our reflections by returning, after a lengthy circular journey, to our paradoxes of security. But at the same time our final remarks will follow, directly and logically, on from our discussion of the conservative and radical perspectives on the problem of law and order.

To begin then our critical presentation of the conventional wisdoms of left and right on the problem of law and order, an important point concerning the nature and as it were academic *raison d'être* of these reflections will need to be clarified. To the informed reader, and especially to those with a specialist training and knowledge of the topics so far discussed, a lot of what has been said and argued here may well appear quite unsensational, platitudinous, derivative, eclectic (if not, indeed, false, confused and wrong-headed). But assuming that some of our foregoing remarks about personal security, the state, morality, crime, political violence, etc., were at all sensible, the question still remains as to why these 'truths' – commonsensical and platitudinous – need have been restated here. What is the momentum of these reflections, what is new and interesting that we can add to the on-going discussion, conducted by experts in the field? The answer to this, reiterating the point made earlier, is that our primary interest in these reflections is in the *conceptual framework* of sundry perceptions, arguments and presentations of the problem of law and order, as distinguished from the 'facts' themselves which in any case need to be ordered and interpreted. Hence our endeavour in the first place to subsume law, order and politics under the category of 'security' and hence also, in the present chapter, the necessity of our commenting at greater length on the fundamental perspectives of left and right which go into and inform the general public discussion of the facts. Without some understanding of the respective conceptual frameworks, basic valuations, unstated assumptions of conservatism and radicalism in this context, the 'problem' of law and order cannot be made fully intelligible. This is for the very good reason that it becomes a problem (or rather two problems, converging on the level of facts maybe but constructed so as to lead to opposite theoretical conclusions) only in terms of these perspectives in the first place. So we ought to make it clear right at this point: we shall not quarrel with the 'findings' of criminologists, the information supplied by historians, sociologists, political scientists, the reasoned arguments and even rhetoric of politicians, all of whom (by and large) present their case coherently *within* the terms of their overall perspective. We shall, furthermore, readily acknowledge the reasonableness, academic legitimacy and indeed great heuristic and practical value of these perspectives; it is surely not an accident that there *are* radical criminologists and conservative politicians. Our concern is with these basic perspectives *as* perspectives, and we shall endeavour to show their intrinsic limitations.

Conservative and radical thinking on law, order and politics (and a great many other things besides) is informed by overall perspectives and paradigms; these, in each case, give the thinking concerned its vitality, attraction, coherence, persuasiveness. On both sides they tend to be unitary perspectives or single perspectives, the advantage of unitariness being clarity, and an obvious, immediate practical orientation. They are 'scientific', 'political' or 'ideological' paradigms, expressing more or less fixed, clearcut, angular world views, coherent (though not always explicit) philosophical convictions about the basic characteristics of human beings, human society, human values, the state and history. In many cases they achieve a commendable degree of precision, they can be made 'operational' and within limits they are predictive. Starting, as the case may be, from rock-hard value foundations or with an 'open mind' their direction is set one way, towards the construction of plausible theories, informed and tested hypotheses, resounding conclusions. They are, or certainly a great majority of them are, practical: having defined the 'problem' and outlined the 'solution', they map out the road for 'action' to follow, whether or not their arguments are openly couched in terms of moral injunctions or technical blueprints. From one side the problem of law and order will be determined as a problem *for* the state and society – okay then, go ahead and reinforce, strengthen, protect state and society, and the problem will be managed, contained. From the other side the problem is *of* the state and society – okay then, change the existing social structure and the existing state, and the problem will go away by itself. It is obvious that the 'plural perspective' adopted in these reflections cannot compete with unitary paradigms on this level; as distinguished from the latter, our conceptual framework is complex, to some extent (let's frankly acknowledge this) parasitic and certainly not 'practical' in the immediate sense. As was said at the very beginning: the intention here is to comment on, elucidate and perhaps explain the problem of law, order and politics in its *total* complexity, in terms of its contradictions and existential paradoxes. The problem of law and order, as commonly understood, *won't go away*, but in order to show this our survey has to take in at one point also the respective paradoxes of relevant unitary perspectives; these conceptual paradoxes join up with the existential paradoxes outlined in the first chapter and thus, through their interpretation and evaluation, we shall (we might, at any rate) achieve a vantage-point applicable at all levels. We shall then be in a position of being able to grasp the problem of law and order as *one* problem. It is here, I think, that a plural perspective definitely scores over its rivals, in showing that unitary views are partial, limited, in the last resort not completely adequate to their self-appointed tasks, simply *because* they are unitary, uni-directional, uni-dimensional. They see the world from where they stand but they cannot see the world *and* themselves in one glance. A plural perspective also has *its* limitations, without the slightest doubt (e.g. its derivative nature, complexity, impracticality, as mentioned above), but at the very least it can supply the critical yeast for the on-going discussion.

As will have been noted, and possibly with consternation by some readers, in the foregoing initial characterization of unitary perspectives the two seemingly separate and (it might be thought) mutually exclusive and antithetical departures, namely 'science' and 'ideology', were rather unceremoniously lumped together. This really should come as no surprise, since our perspective already implicitly involved this classificatory judgment in Chapter 2 where, it will be recalled, the state was described in turns as appearing in the light of traditional political philosophy and of social science, and we more or less concluded that there is no inherent, absolute superiority attaching to either of these two paradigmatic viewpoints. Now it is time to make the point openly and emphatically: in the field with which we are concerned – an understanding of human society in general and the problem of security in particular – there is no absolute distinction between ideology and science. Unlike (perhaps) the natural sciences, social science as a whole tends to be value-impregnated and purposive in its implications, and especially on the level of 'grand theory' it rarely and only precariously achieves what advocates like to call 'scientific value-neutrality' as between opposing world views. Science here reinforces, or weakens as the case may be, ideological convictions, and *vice versa* it is fundamental value-positions which initially direct and govern scientific investigation.

I am, by the way, not using the term 'ideology' here pejoratively and the term 'science' approbatorily; they are taken to mean, respectively, convictions as to the essential nature of human beings and society, and explanatory hypotheses, more or less general, about the connections between various phenomena observed in human behaviour and in social relations. The two converge at almost all points; often, as we know, an ideology will be called scientific and a social science departure will be called ideological. Together – values and causal explanations – they make up what I am calling here basic unitary perspectives. In other words, and with special reference to the present theme, the correct approach for us seems to be the drawing of *vertical* distinctions, between unitary perspectives, rather than horizontal distinctions between 'political rhetoric' on the one hand, and 'science' – jurisprudence, criminology, social psychology, etc. – on the other. Political rhetoric, whether Tory or liberal or socialist, is at least *meant* to be more than hot air; it consists of arguments which consciously employ the 'findings' of social scientists and 'proven' truths about human conduct in society. And social science in its turn, whether meant to be or not, is continually 'hotted up' and embroiled in political debate; it becomes *significant* to the extent to which it can command attention in the public forum and make a visible difference to the plausibility of basic value-positions. Criminology is certainly part of this picture, and its scientific character is by no means denied or deprecated on the realization that the ultimately best way of sorting out criminological theories is by using the vertical distinction: in the last resort there are conservative criminologists and radical criminologists (the same as lawyers, psychologists, historians, etc.). The 'facts' of criminal conduct are neutral and meaningless in themselves; it all depends on how you define your fundamental concepts (i.e. how your general valuation goes). You will be prone to find certain theories as to the 'causes' of crime (or of political disorder) palatable and plausible in accordance with what you believe crime *is*. For example, the *Sunday Times* recently reported (3 June 1984) the findings of two American social scientists (Mednick and Gabrielli) concerning the close correlation between criminality, especially thieving, and genetic structure. The scientists, basing their view on over 14,000 children adopted in a European country between 1927 and 1947, apparently argue 'that a tendency to criminal behaviour may be passed on from parent to offspring.' Interesting and it may well be true. But the question is how could people who are strongly convinced that society as it exists is wicked and that crime is a protest against injustice possibly react to theories like this? And of course it goes the other way round, too. At the end of the day, politics is supreme, in the secular realm of the state where it is revealed as the mediation, synthesis of law and order, and in the intellectual realm as well, being the arbiter of social scientific disputes.

What then are the limitations of unitary perspectives? It is simple: they tend to reduce reality – life, consciousness, society, the state, personal security – to basically unproblematic, neat chunks of intelligible truths which *appear* convincing and coherent because of the reductionism involved. Their stance requires the elimination of paradoxes, the denial of double identities. 'Everything is what it is and not another thing' – is the motto of reductionist, unitary thinking. But the price to be paid for this contrived clarity and simplicity is pretty high, as paradoxes, puzzles, uncertainties, tensions, contradictions, parallel recognition of identities do – inexorably – enter the picture. As soon as one exclusive, reductionist theory is asserted, and the more loudly it is asserted, the opposite also forces itself on the mind: the 'truth' about life, society and security is not a finite number, collection of dead 'propositions', to be tucked neatly away in the cupboard, but rather it is the moving, living, whirling *world* of propositions, or positions, oppositions and reconciliations, of the continual modification and self-transcendence of partial, unitary convictions; truth is not repose but movement, restlessness. This irreducibly complex nature of truth and reality is of course only faintly glimpsed even in terms of a plural perspective, like ours in these reflections, but at least a plural perspective looks in the right direction. Its achievement is the highlighting of paradoxes and parallel identities in a subject matter, and the criticism of views which tend to become oblivious of these. Somebody must stand up and be counted, ally oneself with one or another short-term, partial, unitary truth; but it is all the more important for others therefore to sit down and at least endeavour to do the counting. Our task here is precisely to perform a 'counting' operation, i.e. to highlight the strait-jacket of ideological paradigms concerning 'law and order' and related issues, and to keep on reasserting – what unitary paradigms tend to miss – the *plurality* of the concepts and phenomena that are involved. To recall: we need to grasp the nature of security as paradoxical, the state as having the double identity of power and authority or of order and law, and the converging, interpenetrating but nonetheless distinct identity of crime and politics. Unitary perspectives, as we have already suggested, tend to fall down especially on this last count: it is the inherent tendency of conservative thought to reduce politics to crime, the defiance of order to contravention of the law, and it is the built-in assumption of radical thought which leads it to the elevation of crime to politics, basic immorality to the denial of a particular power settlement. We need then to survey briefly the respective conceptual worlds of these two antithetical perspectives.

If anything the conservative stance on law and order undoubtedly qualifies as 'conventional wisdom'. Without any statistical evidence readily at hand, we can quite confidently say that a great many more people in contemporary societies adhere to this view than to any other, including the radical perspective. Conservatism in this deeper and extended sense is the view, in the first place and not surprisingly, of the 'establishment', the upper and middle strata of society, the church authorities, the media, the police and by far the larger part of the legal profession, the military, business people, headmasters and professors of political philosophy. In addition, and less coherently and firmly perhaps, it also informs the general outlook on life of middle-aged and old people from every social class or stratum, including (probably) the vast majority of the poor and the working class. Conservatives are characterized, in Elder's expression, as people 'sharing the ancient retributive justice approach to law and order as a problem for the state with an ignorant and atavistic electorate, essentially composed of an almost infinite series of Alf Garnetts on Clapham omnibuses.'[1] This again should come as no great surprise. As Macfarlane says: 'Most criminals are working class, but so too are most of their victims. Criminals are not socially or politically conscious. It is ordinary citizens, not the rich and powerful, who suffer most from teenage hooliganism, street violence and petty theft. Not surprisingly, therefore, it is the working class and the lower-middle class in Western states who are the firmest supporters of strong measures against ordinary law-breakers.'[2] And Morgan remarks, in connection with the frequent stoppages by public service workers (like bus-drivers) as a response to violent hooliganism: 'The most tragic paradox of modern British society involves the demand for protection, even the plea, for social survival, from just those who have been credited with a desire to overthrow the social order.'[3] What radical theorists like Stuart Hall label 'authoritarian populism' is rarely far from the surface and its manifestation is quite acute and spontaneous when direct threats to personal security, to an accustomed life-pattern (however miserable it is, in comparative terms), are perceived. Settlement in truth implies that, perhaps more than any other class, the poor and the workers also are and feel 'settled'; it is their law and their order, too, something to be conserved. The malevolent indifference of strangers is regarded in these circles with more concern and suspicion. John Wainwright writes in *Prynter's Devil*:

> The area – lower working class – the typical 'Coronation Street' – is peopled by a breed both pseudo-gregarious and jealously secretive. When the lights are switched on, the curtains are closed; pedestrians – strangers passing the window – must not see what happens inside the carton. The curtains remain closed until next morning; until the first risers are satisfied that daylight has returned. The upper windows, also – they too, must be curtained against unwanted watchers. Even to open a window for air is to invite a possible listener. This is the most suspicious stratum of non-criminal society; it is one big happy family. . . of backbiters and tale-bearers.

The main conceptual planks of the conservative paradigm are not overwhelmingly difficult to identify: they derive, in the main, from theological tenets and the axioms of classical jurisprudence. In the first place and regarded as a kind of ideological major premise, conservatives believe in an absolutely valid, binding and eternal moral law which sanctions hierarchy, asymmetry in general, and the law and order of established states in particular. The human universe is essentially static and states, as we know them, are eternally in the natural order of things.

Sovereignty, the absolute authority of law, is a human necessity. As one of the founders of modern conservatism, Joseph de Maistre, says: 'It is as impossible to imagine a human society, a people, without a sovereign as a hive and bees without a queen; for, by virtue of the eternal laws of nature, a swarm of bees exists in this way or it does not exist at all.'[4] Now of course there are several, and in concrete detail conflicting, theories of law within the broader conservative paradigm but there also tends to be agreement, albeit implicit, concerning the basic sanctity of laws as defining the absolute moral authority of the state. Conservative thought starts out from an acceptance of the broad social framework and order of the state as something 'natural' and essentially unalterable, and this natural necessity also characterizes the law as such. The Marxist writer E. B. Pashukanis quite correctly and perceptively remarks: 'To the kind of thinking which does not transcend the framework of the bourgeois conditions of existence, this necessity must appear as none other than natural necessity. That is why all bourgeois theories of law are based, consciously or unconsciously, on the doctrine of natural law.'[5] Recently Paul Johnson's statement in *A Tory Philosophy of Law* seems to bear this out: 'The phrase "a society under God and law" is appropriate because parliament is not the primeval legislature. It does not, and cannot, create law from nothing. Rather it inherits, and interprets, a system of moralistic law, much of which is enshrined in the organic corpus of Common Law.'[6] In Sir Keith Joseph's pamphlet, *Freedom Under the Law*, the 'rule of law' is described as an 'exotic plant' which has, however, become the 'birthright' of the people of England, superior to and not to be squandered away for the 'thin stew' of social justice. Law as representing eternal right and morality stands above politics representing temporary demands and sectional interests. Governments which might have been elected by a minority, as Joseph goes on, 'use the majesty of the law to dress up their prejudices and panic expedients', and this undermines respect for the law. 'If some people or groups – be they trade unionists or ratepayers – can enjoy widespread sympathy when they defy politically unpopular laws, the next step is for people to defy any laws they find inconvenient.'[7] The state is both 'above' society and also represents and safeguards all legitimate interests within society impartially; the judiciary and law-enforcement agencies are not essentially concerned with order, with particular disputes arising out of social identities and relationships. Talking about the recent mineworkers' strike and picketing (!) in Britain, Leon Brittan, the then Home Secretary, said to the Police Federation: 'Supporting the side of law is the job of the police. It is utterly different from taking sides in the dispute.'[8]

This leads to the next important feature of conservative thought. With particular, though not exclusive, reference to law and order, it is a characteristic of conservative thinking to recognize only the existence of 'individuals' in society, and correspondingly to deny the relevance here of different social groups. Positively this is manifested in the deeply held conviction that the state, as authority backed by power, functions primarily so as to protect individuals, their personal security expressed in terms of established, customary rights. 'The rule of law', as Joseph says, 'is focused on the individual.' It 'begins with the individual, because individuals are real, whereas society is an abstraction.' 'Without property and individual economic rights, all other rights are insecure.'[9] Negatively this principle is underlined by the even more deeply held conviction that individuals permanently, indefinitely *need* protection as individuals against one another. Human beings, without exception, are naturally frail, fickle, self-regarding and prone to evil. They would, were it not for the might of the state and the fear of punishment, continually attack and act so as to oppress one another; malevolent indifference goes all the way. De Maistre put the point eloquently:

> People complain of the despotism of princes; they ought to complain of the despotism of *man*. We are all born despots, from the most absolute monarch of Asia to the infant who smothers a bird with its hand for the pleasure of seeing that there exists in the world a being weaker than itself. There is not a man who does not abuse power, and experience shows that the most abominable despots, if they manage to seize the sceptre, are precisely those who rant against despotism.[10]

For Patrician Morgan: 'Human vices will always be with us, and they must be tackled all the time and with each generation.'[11] 'The concept that the law-breaker and the downright vicious are sick, conveniently hives off the offensive part of Man as if it were a cancer, or bacterial infection that is not part of his real nature.'[12]

The image of society seen in terms of the conservative perspective is thus revealed as a reduced, two-dimensional one: what we earlier in this book called 'natural individuality' in the conservative perspective *directly* confronts the universality of the law, without any intervening realm of particularities. There is nothing else to the problem of law and order, to the problem of personal security: natural nastiness, viciousness on one side, the law and the inculcated law-abiding habits of people on the other. And here we come upon an interesting point. While the conservative view starts out from a conviction in the *general* tendency of human beings to be 'despots' and to have an 'offensive part' to their nature, nevertheless it typically proceeds by distinguishing very sharply indeed between those who are sufficiently socialized into law-abidingness and those who are not. We are all equal but some are definitely more equal than the others. 'We', the law-abiding majority, have somehow managed to restrain the old Adam in us, and we are threatened by 'them', an indefinite stratum or rather aggregate of individual nasties, vicious hooligans, vile thieves, violent muggers, impertinent burglars, desperate murderers, a menacing and unreformable criminal underworld, a 'class' of clearly undesirables. It is a process of particularization which does not start out from society in its concrete shape, indeed it ignores society for the purposes of drawing the distinction: it is particularization in terms of individuals. The departure is individual volition: deliberate wickedness or an exceptionally high degree of psychological weakness, 'moral insanity', and not determinate social position; most legally recognized criminals happen to be poor but poverty has nevertheless nothing to do with their criminality. They are the 'undeserving' poor, a clearly differentiated type of unsavoury characters. The conservative view tends to go considerably further than the perfectly legitimate exercise of isolating a concept of 'crime' (as was attempted here, in the foregoing chapter) towards typecasting criminals as people. As 'P.C. George' says in Brenton's *Revenge*:

> He starts early, pinching his Dad's fags and his Mum's money for the dinner, and smashing the toys of his brothers and sisters. Next he goes to Borstal for his education, and comes out a right villain, mean and

> hard, a foxy dicy snotty-nosed masturbating little runt.

And his complaint well captures grass-roots conservative sentiment offended by the radical tendency to deny the basic distinction:

> Nowadays it's don't you dare touch me and where's my lawyer. In they come to the station full of the citizen's rights and the police and public service and other left-wing slogans . . . Now the true psychos, the truly vicious nuts and villains don't have names. They look ordinary.

The third main feature of the conservative perspective, joining the belief in the sanctity of law and state and in individual wickedness, is the conviction that punishment is both the necessary and a sufficient means to deal with crime and disorder. Now 'punishment', as we pointed out in Chapter 2, is a wide and flexible notion, and it is by no means confined to such drastic methods as hanging, flogging, imprisonment. It also includes psychiatric treatment and compulsory 'community service' – the essential point is the pitting of the (morally and pragmatically) superior will of the state against the will of the individual. Conservatives tend to believe that punishment, in this extended sense, is an absolute right wielded by the state on behalf of law-abiding society: sick or wicked, individuals breaking the law must be dealt with by recourse to power. Hall and his co-authors, writing from a well-thought-out radical perspective, draw an ingenious distinction between the 'Old Testament' view of conservatives (in the narrower sense) who believe in the absolute evil of crime and the 'New Testament' view of 'liberals' who tend to regard criminals as backward, bored, ignorant unfortunates who must be 'cured' of their deviancy. As the authors rightly stress, the two seemingly opposed views converge on the fundamental level: both are 'conservative' in the broader (and here relevant) sense of accepting the superior legitimacy of state and society as they exist, their broad foundations and major distinguishing characteristics. Liberals who acknowledge that crime is a 'social problem' still maintain that it arises from particular and minor failures and not from 'some major structural fault of the social or moral system'. And in the short-run of course these liberals are quite prepared to backtrack on their 'enlightened' perspective and accept the more old-fashioned view that the *first* task is the preservation of 'public safety' which involves the forcible punishing of individual wrong-doers. Hall *et al.* admit, somewhat ruefully, that these two views together 'command and construct the skeletal syntax' of the general popular perception of state, law, crime and punishment.[13] On balance, the 'Old Testament' variant is more coherent, more robust than its counterpart.

Now further, it is also an important aspect of the conservative perspective that punishment, especially punishment in the narrower, 'painful' sense, is the only means available to society for keeping criminality under control; it is not a very nice thing perhaps, and it doesn't work perfectly but it is *sufficient* to protect the order of the state and the personal security of citizens against wrong-doers. Punishment here is seen to work mainly as deterrent (and of course it is presupposed also to be rightful retribution), and not so much as reform. If deterrence is effective, i.e. the detection and sentencing rates are high and penalties are sufficiently stiff, then crime can be prevented. In Conservative MP John Wheeler's view, 'the public should recognize that the best means of containing crime is to encourage ways of preventing it. This is socially desirable. It is also cheaper at the end.'[14] Also: 'The diminished value of social measures suggests that physical ones provide our only *honest* hope of containing crime.'[15] According to the American criminologist James Wilson, the ultimate causes of crime cannot be reached or altered; however, the 'policy analyst' should not be concerned with these but with immediate, short-term and partial remedies. As he puts it: '. . . social problems – that is to say, problems occasioned by human behaviour rather than mechanical processes – are almost invariably "caused" by factors that cannot be changed easily or at all. This is because human behaviour ultimately derives from human volition – tastes, attitudes, values, and so on – and these aspects of volition in turn are either formed entirely by choice or are the product of biological or social processes that we cannot or will not change.'[16] And Wilson concludes on a sombre note:

> Intellectuals, although they often dislike the common person as an individual, do not wish to be caught saying uncomplimentary things about humankind. Nevertheless, some persons will shun crime even if

> we do nothing to deter them, while others will seek it out even if we do everything to reform them. Wicked people exist. Nothing avails except to set them apart from innocent people.[17]

This last quote may serve as an apt and eloquent epitome of the conservative paradigm in its entirety, highlighting its commonsensical basis, undoubtedly the main reason for its popularity, as well as its limitations. The conservative view is certainly best characterized in terms of its intentional 'myopia', its almost exclusive concentration on the here and now, on what goes on at the visible, surface level, and what can be done about disorder and crime immediately. The conservative stance achieves a remarkable degree of clarity and purposiveness in a limited area; the focus is sharp on the 'trouble spots', while the surroundings tend to be ignored and left covered in darkness. As conservative thinking on law and order concentrates on people as 'individuals', so the whole inherent methodology of conservative thought is individualist, at least as it appears to adherents; this is evident in conservative historiography, conservative-oriented clinical psychology and psychiatry, political rhetoric as well as criminology. The individual trees are significant, not the wood; it is details, isolated issues that need highlighting and attention, not the broad contexts in which they occur. The *biggest* context – eternal moral law and the sanctity of the state and social order – is given and beyond dispute, and the details and nuances of criminality and disorder become prominent precisely in this superior 'light' shining on them from above. Stress should be laid on two further points, already touched upon and illustrated in the last passage quoted from Wilson. In the first place the conservative paradigm is characterized by a curious combination of long-term pessimism and of confidence and cheerfulness in the short run. We can never totally eliminate crime but we can and will deal with it now, as it threatens in various particular areas; wickedness is part of human nature and evil persons will always exist but 'crime waves' like the recent one, street mugging as well as political terrorism, are amenable to short, sharp shocks. The war goes on interminably but the next 'battle' against crime can certainly be won. It is interesting to note here how this dualism of long-term, muted gloom and short-term, emphatic glee operates also in a retrospective dimension. Crime and disorder have always existed in history, the 'old Adam' has accompanied us from the very beginning. Yet the present (any present) is something special: the recent crime wave and terrorist wave are 'unprecedented' in their gravity and magnitude, the 'social fabric' is in greater danger of dissolution than ever before, now, unless we take action swiftly and resolutely, 'civilization' itself will go irrevocably to the rocks. No doubt the fostering of 'moral panics' and the accentuation of popular nostalgia after the good, old days (the village bobby, quiet suburban streets, Dixon of Dock Green) can serve very definite conservative political purposes, like higher pay to the police and 'sus' laws – as radical writers are never slow to point out. Nevertheless, there is no reason to believe that moral panics and nostalgia are not genuinely, innocently felt by most people who proclaim them; they are themselves integral, rational aspects of the conservative paradigm as a whole.

The second point to which we might want to draw attention is another kind of dualism, equally interesting: this concerns the conservative belief, as also illustrated by the last quote from Wilson, that it is possible, and of course eminently desirable and the only reasonable thing to do, to set criminals 'apart from innocent people'. While on the one hand the general, unpredictable and random proneness of human beings to criminal conduct will be admitted, indeed emphasized, on the other hand it will be argued that the majority of society is still constituted by 'innocent people' who, once effectively shielded from miscreants and deviants, can and will live peaceably together, in a world of natural social harmony. While there is constant danger outside, on the fringes, and the 'war' against crime and disorder is relentlessly waged, this is to be seen strictly as a *marginal* affair, set against the backcloth of *peace*. Honest people, law-abiding people, orderly people can always in principle get on well together, and their sundry disputes are peaceably 'adjusted' under the law; serious conflicts are absent from the well-established state, and the existence of particular, differentially related social groups and the existence of criminality are mutually irrelevant.

Let us now turn to radicalism (further critical comments on both these major unitary perspectives will be made later). The radical view on law and order and related issues is certainly a minority view but it is by no means the view of a tiny or insignificant minority. Quite the contrary: this perspective, for very good reasons, has a sway and impact which are quite out of proportion to the number of people who seem actually to believe in it and proclaim it. Here there is quality and intellectual *tour de force*, set against the diffused quantity and solid commonsensicality of its antagonist. Conservatism is dominant in the larger, 'public' forums but in scholarly, academic debate (and in rare, but by no means unheard of, situations of acute social conflict) it meets its match, and possibly even more, in radicalism. It is the conflict of the silent majority and the vocal minority. The radical perspective is typically adhered to by those on the extreme edges of society: 'intellectuals' (as Wilson uses the term) at one end, and existentially alienated, 'marginalized' groups at the other end. The majority of intellectuals at least *tend* to be radical, and in the relevant sense: their greater learning and, *ex hypothesi*, keener intellect make them attentive to dimensions not conspicuous in the immediate context. Their gaze is directed far away, to the past and to the future, they are not satisfied with registering immediate effects and symptoms but look for underlying, ultimate causes, they search for inter-connections and 'meanings', they resolutely try to break through the surface and come face to face with the 'roots' of things. And in this area at least, concerning the problem of law and order in society, their as it were 'natural' tendency to radicalism is joined by the outlook of those who *are* the 'roots' and who might find themselves existentially compelled, if not actually and coherently to 'see' beyond the surface, effectively to reach beyond it in their practical, day-to-day conduct. There are, perhaps, in usual circumstances not many of these twisted, gnarled, disturbed, desiccated roots in the deep soil of society who become conscious of their particular situation and turn to radicalism – as there are not many arboreal giants in the forest either. But they are always there and never negligible.

In a less poetic vein, we might venture to suggest that the radical perspective finds its natural home mostly among academic social scientists (as distinguished from 'philosophers'), criminologists, social psychologists, researchers into urban deviance, among those who (as opposed to the police and courts) represent the 'soft embrace' of the state, like social workers and welfare officers, a sizable section of the medical profession (including many psychiatrists) and a much smaller but influential section of the legal profession, i.e. the legal reformers; and at the other extreme among the abjectly poor and literally uprooted, and members of ethnic communities who feel themselves reduced to second-class citizenship and who meet racial prejudice in their daily lives, among unemployed graduates, the lower clergy, women in one-parent families, people with individual grievances against the establishment, conscientious objectors, a number of articulate criminals intent on rationalizing and morally justifying their conduct, and above all among the *young*,[18] especially of the male sex, constitutionally rebellious and cocking a snook at formal rules and embedded customs. It follows from the nature of this varied and internally polarized constituency that radicalism is not, and not meant to be, practically oriented on the problem of law and order in the same sense in which conservatism is pragmatic and practical; the lofty view from the tree-tops as well as the lowly view from the roots (to make just one more use of our rather fanciful analogy) equally demand long-term, sweeping, drastic remedies, real uprooting and replanting.

The radical perspective, like its conservative counterpart, also logically starts out from a definite view of morality, of right and wrong. But whereas conservatives locate morality in heaven, as it were, in unalterable, objective laws which override subjectively perceived human desires and which are built into the existing hierarchies of state and society, radicals take the earth as their starting point: morality is based on, or it is an articulate projection of, human 'needs', 'wants', 'interests', and it is directed to the secular achievement of individual 'happiness'. Goodness is written in the heart and is slowly coming to the head, it is definitely *not* found in the positive law of states, the traditional customs of society, in consciousness distorted by the effects of contingent power settlements. Human beings are good, naturally innocent, sociable; they are made evil only by adverse circumstances. As 'Suzanne' of the Angry Brigade, in the report by Burns: 'My child is a good child, that's all there is to it. There's no such thing as a bad child. The concept of good should never be introduced to a child, it is a complete nonsense. Goodness is something to be taken for granted.'[19] Human goodness, intrinsic human worth, the substantial being of human community constitute the axial centre of historical struggles to make these values fully realized in the actual lives of individuals and in social relations. The human universe is internally fixed, revolving around this notion of the good and happy individual, but *externally* its essential nature is change, movement, progress, the growth of knowledge of things outside and self-knowledge, the emergence of ever newer and more perfect forms of awareness. Morality pertains to human individuals as such, empirically and historically concrete but on this level seen as abstracted from any given social and authority structures; 'human rights', properly speaking, are not the traditional rights of property but rights which protect individual persons against power and which enable them to follow their historical path towards the achievement of full freedom, equality, peace, community, the satisfaction of desires. Evil is not a natural, truly human phenomenon but it does exist historically, it is manifest *now*, in the form of crippling, oppressive, exploitative relationships; 'public wrongs' or 'social injuries' are real but they are to be defined in relation to the needs and interests of historically evolving, morally progressive individuals. Is wrong to be defined, as H. and J. Schwendinger pose the rhetorical question in the collection, *Critical Criminology*, 'by reference to the functional imperatives of social institutions or by the historically determined rights of individuals? In our opinion, the latter is the only humanistic criterion which can be used for this purpose.'[20] Elsewhere it is said: 'Social order cannot be an absolute value: it is subordinate to social change, which clearly can be a disorderly process.'[21] The state and society as they exist are not the repositories of morality and justice but rather obstacles to their historical realization. They themselves – state and society – are subject to constant evaluation and criticism in the light of these general norms and ideals, internally existing in the actual yearnings, desires, aspirations of individuals and externally projected on to a future human community, yet to be realized.

In terms of this – almost cosmic – perspective, institutions existing today are then squarely arraigned and usually pronounced guilty. Crime begins – and almost ends – with actual social arrangements maintained by state power. Schwendinger: 'If the right to be secure in one's own person is to have greater value than social inequalities based on the ownership of property, for example, then one should be prepared to define the use of deadly force on the part of police officers as unjustifiable homicide when this force is used in defence of property.' And: 'If crime is defined by scientists in terms of the *socially* necessary and sufficient conditions for its existence, what would be more logical than to call these social conditions criminal?'[22] Individual criminality – what the *law* brands as crime – is merely the reflection on a miniature scale of the very values on which the existing state and society are based, and is not ultimately distinguishable from legally approved conduct. J. Lea and J. Young say in *What*

Is to Be Done about Law and Order?: 'Out of the heart of the system arise not only the causes of criminality but also the values which make criminality morally possible.'[23] 'The egoism of the speculator at the Stock Exchange is not different from that of the hustler, only the opportunities are much greater; the machismo of the ghetto is scarcely absent from the bar-room talk of upper-class men.'[24] State and society are crime writ large: not only can powerful and socially privileged sections 'bend' the law to suit their own private interests, and thus escape punishment which is ruthlessly meted out to the law-breaking poor, but the law as such, in general terms, is defined to suit the needs of a structure based on inequality, oppression and exploitation. Society tends to corrupt all individuals, from the mighty to the humble; 'capitalism' (as the essential definitional core of state and society in modern times), with its contradictions, inequalities, alienation, leads directly to crime of all sorts; the two are inconceivable without each other. Lea and Young: 'Crime is endemic to capitalism because it produces both egalitarian ideals and material shortages.'[25] R. Quinney in *Class, State and Crime*: 'An understanding of crime in our society begins with the recognition that the crucial phenomenon to be considered is not crime *per se*, but the historical development and operation of capitalist society.'[26]

Criminality is not, as seen by most leading radical writers (from Rousseau and Marx to the recent 'new criminologists'), something good in itself; but it is evil, imperfection, blemish which is caused by greater evils. It is a 'response' basically, though it could be a bad, mistaken response. As the radical writers Lea and Young reasonably argue, in an exercise of perspectival self-correction: 'The radicals are correct when they see crime as a reaction to an unjust society. But they make a crucial mistake: they assume that the reaction to a just cause is necessarily a just one.'[27] Mistake or not, as far as I can see this kind of modification does not really alter the fundamental assumption built into the radical perspective; crime is still 'caused' by factors from the outside, it is still historically contingent and explicable, and in so far as it is pronounced morally wrong *per se*, the responsibility for it still lies ultimately with those in power or with an impersonal 'system'. The radical perspective stretches from a tendency to the 'romanticization' of crime at one extreme (as with the Fourierists, Bakunin, Nechayev, etc.) to its somewhat paternalistic subsumption under determinate social categories. In crime individuals may be acting inhumanly but it is because their humanity was taken away from them in the first place; they act in desperation, irrationally, self-destructively. Angela Davies *et al.* argue: 'The majority of criminal offences bear a direct relationship to property. Contained in the very concept of property, crimes are profound but suppressed social needs which express themselves in anti-social modes of action. Spontaneously produced by a capitalist organization of society, this type of crime is at once a protest against society and a desire to partake of its exploitative content. It challenges the symptoms of capitalism, not its essence.'[28] Put even more embracively in the same book: 'All crime is motivated by simple economic oppression, or the psycho-social effects of an economic order that was decadent a hundred years ago. . . Even the psychology of the sick individual, perpetrator of a "thrill-crime", must ultimately be traced to a sick society.'[29] And Ian Taylor writes in *Law and Order: Arguments for Socialism*: 'Crimes of violence and also crimes against property may have a variety of immediately presenting "causes", but they are always in the end an expression of the desperation produced in individuals and in particular social groups by economic and social inequality.'[30]

On punishment, too, radical views range from the benignly humanitarian (continuous with what Hall calls the 'liberal' outlook, as mentioned earlier) to the firmly antinomian, denying the legitimacy of societal sanction altogether. For radicals punishment is at best 'reform'; it is always suspicious as 'deterrent' (since crime and law-breaking in general are effects of the system itself); as 'retribution' it is always unjustified and an act of immorality *per se.* Since human beings are basically, potentially good, they can in principle always be reformed, improved, educated, and it obviously follows that humane methods are more conducive to this end than coercive ones: counselling, treatment, welfare are much preferred to imprisonment. At worst punishment is of course nothing more and nothing less than the forcible maintenance of the social order, the ultimate weapon of power-holders against the exploited. There is nothing 'universal' and nothing moral in the administration of criminal justice and in law-enforcement. Pashukanis is very clear on the point: 'Criminal justice in the bourgeois state is organized class terror, which differs only in degree from the so-called emergency measures taken in civil war.'[31] And as Michel Foucault argues, in a more sophisticated vein, the apparatus of punishment in the state is uniquely successful in keeping the social order in existence, by separating 'delinquents' from the rest of society. It is not true that recidivism is a failure of the penal system; quite the contrary:

> Can we not see here a consequence rather than a contradiction? If so, one would be forced to suppose that the prison, and no doubt punishment in general, is not intended to eliminate offences, but rather to distinguish them, to distribute them, to use them; that it is not so much that they render docile those who are liable to transgress the law, but that they tend to assimilate the transgression of the law in a general tactics of subjection.[32]

And:

> For the observation that prison fails to eliminate crime, one should perhaps substitute the hypothesis that prison has succeeded extremely well in producing delinquency, a specific type, a politically or economically less dangerous – and, on occasion usable – form of illegality; in producing delinquents, in an apparently marginal, but in fact centrally supervised milieu; in producing the delinquent as a pathologized subject.[33]

The picture is an impressive one and the radical paradigm certainly appears as coherent internally and as compelling as its conservative counterpart. The arguments follow one another in seemingly unassailable logical succession. Human nature is basically, potentially good; moral rules serve human needs and interests; politics as the expression of group conflict takes precedence over law which merely reflects the interests of a group that happens to be in power; social differentiation and asymmetry, themselves immoral and anti-human, give rise to protest which will often take the external form of individual criminality; punishment by the state acts further to *diffuse* this essentially *political* response on the part of the oppressed into self-defeating, ineffectual, inconsequential – indeed, functional from the point of view of the system – forms of action. Criminality in the last resort is nothing but a misplaced, degenerate form of oppositional politics, evoked by the petrified criminality of the legal politics of the state. It is a perfect and of course, for radicals, perfectly vicious circle, but one from which it is nevertheless possible to escape. In direct contrast to the conservative view, and again employing the terminology of our earlier deliberations, radicals might be said to be mindful *only* of particularity or particularization in society, or that they see particularity as the chief or even sole obstacle to the happy embrace of the two extremities, individuality and universality, i.e. individual human persons joining in a universal community. As conservatives do not admit the relevance of particular group relationships to an understanding of crime and disorder, but juxtapose 'natural individuals' *directly* to the putatively perfect universality of the state, so radicals tend to dismiss out of hand, deny, act or argue in oblivion of natural individuality, or rather negate the basic, natural, pre-social character of individuality, as it clashes with universal human morality, and instead endeavour to derive all kinds of immoral conduct *directly* from particularization. Particularity as rigidified into asymmetrical institutions is for radicals the ultimate villain of the peace: human beings *qua* human beings are not guilty of immoral acts, they are indeed as such, in ideal terms, incapable of committing immoral acts. Human beings can be morally 'guilty' only if seen as the embodiments of particularity, as the concrete expression of antagonistic group relationships. Racial discrimination, class exploitation, sexist oppression and the like are the primary, immediate and independent expressions of the immorality residing in particularization, while individual killing, violence, harm, rape, fraud, robberty, theft, dishonesty are its secondary, mediate, dependent consequences.

And further, and again perfectly locically in terms of their overall perspective, radicals will usually argue that it is particularity itself which provides the escape route from the vicious circle, the particularity namely of progressive politics as against the petrified, frozen politics of the state: mobilized particularity against settled particularization. This means the recovery of 'protest' from the morass of criminality, the moralization of despair and dissatisfaction, the political sublimation of social conflict at present consciously experienced on the individual level. And once present asymmetries are transcended, so the radical argument reaches its climax, then the individual and the universal *will* embrace each other; perfectly moral relationships among human beings will go hand in hand with the provision of means to the achievement of individual happiness, and crime will wither away together with moral and legal rules as *externally* imposed. In the short run all we need is vigilance against the recurrence or residues of group-determined immorality. As

Schwendinger: 'All persons must be guaranteed the fundamental prerequisites for well-being, including food, shelter, clothing, medical services, challenging work and recreational experiences, as well as security from predatory individuals or repressive and imperialistic social elites.'[34] As Pashukanis, on the longer vista: 'Only the complete disappearance of classes will make possible the creation of a system of penal policy which lacks any element of antagonism. Moreover, it is very doubtful whether, in such circumstances, there will be any necessity at all for a penal system.'[35] And W. L. McBride looks forward to

> . . . a society of individuals so enlightened that, while they would still be confronted with rules of conduct of all sorts, they would constantly be making conscious choices as to whether to accept or to reject any one of these rules, and no coercion would be exerted over any member's choice. . . It seems to me that this is an ideal limit toward which legislators, judges, philosophers of law, and others ought to work, since this state of affairs would accord most completely with such human values as responsibility, free choice, and respect for persons.[36]

★ ★ ★ ★ ★ ★ ★ ★

This was rather a mixed baggage and I am not entirely unmindful of the danger of distortion creeping into a summary characterization of writers who often violently disagree among one another (e.g. Marxists, pacifist liberals, anti-psychiatrists, etc.) and whose views, almost invariably, appear much more circumspect and reasonable when read at length, in context, than the brief passages, cited here, would suggest. Let us stress the point once more: we are not erecting straw-men here for the purpose of simply knocking them down again, and we are not in the least suggesting that radical writers, or conservative writers for that matter, are misguided or wrong-headed, subject to ridicule or summary dismissal. Quite the opposite: they are right, within the terms of their paradigm. And I think it is reasonable to assert, albeit admitting to some degree of level-mixing and simplification, that these two opposed perspectives *do* exist, recognizable in the debate, each presenting a coherent cluster of fundamental concepts and a number of persuasive arguments deriving therefrom. People here labelled 'conservative', from de Maistre to James Wilson, would obviously differ on a lot of things but (I believe) still agree on basics, on what might be seen as the three salient pillars of conservatism: law above politics, individual proneness to evil, the necessity of punishment. Likewise I think writers who are generally regarded as 'radical' (and who proudly profess themselves to be such) agree at least on *their* minimum, on the three salient pillars of radicalism: the human basis of morality, the historical contingency and social causation of immorality, the possibility of a free, non-coercive community.

To return to radicalism, as with the conservative paradigm it might be worth our while to highlight some interesting features, again resulting in a string of dualisms. We noted the conservative tendency to combine long-term pessimism with short-term optimism. Not unexpectedly, the direct opposite seems to be the case with radicals. Their view is of course – and necessarily – characterized by an overall optimism sometimes of a cosmic magnitude: yes, we will leave this wretched valley of tears, the world of hunger, poverty, exploitation, oppression, dehumanized criminal protesters, prisons, police batons, and move on to a new plane of existence. But at the same time radicals tend to be, and with special reference to the topic of law and order, decidedly tragic, gloomy, apocalyptic in outlook concerning the short term: in their view there is nothing that can be done to eliminate or even minimize crime, disorder, insecurity, short of a thoroughgoing change in social and power relationships (which is of course unlikely to happen tomorrow). Radicals sometimes even display what might appear sardonic pleasure in coolly predicting that the law and order problem will get worse, that it is bound to get worse, that it is 'determined' by escalating class and racial conflicts, that in a way 'we' (i.e. intellectuals, law-abiding middle-class beneficiaries of order, even complacent, settled working-class people in the West) actually deserve what is coming, apt poetic punishment for our collective historical guilt. There is a modicum of gloomy fatalism in Hall: 'Crime is one predictable and quite comprehensible consequence of this process [i.e. the deterioration of the position of the black working-class in Britain] – as certain a consequence of how the structures work, however "unintended", as the fact that night follows day.'[37] There is at least a tiny residue of good-natured *Schadenfreude* in Pearson's excellent observation, denying the historical bases of conservative crisis-mentality: 'Historical myth proposes that our contemporary problems are a break with the past. Historical realism shows that they are not. Indeed, when a government such as Mrs Thatcher's indulges in some old-fashioned class warfare, which will necessarily bite hardest against the under-class, we might even judge it historically appropriate that it should be visited with some old-fashioned "riot".'[38] And there might be just a touch of serene collective self-recrimination in the comment made by Honderich: 'By our ordinary omissions we do as wrong as we might by certain awful acts.'[39] 'What we must accept . . . is that those who engage in violence of the Left have a truth on their side when they respond to the charge that *they* do wrong with the retort that *we* do wrong.'[40] And as the above statement from Geoffrey Pearson indicated, the radical perspective seems to share with the conservative perspective also the retrospective ambiguity concerning the presence of crime and disorder in society. On the one hand, radicals will strenuously argue against moral panics, unprecedented crime waves, melting social fabrics: these things have always accompanied power relations and unequal settlements, there is nothing special in the present. On the other hand, however, in some way most radicals (Pearson and a few others are not included here) find it rather embarrassing to admit historical continuity: after all, it is part of the overall radical stand that the present *is* something special, that capitalism is in a 'crisis', that a worsening law and order situation is an immediate prelude to the big change, a sign of the times. It is of course radicals who ought to welcome and accentuate moral panics, and it is conservatives who ought to endeavour to calm the waters. But there are more general implications of this ideological 'transvestism' which will be dealt with later.

First, a few concluding remarks on the conservative paradigm. The standpoint of these reflections, as has been amply shown in previous chapters, comes very close indeed to the view, or perhaps rather 'instinct', of conservative writers and the rank and file of the silent majority, on the subject of *crime*. In my view it is basically correct to recognize in criminality an elemental, primordial, categorially distinct, irreducible and for all practical intents and purposes enduring phenomenon, a form of immorality which poses a permanent threat to personal security and which it is the paramount duty of the state to control. This duty goes with the absolute right of society to act against individual law-breakers, the overwhelming moral superiority of the state as law over against individuals acting as pure natural individuals. There is an irreducible aspect of 'strangeness' in our society, there is a permanent presence of malevolent indifference, and we must be given constant protection against these. There is no good reason to suppose, as we remarked in the first chapter, that the future in this respect is going to be dramatically different. But this is as far as it goes. The conservative perspective, I think, has a serious and perhaps fatal flaw in it in so far as it implies the tendency to reduce politics, and especially illegal politics, to conduct which is *totally* subject to the law of the state as it exists. Conservatives do not recognize the state as order, do not accept the point that on its external side the state itself is a product of politics, and that consequently political disorder, however unruly, turbulent or violent its immediate manifestations might be, requires a societal (and legal) attitude which is very different from the attitude shown towards criminality. State politics and illegal politics reach in principle a point of moral equivalence which is never the case with crime. A failure to face up to this, morally speaking, amounts to the surreptitious and illegitimate elevation of the state to the plane of divinity, perfect morality. But enough was said about the moral, philosophical dimension in the last chapter. Here it will perhaps suffice to add the pragmatic remark that a rigid, indiscriminately criminalizing attitude is always likely – to put it no stronger – to make political disorder more acute, more threatening, more costly, in terms of expenditure as well as personal security and human lives. When the state, governed under these rigid, one-sided conservative principles, finally and grudgingly gives in to the demands of terrorists, insurrectionists, urban guerillas, ethnic activists, militant trade unions (and the state *does* have this habit of giving in, eventually), this comes alas too late, and in retrospect almost invariably (with a few notable exceptions) a bolder, more imaginative and more conciliatory policy appears to have been the wiser choice. No state, no positive law, no social order stands above the flow of world history.

Concerning the radical perspective, the affinity of the view expressed in the course of these reflections to certain basic radical ideas, again, hardly needs any repetition or extra emphasis. Radicals have, in essentials, the correct approach to politics, including anti-state politics. Unquestionably: the state *is* order, and order does express differential group relations, and these do evoke dissatisfaction, protest, discontent, and dissatisfied groups as groups *do* possess the moral right to overstep the narrow limits of legality in given cases. And I also believe that radicals are saying something extremely important, and something essentially valid, by stressing the human basis and human direction of morality. It is not enough to pay pious lip-service to 'human rights' and the 'dignity of the person' and at the same time go on insensitively or selfishly endorsing structures and relationships which negate these moral values *per se*. The legitimacy, the very moral being, of the state (any state) rests on the presumption that the *state is law*, and this necessarily implies equal citizenship, equitable access to power, a general right to protection against immorality, the establishment of a realm where individuals are regarded and accepted as ends in themselves, not the means to the aggrandizement of others. The person (not the natural individual!) stands in the centre: the person from whom moral conduct is properly expected and who correspondingly rightly demands full moral recognition. Particularization, in its rigidified form of asymmetrical group relations, unquestionably stands in the way; there is, therefore, as radicals assert in a variety of political idioms, an overriding moral injunction, presupposed by the law of the state as it exists, to constantly strive to move *away from order*, in the direction of greater universalization and greater morality all round. But again this is as far as it goes. The radical position, as I understand it, is also flawed and subject to criticism. As the issues involved here are more complicated (and thus theoretically more interesting) than in the case of conservatism, I shall attempt to comment on them more systematically, under two separate headings. Radicals, it seems to me, have some major problems concerning the nature of crime, and their characteristic stance on the moral direction of politics – away from the authoritarian state and towards 'community' – also contains some important ambiguities, in need of being sorted out.

It will not, I hope, sound too exaggerated to say that radicalism is constitutionally unable to grasp the nature of criminality fully, which ultimately stems from the fact that in radical thought human immorality is not afforded 'ontological' status, not recognized for its substantiality. I think this is a logical defect, since immorality, antinomian conduct, the breaking of rules, is presupposed by the idea of morality, the idea of humanity itself, of which it is the reverse or dialectical counterpart. Without immorality we cannot conceive of morality either – the point was argued at some length in the previous chapter. But by 'logical' here I do not mean anything that is remote, academic, impractical, pertaining to metaphysics only; on the contrary this basic insufficiency of radicalism makes its presence felt at numerous points, at the strategic-ideological as well as the tactical-political levels. The presence of criminal wrong-doing in society has posed a problem for most radical thinkers, which they have been able to tackle only by, as it were, leaning over backwards, against the grain of their own theorizing. Apart from the relatively few 'romanticizers' of crime (like Bakunin, the Fourierists, etc.), radicals have tended to take up a double position on crime, arguing both its basic immorality and at the same time its 'positive' character as a form of elemental protest against oppression and social injustice. The position of Marx and Engels here is well known and needs no elaborate commentary. It is, I think, essentially a self-contradictory position, when shorn of its ornamental excrescences. Individual 'ordinary' criminals are condemned outright and in unmistakably moralistic terms; the present criminal content of much of working-class consciousness and conduct is openly acknowledged; in Engels's renowned expression in the *Conditions of the Working Class in England* England, in the present bourgeois and industrializing epoch, has become the 'most criminal country in the world'. At the same time it is this very 'dehumanized' (and dehumanized precisely in the criminal sense) proletariat which is hailed as the future deliverer of humanity, and indeed the very embodiment of humanity. Now the big, underlying theoretical problem here for radicals, as I see it (and Marx's and Engels's difficulties are shared by most), is that the 'criminal response' and 'dehumanization' are not really, or at all, explained in radical terms. Why *should* the oppressed *qua* oppressed respond in such a way? Why is criminality – individual immorality – such an ever-present, natural, spontaneous choice by a number of people, all of whom could in principle have taken the political way? How can original goodness and original innocence be *that* 'corruptible' and 'corrupted' by prevailing conditions? Why should humanity, morality, political radicalism have to be deliberately inculcated into the poor, taking a great effort on the part of radical teachers and expected to take a long time, whereas criminality is here and now, rampant without anybody's conscious effort, a mode of conduct that has to be resisted, combated at every turn? Mass criminalization, as we made the point earlier, can truthfully be ascribed to the responsibility of society. But what lies behind it, namely the criminal tendency as such, the choice of individuals to act like individuals, the human *potential* to act immorally, is in a different category altogether. Here explanations in terms of 'corruption by society' ring decidedly hollow and inadequate; no form of society can be *so* powerful and tragically effective; if basic humanity and original goodness are that volatile, that fickle, that uncertain, then at the end they lose most of their meaning and dynamism as theoretical assumptions. Van den Haag appears to be essentially correct on this point:

> Somehow bad social institutions always seem to corrupt naturally good men. The possibility that naturally bad men corrupt good institutions is rarely considered. None ever satisfactorily explained why naturally good men create bad institutions, and by what means revolutionaries manage to remain uncorrupted so as to lead us into the millennium. [41]

Crime also poses a formidable problem for radicals on a more immediate, tactical or political level. What to do with crime, what is the right attitude to crime, violence on the streets, large-scale individual dishonesty, the personal insecurity which is felt by an increasing number of people? Here it is interesting to note a marked change of tone in radical writing in the last decade or so, with radical writers being less emphatic on 'moral panics' and less dismissive in their attitude to public fears of crime and disorder; there is a more mature position now, with crime being increasingly condemned in terms which are not entirely dissimilar to those found in the conservative armoury. Crime is more or less accepted as a general problem, a problem for the working class. Terry Fields, Labour MP, said in his speech on the Police and Criminal Evidence Bill, in November 1983: 'We have no sympathy with the vicious criminals who are as much menace to the workers as are the big property owners, and whose activities provide the state with excuses for strengthening repressive powers.' [42] Ian Taylor, leading radical criminologist, wrote in the *New Statesman* in 1982: 'We have to retrieve Mannheim's earlier conception of crime as involving both social *and* economic offences *against the common interest*, committed by the advantaged and disadvantaged alike and requiring an equal level of attention by the public and by a socially responsible police force.' [43] Stuart Hall's massive and highly theoretical *Policing the*

Crisis and even more so the remarkably balanced (though still basically radical in terms of its assumptions) volume by Lea and Young, *What Is to Be Done about Law and Order?*, are perhaps the most telling and eloquent examples of this broadening and maturation of position. But I think the dilemma is still there, and perhaps made even more acute, for, while radicals can (and indeed, in political terms, are very wise to) condemn crime and 'vicious criminals' who offend against the 'common interest' in an abstract way, they still find that they have to cling to the notion that crime is 'protest' and that it is 'caused' by social conditions, and that therefore, concretely speaking, criminality should not *always* be condemned but seen, recognized for its positive, forward-looking significance. Radicals of course tend to display a contemptuous attitude towards restrictive and partial 'bourgeois morality', and thus they are almost inevitably driven to a position of looking benignly on *all* forms of moral deviation, including criminality. Furthermore they often see a *continuity* between criminal conduct and revolutionary politics, sometimes even tacitly encouraging crime, and certainly excusing individual criminals; basically immoral or not, here and now crime is still a remote and indirect ally in the great struggle, sharing with revolutionaries at least an opposition to the system, which is immoral itself. My enemy's enemy, even though not a friend, cannot be altogether dismissed as a useful, if perhaps embarrassing, ally. The dualism thus remains.

The practical, psychological problems engendered here are well known and attested to in every great political and social upheaval, from the French Revolution through the Paris Commune to the Bolshevik Revolution: criminality which is positively taken up in the struggle, encouraged (in the form mainly of personal violence, looting, revenge, destruction of property) and heightened by the resulting disorder itself, does not vanish overnight and somehow miraculously get transformed into revolutionary virtue. On the contrary, in a post-revolutionary situation crime becomes an even more acute problem, and of course it is not entirely unknown for criminals, in theory purified by the struggle itself, to end up in positions of great power and continue as criminals, there only for the beer, so to speak. This is of course not the same problem as the generally 'corrupting' effect of power but it is easy to see how the two things can be conjoined, and become mutually reinforcing, in a situation where the crucial distinction between the state as law and the state as order is deliberately blurred (this blurring is, alas, a hallmark of much of modern radical thinking) and hence customary, ordinary *moral* rules, rules prescribing individual conduct, are in a state of suspension. It would probably be too bland and simplistic to assert that the markedly oppressive, corrupt and criminal tendencies of so many successful revolutionary regimes are a direct consequence of their having been genuine 'revolutions' (total upheavals) and of the conjoining of these two kinds of potential immorality – but in the least this should be accepted as a distinct possibility. The really crucial point however, as far as I am able to see, concerns the recognition that established states and societies do represent at least a modicum of humanity, morality, universality (of which criminal conduct is both the logical and the existential opposite), which is not the same as their contingent embodiment of a differential order and which therefore ought not to be fought against and destroyed. Illegal and revolutionary politics, in so far as it allies itself with crime (on whatever level), is always and inescapably in danger of going too far, doing too much, jumping overboard, using an elephant-gun to kill an insect, throwing out the baby with the dirty bath-water. 'Bourgeois' morality may rightly be ridiculed as being too hypocritical, property laws criticized as narrow and inegalitarian, existing justice as partial and discriminatory but this should be no argument against morality in general and as evolving, against laws, against the idea of justice as such. If you like, radical politics does a great disservice to itself in so far as it does not become fully theoretically conscious of the need to struggle on two fronts simultaneously, against the contingent, historical imperfection of states as rigidified systems of order, and against that basic, enduring, ubiquitous form of human immorality of which in our societies (past, present and in all likelihood future) criminal conduct is the main, concrete external embodiment.

This directly leads us to the second point to be considered, namely the radical direction of politics or the radical vision of the society which lies beyond the great dividing line. An obvious but decidedly unsensational remark to make here is that this vision, in the case of most serious radical writers, tends to be left rather vague, abstract, adumbrated more in terms of moralistic outline than concrete institutional detail. Since Marx it has not been very respectable for radicals to indulge in 'utopian' blueprints and descriptions, although many have felt that Marxism historically failed precisely on this point, and needs therefore to be supplemented. The radical vision usually goes by the name of the 'non-coercive society' or the 'community' which has transcended the rigid state form and instead of laws, law-enforcement and punishment is organized along the lines of co-operation, altruism, mutual trust, equality and freedom. Criminality, of course, will have more or less completely vanished from this community. As regards the Marxist position on this, H. Collins gives a useful summary in *Marxism and Law*:

> The supposition that law will always be necessary rests upon beliefs about certain constant qualities of human nature such as greed and selfishness. The theory of alienation includes the assertion that the materially determined content of the human psyche may be fundamentally transformed; under the communist relations of production a novel type of personality will emerge which will be exempt from egocentric lusts for power and wealth. Accordingly the usual reason given by liberal political philosophy for the existence of coercive systems of behavioral control like law will no longer be extant. Men will naturally agree about the proper standards of behaviour and conform to them without the need for sanctions. [44]

In *The New Criminology* by I. Taylor, P. Walton and J. Young it is stated:

> . . . one of the central purposes of this critique has been to assert the possibility – not only of a fully social *theory* – but also of a society in which men are able to assert themselves in a fully social fashion. With Marx, we have been concerned with the social arrangements that have obstructed, and the social contradictions that enhance, man's chances of achieving full sociality – a state of freedom from material necessity, and (therefore) of material incentive, a release from the constraints of forced production, an abolition of the forced division of labour, and a set of social arrangements, therefore, in which there would be no politically, economically, and socially induced need to criminalize deviance. [45]

W. L. McBride, critical even of Lenin's 'conservatism' in *State and Revolution*, paints his vision in boldly: 'If there are some individuals who are committed to the goal of a noncoercive society and who act, as far as possible, in accordance with this goal, then there is no logical argument against the possibility of *all* individuals' sharing this commitment and acting accordingly at some future time.' [46] And: 'If small noncoercive societies actually do exist and "work" for substantial periods of time, then there is no reason *in principle* why the same way of life could not be extended indefinitely over the larger societies of which these are parts.' [47] 'The logic' here may be somewhat suspect but the rationalistic confidence of the author is certainly admirable. This amount of confidence, to be sure, is not shared by many radicals these days, the majority of whom, certainly including the Marxists, see a long and arduous way ahead before this situation can be reached, if it can be reached at all. In *Policing the Crisis*, for instance – a treatise heavily saturated with the somewhat pessimistic short-term scenarios of Gramsci, Althusser and Poulantzas – all that is concretely envisaged is that 'critique' might succeed in weakening the hold of the 'hegemonic' ideas of the ruling class, this being a precondition of any future 'break' with existing power relations. And then? 'Beyond that rupture lie alternatives which are as yet only partially and fitfully glimpsed. . . .' [48]

It is not easy to argue against positions of this kind (whether rationalistically or circumspectly expressed) and in a sense Patricia Morgan is right in saying, with regard to radical criminology: '. . . what is so strenuously insisted on is that social theory continually confront the radical *possibility* of a society without criminalization and without controls. And in a sense, this exhortation can never finally be invalidated.' [49] But again, I think it is somewhat unfair and ultimately self-defeating to attempt to confront the radical vision directly with conservative myopia, and to put too much critical emphasis on the vagueness and moral idealism contained in characteristic radical positions. The radical perspective must, to some extent, be abstract, projective, idealistic, confident; philosophically speaking, abstraction and transcendence are its principal weapons in the arena of ideological conflict. If you advocate an increase in overall human 'freedom', then your position must logically include the conviction that fully liberated human beings, re-humanized particulars, will know *better* than you what kind of organization will be most conducive to happy and trustful living and to the emergence of non-coercive relationships. The trouble, ultimately, with radicalism does not lie in this futuristic idealism. It lies rather in this idealism's being systematically ambiguous, heterogeneous, paradoxical. The radical vision – and this is really the quintessential point to grasp – contains *two* scenarios which are continually confused and conflated, which are fundamentally responsible for the dualistic attitude taken towards criminality, for the non-recognition of the plural character of the state (as law and as order), and for the proneness to immorality evidenced in so many successful revolutionary regimes. In the radical vision there is a radical disjunction, invisible at first precisely because it lies at the 'roots', of two diametrically opposed extremes, two fatally diverging understandings of the moral direction implied in politics and of the 'good society', the non-coercive society and the humanized community of the future. One way or another all our preceding discussion in this volume, and in a more immediate sense our critical remarks on radicalism in the foregoing pages, have led implicitly up to the exposure of this concealed heterogeneity; now is the time to state the point clearly and unequivocally.

The two opposed directions in the radical perspective are those of perfect morality and perfect immorality, perfect legality and complete antinomianism, the push towards the further extension of a universal human consciousness and relations based upon it and simultaneously the pull towards the erosion of universality and the resultant achievement of full individuality. The first direction leads to the superseding of partial social institutions and asymmetrical power relationships by those which are more adequate expressions of morality, of the striving after the good and the right which is implicit in human consciousness and progressively revealed in historical changes and in cultural and political movements. Building on existing ideas and feelings of justice, civility, equality, tolerance, personal freedom and personal security, this direction tends towards the constant broadening and deepening of these bases, towards further and indeed more intensified moralization of natural individuals, towards the creation of conditions where humane living is generally possible, or more precisely conditions which allow for a greater degree of humanization in the lives and activities of more people. This is the direction of *law*, of movement towards the achievement of an ever greater correspondence between the universal moral law and the actual order of communities, a direction which is not at all anti-statist in a really meaningful sense but on the very contrary tending to the further perfection, institutionalization, inculcation into consciousness, of the *true* state, the internal state, the state with genuine moral authority, the legal and moral community which embodies and safeguards the moral interests of individual citizens. This is the direction towards 'civilization', towards more moral respect for the person as such (who, as 'person', is expected to reciprocate by acknowledging, and identifying with, the authority invested in the community), towards the transcendence of particular group conflict – towards, finally, *order* itself, order as renewed, extended, purified. The true mission of the revolutionary, of the radical, as Carlyle once said, 'is Order; every man's is. He is here to make what was disorderly, chaotic, into a thing ruled, regular. He is the missionary of Order. Is not all work of man in this world a *making of Order*?' [50] And in A. P. d'Entreves' apt words: 'Utopias, the models of a perfect society, in which at certain moments of history men sought an escape and refuge from reality, do not imply a denial of order; far from it. They are expressions of an aspiration after a better or different order, after an order which may well be more rigorous and exacting than that which actually exists and is laid down in positive legal systems.' [51]

But to this we must contrapose the simultaneously present direction within the radical perspective which goes towards individual liberation and immediate gratification, towards spontaneity, towards the apotheosis of emotion, impulse, instinct, towards the reassertion of the natural individual existing beneath. This direction leads not to the perfection of morality, of rights, law, state but to their very denial, to an advocacy of the complete abolition of rules binding on human conduct. It is expressive of a deep contempt for law and for morality and for all kinds of restrictions, involving the square negation of the very idea of wrong, of sin, crime, guilt, imperfection, it tends to the ridiculing of all customs, all traditions, all modesty and civility, all justice and in the last resort all genuinely 'human' relations. It negates order directly, for the sake of negating it, in a spirit of eternal and total rebellion, in an effusion of natural force and immediate vitality; it poses violence against persuasion, haste against patience, inflamed rhetoric against arguments, spontaneous demonstration and revelation against political work. This direction involved in the radical perspective then *is* truly 'anti-authoritarian' and anti-statist; it is in the proper and literal sense 'individualist', divinizing the natural individual who here *becomes* the human community, who does not accept any order, any structure, any system, any law or any government but who revels in, achieves self-realization and aggrandizement in, perfect chaos and disorder.

The occasional hyperbola employed in this presentation of the two directions might perhaps be forgiven; at any rate, it is not intended to argue here that the two opposed stances within radicalism are *equally* important or equally emphasized in the literature. Far from it. The first or 'moral' direction gets by far the greater proportion of the limelight. But it can scarcely be denied that in radical thought, especially from the eighteenth-century Enlightenment onwards, there has been a pretty strong 'immoralist' undercurrent, influential on all levels. In a pure form, immoralism has of course rarely been advocated (perhaps Nietzsche comes nearest, or Stirner, but again their *political* radicalism is questionable), but the ideas belonging to the current have played an important role in the unfolding of doctrines of modern socialism, communism or anarchism as well as in the actual conduct of anarchists, communists, socialists. I believe – obviously – that this second tendency within radicalism is wrong, false, negative, self-defeating, disastrous, detrimental to progress and seriously damaging to the positive, *moral* cause of radicalism. I will not attempt to argue this now on a philosophical level, as it has already been done earlier in these reflections (with special reference to our discussion on the distinction between 'criminal' and 'political'). But maybe one or two further remarks are called for, concerning the practical level, the political strategy and tactics of radicalism. It seems to me, however naive this may sound, that radical movements have everything to gain by encouraging a sense of *basic morality* among their followers and the public at large, building on an elemental sense of 'decency' (in the Orwellian sense) undoubtedly present in human consciousness and in everyday conduct. This should mean, among other things, paying serious and genuine regard to humdrum and traditional, 'ordinary' moral rules, to the 'old-fashioned' values of personal modesty, fidelity, integrity, to the sanctity of life, to responsibility for individual conduct, to respect for the underlying 'law' present even in asymmetrically ordered societies, to 'politics' in a genuine sense. Political revolution thus ought not to be confused with some kind of 'moral' revolution, with 'cultural' revolution – these latter do not signify or refer to anything that is really going on in the world, they are fictitious and fantastic entities. Moral upheavals are not revolutionary but counter-revolutionary, they are retrograde rather than progressive, they are empty and misleading expressions of the enduring and unproductive rebelliousness of the 'old Adam'. Immoralism *means* immorality, the descent to criminality. Political revolution should instead be predicated on a full acceptance and avowal of moral *continuity*, and this acceptance should always be informing radical political action. Disregard for moral rules, the encouragement of rebelliousness and turbulence and chaos in everyday life might seem advantageous in the short term but in the longer run they inevitably lead to a dead end. There are several roads to crime.

So much for radicalism. We have now to broaden the discussion and endeavour to make a few comments on the two basic unitary perspectives of conservatism and radicalism as they appear, so to speak, *together*, displaying the same kind of limitations and inadequacies, which accrue to them on account of being unitary. We have argued in this chapter that both the conservative and radical paradigms are restrictive and reductionist; in both cases what we observe is a more or less systematic blurring, ideological obliteration of *one* out of three dimensions which make up human consciousness and social life: conservatives tend to blot out particular group divisions in society (except as they figure within and under the state's positive law), while radicals appear to be oblivious of natural individuality (except as derived, contingently, from existing particularities). Now the elimination of this – in each case disturbing – third category necessarily leads to a close approximation and joining of the other two: that is, for conservatives human individuals appear as being directly involved in the moral universality of the law (which they all 'ought' to obey, whatever the circumstances), and for radicals 'concrete' human beings, i.e. members of various social groups, appear to have the potential ability to draw together and form the truly universal, moral community, once a given entrenched power settlement is broken. In both cases the relationship is seen as *unproblematic* in principle (though it might be highly problematic in practice), the situation is 'clear' and 'simple': there is no reason why 'people' could not live in peace together, tranquilly going about their activities, related to one another by ties of morality and common humanity, *either* 'under the law' (conservatism) *or* 'beyond the law' (radicalism). Thus there is, once the surface waves of ideological opposition are washed away, an underlying and subconscious assumption shared by both radicals and conservatives, namely the assumption of the 'peaceful society'. Both perspectives assume that underneath the turbulence and conflict and imperfection there is something hard, smooth, fully intelligible about human character and society, that the problem of personal security, of law and order in general, is in principle capable of resolution. Conservatives and radicals, however strange this might sound at first, both believe in a bottom layer of *natural harmony* in human affairs. For conservatives state, society and positive law are all right, in essential terms, and there is just the relatively small business of keeping a minority of crooks, murderers, fanatics under tight control. For radicals human character is all right, in essentials, and there is just the (theoretically speaking) minor matter of altering the institutions of society. Unitariness, reductionism in both cases manages to spirit away that which is troublesome in thinking.

The common assumption of natural harmony in human society signifies, on the negative side, a view of crime, or criminality, which is shared by radicals and conservatives. Conservatives, as has been said before, are correct in pinpointing the basic immorality of crime. Radicals are correct in calling attention to the imperfection of existing order and the resultant social preconditions of much that passes under the label of criminality. But whether crime is said to result from depravity or from deprivation, on this shared assumption it appears something which is wholly *negative* in character, something to be deeply disturbed about, something to be eliminated or tightly controlled, something to be sharply distinguished from paradigmatic, normal, ordinary human conduct, whether it is the conduct of the majority today (conservatism) or the conduct of all tomorrow (radicalism). Conservatives are always worried about, and do not understand, the *spatial* dimension of crime, its extent, its ubiquity, its constant shading into normal conduct, its interpenetration of social and political life at all levels. Radicals are worried about, and really fail to face up to, the *temporal* dimension of crime, its continual reappearance in novel cultural and institutional settings. What this common assumption about criminality tends to overlook – and what makes crime (as we said earlier) *the* prime problem of political philosophy – is that criminality, while signifying and equivalent to basic immorality, is also basically *human* and thus, in all likelihood, not really capable either of elimination or of isolation. Within and interpenetrating its essential negativity, crime has a positive element, too: it is *fun*, elemental, natural, irrepressible like the wind or flooding waters. As it is human to have a sense of right and wrong, it is also human to be turbulent, negative, self-contradictory, deviant, to cock a snook at society (*any* society), to brush against the rules, however enlightened and 'internalized', to act consciously or impulsively against one's own sober 'human' interest, to remain and burst out from time to time as an *individual.* It may well be true, as Foucault, Erikson and others have argued, that established societies need the category of 'delinquency' or 'deviance' in order to keep the majority in check. But it may also be true that human character itself needs these very same external categories in order to *become* delinquent, deviant, violent, criminal! Very few most of the time, very many some of the time. It may be, as Taylor, Walton and Young write in *The New Criminology*, that what is today 'criminalized' and labelled 'deviant' is really the assertion of 'human diversity'. But the authors' conclusion: 'The task is to create a society in which the facts of human diversity, whether personal, organic or social, are not subject to the power to criminalize', [52] does not necessarily follow. It is just possible that the very *point* of some kind of 'diversity' is precisely to *be* criminalized, to be outside, in total opposition. Security is the chief human good, it means freedom, peace, civil relations, happiness – but this would scarcely be so if *insecurity*, too, with all its implications, were not a part of the total picture.

Going further, it may be surmised that the nature of the ground shared by the opposed perspectives of conservatism and radicalism has also something to do with the phenomenon of 'transvestism', fleetingly referred to earlier. This transvestism is really an amusing and edifying spectacle, easily observed in the ramifications of the on-going debate on law and order; this debate increasingly reveals (in Britain at any rate) a crazy, topsy-turvy ideological world, a constant game of musical chairs, changing places, phrases, garments, arguments. This might not be so, if underneath the ideological clothing the antagonists did not really have a similar, or the same, body. There is of course this basic similarity, namely the assumption of natural harmony. This basic harmony is threatened, hence the 'problem' of law and order. But what threatens it? It is a small bunch of wicked criminals, fanatics, terrorists – so conservatives *should* argue. Or it is the established institutions of state and society – as radicals *should* assert. But in reality this is not always what happens. It is quite easy sometimes, so it seems, to push the conservative position to a point where it becomes, in theoretical terms, almost indistinguishable from the radical position, and *vice versa*. Conservatives, who normally assume social peace and tranquillity in existing society and who are supposed to be defending established values, can become strident conflict theorists and bitter critics of their own order. Radicals, with their basic defining characteristic of thoroughgoing social criticism and their underlying belief in social conflict, can on the other hand become the staunch defenders of tradition and the establishment. Concerning conservatism, two points might be worth making, by way of illustration. Firstly, the increasing use of military metaphors and phrases by leading conservative writers and politicians has been noted. It is now 'crime-fighting' rather than 'peace-keeping', the 'war' against crime and disorder, 'battles' to be won and lost, 'emergency' situations. 'You here today are in the front line of the battle against crime' – as the Home Secretary declared in his speech to the Police Federation in 1984. There might be telling reasons for the employment of such language but nevertheless it does mean that conservatives are beginning to play the radical game. The assertion that, as Peter Calvert has put it, 'the war on crime *is* a war', [53] is tantamount to the admission, however well concealed, that there is something fundamentally wrong with the existing set-up, that there is an underlying and inexorable conflict in society, that the silence of the silent majority is no longer enough or cannot be counted on – we may recall here Spinoza's brilliant observation, quoted in the previous chapter, concerning the significance of increasing criminality and disorder. Secondly, and on a more rarefied level, conservative-inspired strictures on delinquency and on 'progressive' educational and penal policies might well be read as deep, implicit, and presumably unintentional criticisms of the very society, the very establishment, which produced these phenomena in the first place. Patricia Morgan's excellent volume, *Delinquent Fantasies*, is I think a case in point where the author thus accounts for the rise and spread of the 'delinquent syndrome':

> The breakdown of socialization and social controls began with the adult's embarrassment at prescribing norms for children; their withdrawal from the children's world, and the parallel abdication of the schools. The vicious spiral is accelerated by the hamstringing of the community . . . [54]

Now if this is not exactly playing the radical game, at least statements like this serve to open the ranks before the onslaught of radicals who of course know very well *why* adults should have been 'embarrassed' to inculcate their values and why social agencies like schools should have 'abdicated': it is because existing society itself is rotten to the core, the defenders of order increasingly become conscious of their guilt, capitalism is confronted by a 'legitimation crisis'. In this connection it might be noted further and with some glee how easily Morgan, in her on the whole well-argued defence of Western liberal-democratic society, is pushed into a position where she almost comes to uphold, as the model of a well-ordered and undelinquent society, an order which is the very negation of Western liberal values, namely the Soviet Union. As she says, having approvingly observed how in Marxist revolutions the criminal 'riff-raff' have been swept away and how today in the Soviet Union vandalism, drunkenness and crime are relatively successfully controlled:

> It is easy to conclude that the price paid for this security is the oppressiveness of the Russian political system. It is doubtful whether the liberty of the Russian people would be increased by a rise in street crime. Our surfeit of crime often works to undermine our claims to be a defender of individual freedom. [55]

With some radical writers the opposite seems to be the case: they have begun donning the clothes of conservatives, traditionalists, the staunch defenders of established values, customs and institutions. They, who (one presumes) ought to think in terms of an underlying, on-going social war and thus ought to welcome the intensification of struggle, the polarization of class conflict, the crisis of historical institutions and even the increase in police 'repression' and the rise of 'fascism' (as being the necessary prelude to the big change), yet often talk as if – in a strange way – they actually feared these developments. Conservatives are now the ones who innovate and cause upheaval and boldly take a leap ahead; it is radicals who look to the past for inspiration and jealously guard time-honoured institutions. Gerald Bermingham, Labour MP, on the Police and Criminal Evidence Bill:

> Do we really want the type of society in which people are lifted on suspicion, detained on suspicion, interrogated on suspicion and detained in custody because an application has been to a magistrate's court that further evidence might be obtained which could lead to further interrogation? That is not English justice as I and many other members of my profession have known it for a long time. That is the first step on the road to a centralized police state. [56]

E. P. Thompson, doyen of Marxist historians and theorists in Britain, captured the academic limelight recently in his thought-provoking collection of essays, *Writing by Candlelight*, a book which is conspicuous for its firm traditionalism and historical realism. Thompson strongly repudiates the idea, often attributed to and espoused by some Marxists, that the state is solely and simply a repressive organ; the rhetoric which 'often goes along with a wholesale dismissal of *all* law and *all* police, and sometimes with a soppy notion that *all* crime is some kind of displaced revolutionary activity.' [57] Further he writes, on a topic which is more directly relevant here, about 'a very ancient cultural tradition in Britain of bloody-mindedness towards the intrusion of authority'. [58] Nostalgically: 'Seventeenth-century yeomen did not give their children into the hands of the parish beadle, nor, in the eighteenth century, did London tradesmen and artisans matriculate beneath the lecterns of the Bow Street Runners.' Foreign observers saw for over three hundred years 'the peculiar jealousy of the British people towards the central powers of the state . . . their indiscipline and their sensitivity as to the citizen's rights of privacy.' [59] And as to the present, Thompson impassionedly concludes that it is radicals, 'libertarians'

> . . . who are trying to *uphold these institutions*, whereas it is the police lobby and its numerous supporters who are trying to discredit them. Not the law-and-order brigade but the defenders of civil liberties are

> attempting to uphold the constitution and the rule of law. [60]

Again, it is not our intention here to argue against the particular points made by Thompson and other radical writers on the issue of increasing state powers and the erosion of traditional institutions; there is certainly *something* worrying about prevailing tendencies to centralize and rationalize the 'war effort' against crime and disorder. Neither would we have much quarrel with the highly sophisticated and mature view of the state upheld by Thompson (in the company of other contemporary Marxist writers, like Claus Offe and Ralph Miliband); indeed, there is a tiny corner in which this moderate Marxist perspective and the 'plural perspective' espoused in these pages would rendezvous for a stolen embrace. But it seems to me quite obvious that there are grave theoretical problems in reconciling this realist, traditionalist, almost openly nostalgic position with the underlying premises of radical thought, with special reference to Marxism. Hugh Collins, I think, is essentially correct in seeing in the arguments of Thompson and others a position which threatens 'to slide into a wholesale acceptance of the Rule of Law.' [61] 'There is', Collins goes on, 'an unresolved contradiction in the Marxist position in so far as it includes a blanket concern for legality and liberty as well as an attack on the Rule of Law.'[62] Belief in the Rule of Law, in the sanctity and moral superiority of the law (as against fickle and temporary majorities) is, of course, as we have seen earlier, an integral aspect of the conservative paradigm, and it goes logically, coherently with other fundamental conservative values and beliefs, like objective and eternal moral truths, an essentially static social universe, and individual proneness to wrong-doing. But it does not coherently fit any radical paradigm worth its name. And this is an appropriate moment to recall, by way of concluding our foregoing critical discussion of the 'conventional wisdoms' of right and left, a remark made in the first chapter. Transvestism is mutual; yet at the same time one is almost inevitably led to observing the *overall* ascendancy of conservative thinking in ideological debate these days, not only on the issue of 'law and order' (where the very terms come from the conservative armoury) but on a host of other things as well, e.g. the acceptance of 'market socialism', 'discipline' and 'standards' in education, income policies, etc. On the whole it might seem, and with obvious and particular reference to the question discussed here, that radicalism has somehow lost its soul, its confidence in the future; it has become stagnant, almost backward-looking, lost in the wilderness, sharing in the gloom as well as in the doom. Conservatives call the tune. Not so long ago, in the 1950s and 1960s in particular, ideologies vied in endeavouring to appear 'progressive'. Recently they have been vying to cast a more traditional image than their rivals.

★ ★ ★ ★ ★ ★ ★ ★

And so we can now conclude on the whole enterprise behind us, on our meandering ambulation through some of the vexed and far-reaching issues conjured up by the problem of personal security in our modern societies. 'Reflections' perhaps need not involve perfectly rounded, neatly tailored and coiffured arguments, the crescendo of an orchestral coda, a final and triumphant crossing of t's and dotting of i's. Yet there has been some sort of a direction in our meditative-argumentative journey and a destination to be reached, not perhaps with a noisy climax but informed by a quiet conviction. Our destination is our departure: the paradoxes of security. Now, however, we can perhaps comment more meaningfully on the issues involved, having delved into the subject somewhat and having, in this present chapter, gone a certain distance in engaging in ideological criticism. The critical comments above were certainly not meant to be wholly negative, not just a protracted string of back-biting, digressive remarks. What I think our survey, however uneven and selective it may have been, has conclusively shown is that the problem of security cannot be reduced either to a political problem or to a legal problem. There is more to disorder, to political illegality and violence than crime, and there is more to criminality than a response to the injustice of a particular social and legal order. Turning it the other way round, our conclusion must be therefore that there is *more* to the adequate provision of personal security than marshalling the external, visible power of the state, and also *more* to it than creating a new kind of society or progressing beyond the state to 'community'. The state, as imperfect, cannot alone provide security: its underlying weakness is revealed by the presence of order and the presence of politics, within and without, legal and illegal. And human beings, as imperfect, cannot reasonably be expected to lose their natural individuality entirely in a new kind of community; the weakness of this anticipation is indicated by the singular lack of success hitherto in the creation of orderless, crime-free social and political structures. If we now, in a rather ambitious manner, attempt to epitomize the conservative and radical perspectives under the respective labels of 'state' and 'community', then what becomes apparent is their mutual interpenetration on a conceptual level: while neither community nor state as such, in rigid isolation, can deal adequately with the problem of security in society, together they not only can (up to a point) but must; there is nothing else but a *synthesis* of state and community, of conservatism and radicalism, that can rise to meet the problem of crime and disorder. There is no total or final solution to the problem of law and order but there may be a partial, uncertain, temporary way of containment or management, and the road to it seems to lie in the adoption of a synthetic (i.e. plural) perspective, which means learning both from radicalism and from conservatism. Once stated, of course, this is not only obvious but rather stale, unsensational and seemingly pointless; isn't this what every person of good will and good sense has been saying up to now? And with what success? Fortunately, however, in this book we are not concerned with the selling of patent medicines and we shall not sink to the solecism of trying to tell policemen, judges, governments, criminals, terrorists what to do. Our concern rather – and this may not be a wholly platitudinous, wholly pointless exercise – is with attempting to clarify what it means actually to say that the provision of personal security requires the presence of both 'state' and 'community'.

To resort again to the kind of 'existentialist' language we employed in the introductory chapter: as an individual person I am vulnerable and always shall be vulnerable; in my social relationships I am confronted with a certain amount of strangeness and that strangeness will remain; some people some of the time will be indifferent to my welfare and this indifference can always be combined with malevolence on their part. It is always possible for others to show hostility to me in their conduct. Therefore, in most circumstances the maintenance of my security, my way of life, requires that I should be able to rely on power that augments or replaces my own strength. This power is provided by the state, by agencies 'outside' which nevertheless relate to me directly, internally: the power of the state rests on its authority and this authority stems ultimately from my own will as a moral person. (So far traditional political philosophy: Hobbes, Hegel and the rest of them.) But it is obvious that reliance on the state, on power outside, cannot go all the way. If the state is weak, limited, its power circumscribed, then it cannot defend me. Law and order then will remain empty formalities or at best very minimal and inadequate safeguards. If on the other hand the state is too strong, total, possessing overwhelming power, then it might be able to defend me against other threats but at the same time, and by the same token, it will also become a threat to my personal security. In this case it is my 'will' authorizing the state which itself will become illusory, vacuous and merely formal. The point is – and this is rather an important point, spelt out clearly for the first time in our endeavour – that in either case my security will require something else, besides the state. It will require 'community': that is, reliance on other people around me who are not related to me through power but by ties of affinity, amity, sentiment, benevolence, shared interests. Moreover it will also require that I act consciously with and for this community, that I identify with it. My relation to the state as a citizen, and through the state to my fellow citizens in society, is a substantial and meaningful relation only if at the same time I also relate to other people, not as citizen but as friend, family, comrade, etc. As an 'individual' and isolated person I have no standing whatsoever against the state, I become wholly absorbed, vanish in the void. And this absorption – a logical certainty – spells the end of my 'security'. I will at this point cease to be a person, a distinct and unique centre of consciousness: Big Brother will look after me completely but it is no longer 'me', it is simply an emanation of Big Brother. The 'problem' of personal security at this point becomes entirely meaningless.

But now look at it from the other side. The state requires community. But community also requires the state. Suppose that – and it is a tall order – people around me can trust me as completely, as unreservedly as I can trust them, we are friends, sisters, brothers, comrades-in-arms, spontaneously co-operating, totally altruistic in our relationships. Strangeness is now totally overcome, and so are indifference and malevolence. Power withers away, there is absolutely no need for law, judges, adjudication, enforcement, punishment. In this case, again, 'personal security' becomes devoid of meaning. I am submerged in the community, entirely one with it, it fills my consciousness and directly defines my thoughts and my conduct, I move with its ebb and flow. There is no 'me' which would remain distinct and unique in my human surroundings, no 'person' who is individually conscious of a way of life to be purposely followed and which might be contingently threatened from outside. There is now complete indetermination, complete arbitrariness, unlimited freedom – not for me, however, as a person who has ceased to exist but for the community in which I have been dissolved. The situation is *exactly* the same as with the unlimited state, with the complete reliance on power. It might be argued that in the latter case absorption, submergence is a 'negative' process, whereas in the former case it is something 'positive', but this would be erroneous. Whichever way you arrive at it, community or state, you as a person disappear from the scene. As with living under unlimited power you cannot tell when the power which is supposed to be protecting you is being turned against you, so living in a total community means that you can never tell when this community ceases to be 'community' in the required sense. Loving Big Brother is no different from 'loving' all little brothers and sisters. The total state, because it is total, is also community: community, because it is total, is also 'state' in that it expresses overwhelming power. So supposing that as a 'communal unit', as a friend, lover, altruistic co-operator, you still have some modicum of individual consciousness left, still feel and think as a person, and consequently still have some interest in and desire for security? What do you do? You will seek, one way or another, relationships which are *not* 'communal' relationships, not intimate, not sentimental, not spontaneous; you will want some sort of formalization, indeed some form of 'strangeness' to be introduced into the community, something cold to temper the consuming heat of immediate human ties, something that gives you distance from your dear fellows. You will need, in the last resort, some kind of *power* to countervail the power of community. So we are back where we started: community leads back to the state.

In this staccato manner perhaps we have succeeded in indicating the absurdities to which the exclusive pursuit of extreme statism, legalism (conservatism) and of extreme communalism, moralism (radicalism) will logically lead. They lead to the same result, to the disappearance of personality and of personal security. Now if finally we make the assumption – audacious, outlandish, eccentric, extravagant – that human beings *do* have individual personalities and consciousness, and that they will want to *go on* as individual persons in this sense, and remain conscious of the need to maintain their security, their freedom, their way of life, unique concerns, desires, fears, interests, then it inevitably follows that radicals and conservatives are only partially right, that the correct approach is the synthetic one, that state and community must co-exist and develop together, side by side. But there is yet a further point to be made, and it is here that we come, once again, face to face with the ineluctable paradox involved in the quest after personal security. State and community together make up society and since neither community nor state is adequate on its own to provide for personal security (indeed, each can become potentially a source of insecurity), it seems to follow that 'society' as such, in its most general sense, is inadequate for the task. Two halves, faulty and jagged, can only make up a whole which is faulty and jagged. Therefore, in the final resort, my personal security is my own personal affair, and I cannot entirely relinquish its management to anybody outside, friends or officials. If I want to avoid total absorption, total abdication, then I must consciously and actively 'relate' as a distinct individual, to my citizenly ties as well as to my communal ties. I must act, be a constant co-producer of my own security, and then just as my *natural* limitations mean that I must accept the eternal uncertainty of my personal safety, so my *moral* limitations mean that I can never existentially guarantee the perfect security of others. So our paradoxes remain to the very end.

Notes

1 Paradoxes of Security

1. I. Taylor, *Law and Order: Arguments for Socialism*, London, Macmillan, 1981, p. 89. (N.B. Italics in direct quotes are always in the original.)
2. P. Marsh, *Aggro: the Illusion of Violence*, London, Dent, 1978, p. 142.
3. T. Hobbes, *Leviathan* (1651), London, Dent (Everyman's Library), 1973, p. 65.
4. J. E. Conklin, *The Fear of Crime*, New York, Macmillan, 1975, p. 7.
5. ibid., p. 25.
6. J. Lea and J. Young, *What Is to Be Done about Law and Order?*, Penguin Books, 1984, p. 54.
7. ibid., p. 55.
8. Marsh, op. cit., p. 105.
9. P. Morgan, *Delinquent Fantasies*, London, Temple Smith, 1978, p. 13.
10. ibid., p. 15.
11. ibid., p. 249.
12. E. van den Haag, *Punishing Criminals*, New York, Basic Books, 1975, p. 159.
13. L. J. Macfarlane, *Violence and the State*, London, Nelson, 1974, p. 101.
14. H. Arendt, *Between Past and Future: Six Exercises in Political Thought*, London, Faber and Faber, 1961, p. 93.
15. van den Haag, op. cit., p. 155.
16. G. Ionescu, *Politics and the Pursuit of Happiness*, London, Longman, p. 181.
17. P. H. Johnson, *On Iniquity: Some Personal Reflections Arising out of the Moors Murder Trial*, London, Macmillan, 1967, p. 130.
18. R. Nisbet, *Twilight of Authority*, London, Heinemann, 1976, p. 60.
19. Morgan, op. cit., p. 9.
20. T. R. Gurr, *Why Men Rebel*, Princeton, N. J., Princeton University Press, p. 26.
21. N. C. M. Elder, 'Conclusion', in P. Norton, ed., *Law and Order and British Politics*, Aldershot, Gower, 1984, p. 207.
22. M. Laver, *The Crime Game*, Oxford, Martin Robertson, 1982, p. 172.

2 The State as Law and Order

1. H. L. A. Hart, *The Concept of Law*, Oxford, Clarendon Press, 1961, p. 158.
2. ibid., p. 167.
3. I. Eibl-Eibesfeldt, *Love and Hate: on the Natural History of Basic Behaviour Patterns*, trans. by G. Strachan, London, Methuen, 1971, p. 93.
4. K. Lorenz, *On Aggression*, trans. by M. Latzke, London, Methuen, 1966, p. 194.
5. L. L. Fuller, *The Morality of Law*, rev. ed., New Haven, Yale University Press, 1969, p. 115.
6. Macfarlane, op. cit., p. 59.
7. A. P. d'Entreves, *The Notion of the State*, Oxford, Clarendon Press, 1967, p. 228.
8. G. K. Chesterton, *The Defendant*, London, Dent, 1901, p. 161.
9. Laver, op. cit., p. 111.
10. J. de Maistre, *Works*, trans. by Jack Lively, London, Allen and Unwin, 1965, p. 191.
11. ibid., p. 192.
12. M. P. Golding, *Philosophy of Law*, Englewood Cliffs, N. J., Prentice-Hall, 1975, p. 73.
13. Weekly Hansard, No. 1233 (HMSO), p. 462.
14. Golding, op. cit., p. 87.
15. ibid. p. 88.
16. Johnson, op. cit., p. 25.
17. E. Durkheim, *Selected Writings*, trans. by A. Giddens, Cambridge, C.U.P., 1972, p. 125.
18. ibid., p. 126.
19. van den Haag, op.cit., p. 11.
20. R. P. Rhodes, *The Insoluble Problems of Crime*, New York, John Wiley, 1977, p. 257.
21. J. Alderson, *Policing Freedom: a Commentary on the Dilemmas of Policing in Western Democracies*, London, Macdonald and Evans, 1979, p. 111.
22. M. Foucault, *Discipline and Punish: the Birth of the Prison*, trans. by A. Sheridan, London, Allen Lane, 1977, p. 49.
23. L. Siedentop, 'Political Theory and Ideology: the case of the State', in D. Miller and L. Siedentop, eds., *The Nature of Political Theory*, Oxford, Clarendon Press, 1983, p. 58.
24. ibid., p. 72.
25. G. W. F. Hegel, *The Philosophy of Right* (1821), trans. by T. M. Knox, Oxford, Clarendon Press, 1962, p. 105.
26. Quoted in the *New Statesman*, 19 April 1985.
27. A. T. Turk, *Political Criminality: the Defiance and Defense of Authority*, Beverly Hills, Sage Publications, 1982, p. 22.
28. J. H. Skolnick, *Justice without Trial: Law Enforcement in Democratic Society*, New York, John Wiley, 1967, p.4.
29. ibid., p. 243.
30. R. V. G. Clarke and J. M. Hough, eds., *The Effectiveness of Policing*, Farnborough, Gower Publications, 1980. 'Foreword' by M. Banton, p. 9.
31. H. Davies, *The Glory Game*, London, Sphere Books, 1973, p. 107.
32. E. B. Pashukanis, *Law and Marxism: a General Theory* (1929), trans. by B. Einhorn, London, Ink Links, 1978, p. 174.
33. Turk, op. cit., p. 16.
34. T. Benn, *Arguments for*

Socialism, ed. by C. Mullin, London, Jonathan Cape, 1979, p. 151.

35. Conklin, op. cit., p. 26.
36. Laver, op. cit., p. 48.
37. P. King, *The Ideology of Order; a Comparative Analysis of Jean Bodin and Thomas Hobbes*, London, Allen and Unwin, 1974, p. 279.
38. ibid., p. 284.
39. ibid., p. 285.
40. d'Entreves, op. cit., p. 222.
41. E. Gellner, *Nations and Nationalism*, Oxford, Blackwell, 1983, p. 73.
42. P. Selznick, *Law, Society and Industrial Justice*, New York, Russell Sage, 1969, p. 28.
43. For the meaning of these terms, see A. Megill, *Prophets of Extremity*, Berkeley, University of California Press, 1985. Introduction and *passim*.
44. G. W. F. Hegel, *Science of Logic* (1816), tans. by W. H. Johnston and L. G. Struthers, London, Allen and Unwin, 1929, Vol. II, p. 398.
45. G. Simmel, *Conflict* (1908), trans. by K. H. Wolff, Glencoe, Ill., The Free Press, 1955, p. 65.
46. R. Clutterbuck, *Britain in Agony: the Growth of Political Violence*, Penguin Books, 1980, p. 307.
47. ibid., p. 310.
48. S. Hall *et al.*, *Policing the Crisis: Mugging, the State, and Law and Order*, London, Macmillan, 1978, p. 139.
49. ibid., p. 142.
50. ibid., p. 149.
51. S. D. Cook, 'Coercion and Social Change', in J. R. Pennock and J. W. Chapman, eds., *Coercion* (NOMOS XIV), Chicago, Aldine-Atherton, 1972, p. 133.
52. Hegel, *Philosophy of Right*, op. cit., p. 156.
53. M. J. Oakeshott, *On Human Conduct*, Oxford, Clarendon Press, 1975, p. 152.

3. Criminal and Political

1. B. Lenman and G. Parker, 'The State, the Community and the Criminal Law in Early Modern Europe', in V. A. C. Gatrell, B. Lenman and G. Parker, eds., *Crime and the Law: the Social History of Crime in Western Europe since 1500*, London, Europa Publications, 1980, p. 31.
2. van den Haag, op. cit., p. 47.
3. Quoted in G. Carr, *The Angry Brigade: the Cause and the Case*, London, Gollancz, 1975, p. 68.
4. *Report of the Commission to Consider Legal Procedures to Deal with Terrorist Activities in Northern Ireland*, Cmnd. 5185, December 1972, ch. 3, par. 5.
5. ibid., par. 6.
6. J. Bowyer Bell, *A Time of Terror: How Democratic Societies Respond to Revolutionary Violence*, New York, Basic Books, 1978, p. 40.
7. Quoted in E. Hyams, *Terrorists and Terrorism*, London, Dent, 1975, p. 28.
8. F. Burton, *The Politics of Legitimacy: Struggles in a Belfast Community*, London,

Routlege and Kegan Paul, 1978, p. 89.
9. Carr, op. cit., p. 76.
10. Alderson, op. cit., p. 111.
11. H. L. Packer, *The Limits of the Criminal Sanction*, London, 0.U.P., 1969, p. 364.
12. J. Q. Wilson, *Thinking about Crime*, New York, Basic Books, 1975, p. 204.
13. J. Raz, *The Authority of Law*, Oxford, Clarendon Press, 1979, p. 238.
14. Morgan, op. cit., p. 130.
15. D. Lyons, *Ethics and the Rule of Law*, Cambridge, C.U.P., 1984, p. 153.
16. Golding, op. cit., p. 55.
17. van den Haag, op. cit., p. 118.
18. Johnson, op. cit., p. 61.
19. R. F. Sparks *et al., Surveying Victims*, Chichester, John Wiley, 1977, pp. 100–103.
20. *A Report on the Attitudes and Opinions of the Public towards the Humberside Police*, Keith Gordon Services, Hull, February 1984, p. 18.
21. C. Rook, *The Hooligan Nights* (1899), London, 0.U.P., 1979, p. 11.
22. N. Lucas, *Britain's Gangland*, London, Pan Books, 1969, p. 110; see also J. Pearson, *The Profession of Violence: the Rise and Fall of the Kray Twins*, Frogmore, Panther Books, 1973. What limited the Krays' building an empire of crime, the author argues, 'was not the law but their stupidity' (p. 263).
23. Gatrell, op. cit., p. 40.
24. J. Davies, 'The London Garotting Panic of 1862: a Moral Panic and the Creation of a Criminal Class in Mid-Victorian England', ibid., p. 211.
25. V. A. C. Gatrell, 'The Decline of Theft and Violence in Victorian and Edwardian England', ibid., p. 249.
26. G. Pearson, *Hooligan: a History of Respectable Fears*, London, Macmillan, 1983, p. 236.
27. e.g. '. . . to the extent that the relevant public gain an increased confidence in the law enforcement agencies and have ready access to them, with few deterrents to reporting crime, to that extent will an augmented, more efficient and sympathetic police force be likely to *create a crime wave* of tidal proportions!' (A. K. Bottomley and C. Coleman, 'Law and Order: Crime Problem, Moral Panic, or Penal Crisis?', in Norton, op. cit., p. 43.)
28. Wilson, op. cit., p. 47.
29. Nisbet, op. cit., p. 62.
30. A. Montagu, *The Nature of Human Aggression*, New York, 0.U.P., 1976, p. 309.
31. ibid., p. 324.
32. Gurr, op. cit., p. 33.
33. Eibl-Eibesfeldt, op. cit., p. 30; cf. 'Not only do people evidently and constantly act and feel in ways to which they have never been conditioned, but the very idea that anything so complex as a human being could be totally plastic and structureless is unintelligible.' (M. Midgley, *Beast and Man: the Roots of Human Nature*, Hassocks, Harvester Press, 1979, p. 19.)
34. Eibl-Eibesfeldt, op. cit., p. 79.
35. Rook, op. cit., p. xxii.
36. ibid., p. 2.
37. Lorenz, op. cit., p. 38.
38. Marsh, op. cit., p. 33.

39. Macfarlane, op. cit., p. 115.
40. Davies, op. cit., p. 105.
41. Marsh, op. cit., p. 11.
42. Johnson, op. cit., p. 61.
43. Morgan, op. cit., p. 170.
44. Rhodes, op. cit., p. 16.
45. cf.: 'If this long, connected history of respectable fears tells us anything at all, then it is surely that street violence and disorder are a solidly entrenched feature of the social landscape.' Pearson, op. cit., p. 242.
46. M. Banton in Clarke and Hough, op. cit., p. xi.
47. Durkheim, *Selected Writings*, op. cit., p. 127.
48. Conklin, op. cit., p. 68.
49. Macfarlane, op. cit., p. 103.
50. Morgan, op. cit., p. 171.
51. E. Durkheim, *The Rules of Sociological Method* (1895), trans. by S. A. Solvay and T. H. Mueller, Glencoe, Ill., The Free Press, 1958, p. 67.
52. ibid., p. 71.
53. ibid., p. 72.
54. K. T. Erikson, *Wayward Puritans: a Study in the Sociology of Deviance*, New York, John Wiley, 1966, p. 17
55. ibid., p. 18.
56. Sparks, op. cit., p. 227.
57. B. de Spinoza, *The Political Works*, trans. by A. G. Wernham, Oxford, Clarendon Press, 1958, p. 309; cf. Hegel, *Philosophy of Right*, op. cit., par. 241.
58. Laver, op. cit., p. 145.
59. ibid., p. 146.
60. T. Honderich, *Violence for Equality: Inquiries in Political Philosophy*, Penguin, 1980, p. 196.
61. Bowyer Bell, op. cit., p. 19.
62. H. Arendt, *On Violence*, London, Allen Lane, 1969, p. 68.
63. Bowyer Bell, op. cit., p. 16.
64. Marsh, op. cit., p. 114.
65. A. Arblaster, 'Terrorism: Myths, Meaning and Morals', *Political Studies*, Vol. XXV, No. 3, September 1977, p. 422.
66. E. Moxon-Browne, 'Terrorism in Northern Ireland: the Case of the Provisional I.R.A.', in J. Lodge, ed., *Terrorism: a Challenge to the State*, Oxford, Martin Robertson, 1981, p. 154.
67. P. Furlong, 'Political Terrorism in Italy: Responses, Reactions and Immobilism', in ibid., p. 59.
68. D. Miller, 'The Use and Abuse of Political Violence', *Political Studies*, Vol. XXXII, No. 3, September 1984, p. 413.
69. Clutterbuck, op. cit., p. 311.
70. R. Mark, *In the Office of Constable*, London, Fontana, 1978, p. 325.
71. P. Singer, *Democracy and Disobedience*, Oxford, Clarendon Press, 1973, p. 122.
72. ibid., p. 123.
73. ibid., p. 124
74. A. Y. Davis *et al.*, *If They Come in the Morning: Voices of Resistance*, New York, The Third Press, 1971, p. 24.
75. Hyams, op. cit., p. 170.
76. Quoted in Carr, op. cit., p. 63.
77. J. Harris, *Violence and Responsibility*, London, Routledge and Kegan Paul, 1980, p. 12.
78. van den Haag, op. cit., p. 213.
79. Weekly Hansard, No. 1283 (HMSO), p. 469.
80. Harris, op. cit., p. 53.
81. Miller, op. cit., p. 404.
82. Hall, op. cit., p. 302.

83. cf. R. N. Berki, 'Marcuse and the Crisis of the New Radicalism: from Politics to Religion?', *The Journal of Politics*, Vol. 34, No. 1, February 1972.
84. A. Burns, *The Angry Brigade: a Documentary Novel*, n.d. (ISBN 085031 1128), p. 8.
85. ibid., p. 69.
86. ibid., p. 9.
87. ibid., p. 24.
88. ibid., p. 156.
89. ibid., p. 164.
90. ibid., p. 167.
91. B. Baumann, *Terror or Love? the Personal Account of a West German Urban Guerilla*, London, John Calder, 1979, p. 19.
92. ibid., p. 20.
93. ibid., p. 116.
94. ibid., p. 120.
95. cf. G. Pridham, 'Terrorism and the State in West Germany during the 1970s: a Threat to Stability or a Case of Political Over-reaction?', in Lodge, op. cit., p. 29.
96. Burns, op. cit., p. 166.
97. Baumann, op. cit., p. 116.
98. Carr, op. cit., p. 86.

4 Conventional Wisdoms

1. Elder, op. cit., p. 197.
2. Macfarlane, op. cit., p. 66.
3. Morgan, op. cit., p. 270.
4. de Maistre, op. cit., p. 98.
5. Pashukanis, op. cit., p. 68.
6. P. Johnson, *A Tory Philosophy of Law*, London, Conservative Political Centre, 1979, p. 6.
7. Sir Keith Joseph, *Freedom Under the Law*, London, Conservative Political Centre, 1975, p. 13.
8. Home Secretary's speech at the Joint Central Conference of Police Federations of England and Wales, Scarborough, 23 May 1984.
9. Joseph, op. cit., p. 6.
10. de Maistre, op. cit., p. 118.
11. Morgan, op. cit., p. 53.
12. ibid., p. 59.
13. Hall, op cit., pp. 168–9.
14. J. Wheeler, *Who Prevents Crime?*, London, Conservative Political Centre, 1980, p. 16.
15. ibid., p. 21.
16. Wilson, op. cit., p. 50.
17. ibid., p. 209.
18. See Sparks, op. cit., p. 129; Humberside Police, op. cit., p. 26.
19. Burns, op. cit., p. 22.
20. H. and J. Schwendinger, 'Defenders of Order or Guardians of Human Rights?', in I. Taylor, P. Walton and J. Young, eds., *Critical Criminology*, London, Routledge and Kegan Paul, 1975, p. 132.
21. M. Shaw, 'Marxism and the Problem of Law and Order in Britain', in Norton, op. cit., p. 180.
22. Schwendinger, op. cit., p. 135.
23. Lea and Young, op. cit., p. 42.
24. ibid., p. 43.
25. ibid., p. 96.
26. R. Quinney, *Class, State and Crime*, New York, Longman, 1980, p. 39.
27. Lea and Young, op. cit., p. 97.
28. Davis, op. cit., p. 27.
29. ibid., p. 143.
30. Taylor, op. cit., p. xv.
31. Pashukanis, op. cit., p. 173.
32. Foucault, op. cit., p. 272.

33. ibid., p. 277.
34. Schwendinger, op. cit., p. 133.
35. Pashukanis, op. cit., p. 175.
36. W. L. McBride, 'An Overview of Future Possibilities: Law Unlimited?', in J. R. Pennock and J. W. Chapman, eds., *The Limits of Law* (NOMOS XV) New York, Leiber-Atherton, 1974. p. 34.
37. Hall, op. cit., p. 390.
38. Pearson, op. cit., p. 237.
39. Honderich, op. cit., p. 96.
40. ibid., p. 97.
41. van den Haag, op. cit., p. 264; cf. de Maistre, op. cit., p. 134.
42. Weekly Hansard, No. 1288 (HMSO), 1984, p. 55.
43. I. Taylor, 'Is Crime Here to Stay?', *New Statesman*, 12 November 1982, p. 12.
44. H. Collins, *Marxism and Law*, Oxford, Clarendon Press, 1982, p. 120.
45. I. Taylor, P. Walton, J. Young, eds., *The New Criminology: for a Social Theory of Deviance*, London, Routledge and Kegan Paul, 1973, p. 270.
46. W. L. McBride, 'Noncoercive Society: Some Doubts, Leninist and Contemporary', in Pennock and Chapman, *Coercion*, op. cit., p. 188.
47. ibid., p. 190.
48. Hall, op. cit., p. 176.
49. Morgan, op. cit., p. 184.
50. T. Carlyle, *On Heroes, Hero-Worship, and the Heroic in History* (1848), Boston, Ginn & Co., 1901, p. 233.
51. d'Entreves, op. cit., p. 154.
52. *The New Criminology*, op. cit., p. 282.
53. P. Calvert, *A Study of Revolution*, Oxford, O.U.P., 1970, p. 17.
54. Morgan, op. cit., p. 264.
55. ibid., p. 222.
56. Weekly Hansard, No. 1288 (HMSO), 1984, p. 49.
57. E. P. Thompson, *Writing by Candlelight*, London, Merlin, 1980, p. 166.
58. ibid., p. 178.
59. ibid., p. 204.
60. ibid., p. 210.
61. Collins, op. cit., p. 144.
62. ibid., p. 146.

Select Bibliography

J. Alderson, *Law and Disorder*, London, Hamish Hamilton, 1984.

J. Alderson, *Policing Freedom: a Commentary on the Dilemma of Policing in Western Democracies*, London, Macdonald and Evans, 1979.

A. Arblaster, 'Terrorism: Myth, Meaning and Morals', *Political Studies*, Vol. XXV, No. 3, September 1977.

H. Arendt, *On Violence*, London, Allen Lane, 1969.

D. H. Bailey, ed., *Police and Society*, Beverly Hills, Sage, 1977.

B. Baumann, *Terror or Love? The Personal Account of a West German Urban Guerilla*, London, John Calder, 1979.

J. Bowyer Bell, *A Time of Terror: How Democratic Societies Respond to Revolutionary Violence*, New York, Basic Books, 1978.

A. Burns, *The Angry Brigade: a Documentary Novel*, n.d. (ISBN 085031 1128).

F. Burton, *The Politics of Legitimacy: Struggles in a Belfast Community*, London, Routledge and Kegan Paul, 1978.

P. Calvert, *A Study of Revolution*, Oxford, 0.U.P., 1970.

G. Carr, *The Angry Brigade: the Cause and the Case*, London, Gollancz, 1975.

W. J. Chambliss and R. B. Seidemann, *Law, Order and Power*, Reading, Mass., Addison-Wesley, 1971.

R. V. Clarke and J. M. Hough, eds., *The Effectiveness of Policing*, Farnborough, Gower Publications, 1980.

R. Clutterbuck, *Britain in Agony: the Growth of Political Violence*, Penguin, 1980.

H. Collins, *Marxism and Law*, Oxford, Clarendon Press, 1982.

J. E. Conklin, *The Impact of Crime*, New York, Macmillan, 1975.

T. A. Critchley, *The Conquest of Violence: Order and Liberty in Britain*, London, Constable, 1970.

A. Y. Davis *et al.*, *If They Come in the Morning: Voices of Resistance*, New York, The Third Press, 1971.

A. P. d'Entreves, *The Notion of the State*, Oxford, Clarendon Press, 1967.

D. Downes, *Law and Order: Theft of an Issue*, London, Fabian Society, 1983.

E. Durkheim, *Selected Writings*, trans. by A. Giddens, Cambridge, C.U.P., 1972.

E. Durkheim, *The Rules of Sociological Method*, trans. by S. A. Solvay and T. H. Mueller, Glencoe, Ill., The Free Press, 1958.

I. Eibl-Eibesfeldt, *Love and Hate: on the Natural History of Basic Behaviour Patterns*, trans. by G. Strachan, London, Methuen, 1971.
K. T. Erikson, *Wayward Puritans: a Study in the Sociology of Deviance*, New York, John Wiley, 1966.
M. Foucault, *Discipline and Punish: the Birth of the Prison*, trans. by A. Sheridan, London, Allen Lane, 1977.
L. L. Fuller, *The Morality of Law*, New Haven, Yale University Press, 1969.
V. A. C. Gatrell, B. Lenmann and G. Parker, eds., *Crime and the Law: the Social History of Crime in Western Europe since 1500*, London, Europa Publications, 1980.
M. P. Golding, *Philosophy of Law*, Englewood Cliffs, N. J., Prentice-Hall, 1975.
T. R. Gurr, *Why Men Rebel*, Princeton, N. J., Princeton University Press, 1970.
E. van den Haag, *Punishing Criminals*, New York, Basic Books, 1975.
J. Habermas, *Legitimation Crisis*, trans. by T. McCarthy, London, Heinemann, 1976.
S. Hall *et al.*, *Policing the Crisis: Mugging, the State, and Law and Order*, London, Macmillan, 1978.
J. Harris, *Violence and Responsibility*, London, Routledge and Kegan Paul, 1980.
H. L. A. Hart, *The Concept of Law*, Oxford, Clarendon Press, 1961.
T. Honderich, *Violence for Equality: Inquiries in Political Philosophy*, Penguin, 1980.
E. Hyams, *Terrorists and Terrorism*, London, Dent, 1975.
G. Ionescu, *Politics and the Pursuit of Happiness*, London, Longman, 1984.
P. Johnson, *A Tory Philosophy of Law*, London, Conservative Political Centre, 1979.
Sir Keith Joseph, *Freedom Under the Law*, London, Conservative Political Centre, 1975.
E. Kamenka, R. Brown and A. E. S. Tay, eds., *Law and Society: the Crisis in Legal Ideals*, London, Edward Arnold, 1978.
P. King, *The Ideology of Order: a Comparative Analysis of Jean Bodin and Thomas Hobbes*, London, Allen and Unwin, 1974.
M. Laver, *The Crime Game*, Oxford, Martin Robertson, 1982.
J. Lea and J. Young, *What Is to Be Done about Law and Order?* Penguin, 1984.
J. Lodge, ed., *Terrorism: a Challenge to the State*, Oxford, Martin Robertson, 1981.
K. Lorenz, *On Aggression*, trans. by M. Latzke, London, Methuen, 1966.
D. Lyons, *Ethics and the Rule of Law*, Cambridge, C.U.P., 1984.
L. J. Macfarlane, *Violence and the State*, London, Nelson, 1974.
P. Marsh, *Aggro: the Illusion of Violence*, London, Dent, 1978.
R. Miliband, *Capitalist Democracy in Britain*, Oxford, O.U.P., 1982.
D. Miller, 'The Use and Abuse of Political Violence', *Political Studies*, Vol. XXXII, No. 3, September 1984.
P. Morgan, *Delinquent Fantasies*, London, Temple Smith, 1978.
J. Muncie, *The Trouble with Kids Today: Youth and Crime in Post-War Britain*, London, Hutchinson, 1984.
R. Nisbet, *Twilight of Authority*, London, Heinemann, 1976.

P. Norton, ed., *Law and Order and British Politics*, Farnborough, Gower Publications, 1984.

M. Oakeshott, *On Human Conduct*, Oxford, O.U.P., 1975.

H. L. Packer, *The Limits of the Criminal Sanction*, Oxford, O.U.P., 1969.

E. B. Pashukanis, *Law and Marxism: a General Theory*, trans. by B. Einhorn, London, Ink Links, 1978.

G. Pearson, *Hooligan: a History of Respectable Fears*, London, Macmillan, 1983.

J. R. Pennock and J. W. Chapman, eds., *Coercion*, Chicago, Aldine-Atherton, 1972 (NOMOS XIV).

J. R. Pennock and J. W. Chapman, eds., *The Limits of Law*, New York, Leiber-Atherton, 1974 (NOMOS XV).

T. Platt and P. Takagi, eds. *Crime and Social Justice*, London, Macmillan, 1981.

L. Radzinowicz, *Ideology and Crime: a Study of Crime in its Social and Historical Context*, London, Heinemann, 1966.

J. Raz, *The Authority of Law*, Oxford, Clarendon Press, 1979.

R. P. Rhodes, *The Insoluble Problems of Crime*, New York, John Wiley, 1977.

P. Selznick, *Law, Society, and Industrial Justice*, New York, Russell Sage, 1969.

J. N. Shklar, *Legalism*, Cambridge, Mass., Harvard University Press, 1964.

G. Simmel, *Conflict*, trans. by K. H. Wolff, Glencoe, Ill., The Free Press, 1955.

P. Singer, *Democracy and Disobedience*, Oxford, Clarendon Press, 1973.

J. H. Skolnick, *Justice without Trial: Law Enforcement in Democratic Society*, New York, John Wiley, 1967.

R. F. Sparks *et al.*, *Surveying Victims*, Chichester, John Wiley, 1977.

I. Taylor, *Law and Order: Arguments for Socialism*, London, Macmillan, 1981.

I. Taylor, P. Walton and J. Young, eds., *Critical Criminology*, London, Routledge and Kegan Paul, 1975.

I. Taylor, P. Walton and J. Young, *The New Criminology: for a Social Theory of Defiance*, London, Routledge and Kegan Paul, 1973.

E. P. Thompson, *Writing by Candlelight*, London, Merlin Press, 1980.

A. T. Turk, *Political Criminality: the Defiance and Defense of Authority*, Beverly Hills, Sage Publications, 1982.

J. Wheeler, *Who Prevents Crime?* London, Conservative Political Centre, 1980.

J. Q. Wilson, *Thinking about Crime*, New York, Basic Books, 1975.

Index